Directing the Movies
in Your Subconscious Mind

Remove the Blocks That Stop Your Success in Any Area of Life

Jim Britt

STAY IN TOUCH WITH JIM BRITT

www.JimBritt.com

www.CrackingTheRichCode.com

www.PowerOfLettingGo.com

www.TheRichCodeClub.com

www.JimBrittCoaching.com

Email or to hire Jim as a speaker: support@JimBritt.com

THE RICH CODE CLUB

FREE members site.

www.TheRichCodeClub.com

Jim Britt

All Rights Reserved

Copyright 2020

Cracking the Rich Code, LLC

10556 Combie Road, Suite 6205

Auburn, CA 95602

The use of any part of this publication, whether reproduced, stored in any retrieval system, or transmitted in any forms or by any means, electronic or otherwise, without the prior written consent of the publisher, is an infringement of copyright law.

Directing the Movies in Your Subconscious Mind

Remove the Blocks That Stop Your Success in Any Area of Life

ISBN: 978-1-64153-362-1

DEDICATION

*To those rare individuals that are willing to
look inside versus outside to discover their true greatness.*

About Jim Britt

Jim Britt is an award-winning author of 13 best-selling books and numerous #1 International best-sellers. Some of his many titles include Rings of Truth, Do This. Get Rich-For Entrepreneurs, Unleashing Your Authentic Power, The Power of Letting Go, and Cracking the Rich Code Series.

Jim has served as a success strategist to over 300 corporations worldwide and was recently named as one of the world's top 50 speakers and top 20 success coaches. He was presented with the "Best of the Best" award out of the top 100 contributors of all time to the Direct Selling industry.

He has presented seminars throughout the world sharing his success strategies and life enhancing realizations with over 4,000 audiences, totaling more than 1,500,000 people from all walks of life.

Early in his speaking career he was Business partners with the late Jim Rohn for eight years, where Tony Robbins worked under Jim's direction for his first few years in the speaking business.

As a performance strategist, Jim leverages his skills and experience as one of the leading experts in peak performance, entrepreneurship and personal empowerment to produce stellar results. He is pleased to work with small business entrepreneurs, and anyone seeking to remove the blocks that stop their success in any area of their life.

One of Jim's latest online programs "Cracking the Rich Code" focuses on the subconscious programs influencing one's financial success, that keeps most living a life of mediocrity. This four-month program is designed to change one's money programming and relationship to money to that of the wealthy. More at www.JimBritt.com

What Other Professionals Say About Jim Britt

"Success is predictable if you know what determines it. Jim Britt offers valuable insights and strategies that will challenge you to leap beyond your current comfort level and stand up and be heard. If you want to strengthen your life, your mindset, your income and your effectiveness overall, Jim presents profound ideas in the most-simple, clear and easy to grasp manner. He offers practical wisdom for today's complex world."

Kevin Harrington, Star of the hit TV show Shark Tank

***

"Jim Britt's insights into the psychology of wealth will give you the focus, clarity and purpose to refine your financial plan and make the right choices for your business, your finances and your life."

Tony Robbins, NYT Best Selling Author, World's#1
Success Strategist, Motivational Speaker

***

"Jim Britt has been a friend and business associate for over 30 years. His work as a success coach, trainer and entrepreneur is remarkable. Work with Jim if you are interested in great success."

Jim Rohn, Best Selling Author, Top Inspirational Speaker

***

"I've known Jim since the mid 70's. He is a giant of a man and a giant thinker. If you ever get a chance to work with him do not hesitate. He delivers powerful, lasting, life-changing, results."

Mark Victor Hansen, Co-creator of Chicken Soup for the
Soul

***

"They say that success leaves clues. After reading Jim Britt's book Rings of Truth you'll know what those clues are and how to use them. You'll want to keep it near you for quick reference, because you'll likely want to read it again and again on your way to success."

> T. Harv Eker, NYT Best-selling Author, Secrets of the Millionaire Mind

***

"Jim Britt is an inspiring speaker and result-producing coach and mentor. He offers hope for a better future and the tools to make it happen."

> Dr. Denis Waitley, Best Selling Author, Psychology of Winning

***

"Because of the work that Jim Britt does and the methods and techniques he uses to change your story and how you see yourself, it has enabled me to build my career and to make it against all odds."

> Les Brown, World Renowned Motivational Speaker

Preface

We're all playing a high stakes game called life. You have only one life in which to do everything you will ever do. So, it is in your best interest to step up, get focused, let go of those things holding you back and find the fastest way to move on your bucket list.

In order to make rapid changes, the most important thing is to learn to suspend your beliefs and look for the real truth behind your actions and results.

It starts with believing in yourself. You must risk believing in yourself and the decisions you make if you want to move toward the life you desire. If you want more money, more fulfilled relationship, better health, or whatever, you have to risk making the assumption that you can become successful to whatever level you choose. Otherwise you risk settling for only a small fraction of what life could provide for you.

I'm not talking about taking a big chance, but rather giving yourself a chance. The solutions you'll find in this book are not to challenge the odds of success but rather to challenge your limiting beliefs about success. Until you challenge your limiting beliefs of what you think you can achieve, you'll never know how far you can go.

Remember, a belief is something that you have decided is true, but the reality is, it may not be true at all. All beliefs are limiting. A belief is simply a ceiling you place on yourself. The idea is to learn to suspend your beliefs and look for the real truth. Instead of deciding whether something will or will not work, look for evidence proving beyond any doubt that it can, or it cannot work. And if you decide that it can work, act as if your success is absolutely guaranteed.

I have a very simple philosophy when it comes to getting things done. Once a decision is made, then every action you take is either going to move toward your objective or further away. If you are going to go all out to achieve a goal, might as well get it done in the fastest way possible.

If this philosophy sounds appealing, you are in the right place. You have to say goodbye to conventional ways of thinking, false assumptions, old programming, mediocrity, and low expectations; surrender the self-limiting and self-sabotaging beliefs you have clung to regarding living the life you want. They have no place in your life unless you want to stay exactly where you are now. They only serve to sabotage your performance, scare you into quitting, and put you in the slow lane to success.

Over the years, I've learned to discipline myself by focusing only on the behaviors and strategies that gave me the biggest results in the shortest amount of time. And, if you want rapid rewards, you must learn to do the same. The great part about life is that you have a choice as to how you spend your time each day. So, doesn't it make perfect sense to concentrate your energy on the strategies that will give you the biggest breakthrough and results?

Time ruthlessly passes us by. It waits for no one. It is an unrecoverable asset, and unlike any other asset or resource, it cannot be reproduced, bought, sold, borrowed, stolen, saved, or modified in any way. All of us have the same 24 hours every day. When you spend an hour, you have one less to spend. All we can do is make use of it. But the reality is that most spend 90% of their time focused on what they don't want instead of what they do want. That's the reason why we need to learn how to compress its use, to get more results faster, to shorten and reduce the length of time it takes to achieve your objectives.

Bottom line: Time can only be used or wasted, and that's your choice. If you want to become better at anything, you need to learn how to use time to upgrade your execution skills, so that you can shorten the path and accelerate your rate of success.

Learn from the past, yes. Plan for the future, yes, but stay focused on the present moment where the action takes place. Time is a shopping spree. The Clock is ticking. When you spend a minute, you have one less to spend! Happy shopping!

Let's get started, shall we?

Table of Content

About Jim Britt v
What Other Professionals Say About Jim Britt vi
Preface viii
Chapter 1: The Law of Cause and Effect 1
Chapter 2: The Secret to Happiness 18
Chapter 3: Letting Go 37
Chapter 4: Self-Observation 54
Chapter 5: The Addictive Cycle 69
Chapter 6: Releasing Emotional Addictions 80
Chapter 7: Look for the Truth 90
Chapter 8: How to Change a Belief 100
Chapter 9: The Frequency of Emotions 117
Chapter 10: Intention and Faith 131
Chapter 11: Emotional Clearing 148
Chapter 12: Suppression and Repression 155
Chapter 13: Releasing Attachments 172
Chapter 14: Language and Feelings 190
Chapter 15: Letting Go of the Need for Acceptance 204
Chapter 16: Letting Go of Control 217
Chapter 17: What is Love? 235
Chapter 18: Loverage 245
Afterword 247

ONE

The Law of Cause and Effect

We all have moments when everything we do seems to work. It is during these times that great insights occur. We feel abundant, happy, and trusting of life. We are refreshingly still inside. We are receptive and open to receive. Our usual nagging "mind chatter" is quiet and our energy is flowing freely. In this state, we are able to experience our true nature and the full beauty of our surroundings. We feel alive, balanced, and purposeful.

You've felt it. Maybe when you were walking in the woods and experiencing nature.

Maybe you've felt it with a goal you set for yourself; you get inspired and feel like nothing can stop you.

Then suddenly, without any notice, this vibrant state disappears as mysteriously as it came. Your soaring spirit and creative abilities seem to fall back to sleep, as you drift back into your old identity. You begin to once again buy into the mind chatter, the self-talk of doubt, fear, and uncertainty. Does this sound familiar at all? You've experienced it, I'm sure.

Come along with me for a moment. Imagine for a moment how you would feel if your heart and mind were completely clear of all stressful thoughts and feelings. Imagine being in that place of overwhelming certainty and creativity. Imagine how that would feel. Imagine that everywhere you went, you were completely relaxed, non-judgmental, and certain that the whole world was totally friendly and supported you in every way.

Take a moment and recall yesterday. How would it have felt if you had known that everyone you contacted was sending you love and total support, and that you radiated that same energy out to others?

No matter what people said, or how they said it, you could recognize their true meaning. Think of how centered and confident you would have felt and how little you would have needed from the outside world.

Do you realize that absolutely nothing stands between you and this experience except your own beliefs and expectations of how life or others should be? You know what I mean…those silent whispers that draw you back into past or future anticipations.

I remember a man who attended my leadership program in Toronto a few years back. When it was over, he remained seated while everyone else left the room. I noticed that he looked a bit confused, so I walked over and asked him how he had enjoyed the weekend.

He complimented the program but added that he was dealing with a very serious problem.

I asked if I could help. After a few minutes of conversation, he told me that he thought he had a split personality, and he wasn't sure what to do about it.

He explained, "I have been to dozens of seminars and workshops, and when each program ends, I always feel the same way that I feel now, like I can accomplish anything I want! But," he said, "I also know that when I get home, or maybe in the next day or so, my *other* personality will take over. The voice inside my head will begin pulling me back into my *other* identity, and very soon I will be right back where I started."

I spent some time with him explaining that this feeling of duality was not unique to him, but that everyone experienced it to one degree or another. I told him he was fortunate to realize this because most people never do. They just go on about their business, seminar after seminar, hoping for a different result next time. What he was really experiencing was coming face-to-face with his own past subconscious programming and core beliefs, created by past experiences.

You see, we all have subconscious programming, both positive and negative, that create second-nature habit patterns. In other words, we use them so much that we don't even realize we are using them. On a positive side, it would be difficult to live our lives without some of these habit patterns, like walking and talking. Driving your car is another good example. You don't get into your car and have to re-learn how to drive it. It's second nature.

On the negative side, we also engage in habit patterns that have become second nature, and we don't know we are doing it. Here's a good example. I recently spoke with a gentleman who expressed to me that he had not been able to pay his bills on time or fully for twenty-five years.

My response was, "Wow! What do you plan to do about it?"

He said, "I am thinking about cutting my overhead."

I responded back, "Well there is nothing wrong with cutting your overhead, but within a few months, you'll be right back to not being able to pay your bills on time or fully each month."

Sounding a bit confused by my statement, he snapped back, "Why would you say that?"

I said, "Because you are addicted to that behavior, and until you figure out how to break the addictive cycle, or someone helps you break it, you will continue the same behavior until your life ends."

Just like the man who had so many experiences attending seminars and workshops, then immediately falling back into his old ways, this gentleman had actually developed a core belief that the same thing was going to happen each time. And each time he tries and fails, the stronger the addiction, or core belief, becomes.

His other personality was nothing more than his core beliefs developed from past subconscious programming, strengthened by repeating the habit pattern that had become second nature to him. That other personality was nothing more than old beliefs, feelings, and emotions surfacing, needing to be released before he could truly move forward.

He attended my workshop because he wanted something different in his life. At the same time, his new vision came face-to-face with his existing programming and belief that it was only going to last for a few days.

Unless you understand what is happening, your dominate programming will always win out over your current decision. That's why so many people feel stuck and can't seem to move forward.

The first step is becoming aware of what is happening, and that it is not leading you in the direction you want to go. Then, stop for a moment and observe what actions you take from that moment forward. Will acting on the feeling or emotion take you in the direction you want to go? It's a battle going on between your subconscious programming and the vision of how you want your life to be. It is like two frequencies coming in on the same channel, all you get is static and misinformation. The only way to handle the situation is to either sink back into your old frequency by honoring your fear, or let go of the old and stay tuned to the new.

Here's another way to look at it. Let's say you have had the experience of wanting something but never got it, and as a result, you have developed a belief that it may never happen. The intense desire then meets the fear of never having it, and this creates a mixed message to the subconscious. Because it is not clear and concise, the subconscious doesn't act upon it as real.

So can you see why getting "pumped up" or "motivated" at a seminar, and not dealing with the real issue—the feelings and emotions that support the limiting belief—is always incomplete and short lived?

Here's another way to look at it. Let's say that a really cute stray puppy shows up at your back door looking hungry. What do you do? You feed it, don't you? Then what happens?

Right, it comes back! And of course, it keeps coming back as long as you continue feeding it. And pretty soon, it's no longer a cute little puppy, but has turned into a huge Great Dane that eats a lot more food than you ever imagined, and you don't know how to get rid of it. You have grown attached, and so you decide to keep it around anyway and just suffer with the added expense and trouble.

Many of your experiences start out in much the same way, as simple little programs. But then, as you feed them, as you begin to pay more attention to them, as you focus on them and suppress them more and more, they become stronger and stronger. Eventually these little programs can and will run your life. But, because you have grown so attached to them, even though you don't want them in your life, you keep them around anyway.

As an example, let's say that as a child you were told repeatedly that your room was a mess and that you were incapable of keeping yourself organized. You were told this over and over, by the parents you admired and loved. So of course you believed them, didn't you? After all, they are the authority figure and must know more than you; they must be right. They know more than you, so how could you question the person you admire and look up to the most?

You are now an adult, and you find that your room is still a mess. In fact, your whole life is disorganized. Or you might even find that the opposite is true. Because you were told so often that your room was a mess, you now over-compensate. Because of your need to be accepted, you are now an obsessive-compulsive, cleaning fanatic!

These programs can literally run your life. We all have them and how you deal with them will determine how you experience life. You keep old programs alive by feeding them, just like the stray puppy. What do you feed them? You feed them with emotions you refuse to let go of, like the frustration of not being able to get rid of them.

Whatever you focus your attention upon will always grow stronger. If you are focused on lack, you will experience more lack. If you are focused on being lonely, you will experience more loneliness in your life. If you focus on needing money, you will always need more money. On the other hand, if you are focused on love, prosperity, and abundance, you will begin to experience those things.

You create *your* world based on your view of *the* world. The problem is that most look at the world through rose-colored glasses of the past. That is the only way it can work. It is the Law of Cause and Effect. We don't attract our circumstances, as most believe, we realize them by our own creation. We cause the effect. This it is always, and without question, working. Just look at your life honestly, and you'll see the truth of what you have created. If you connect the dots backward through your life, you'll see exactly what actions you took that led you to where you are today.

A law is something that works the same way every time we apply it. That's the way the Law of Cause and Effect works; and it never fails.

So, when a negative emotion surfaces, realize that it is simply the feeling—or trapped energy—surfacing, offering you the perfect opportunity to let go, to move past it, and to make the changes in your life that you desire.

Don't get upset with yourself for what you've created. It is what it is. You can't change where you are. However, you can change what happens from this point forward.

The more you become upset with yourself for where you are or how life is treating you, the stronger the programs become and the more you create the same. There is no need to be upset. Just look at your upset as something that is happening. Not good or bad, just simply something that is happening that you need to deal with in order to move past it. Because before long, if you don't deal with these upsets as they arise, just like the stray dog, they grow up and take over your life. They become a stubborn attachment to a one-sided point of view, formed by your own conditioned beliefs and perceptions of how you think life should be. Over time, by identifying with your old beliefs and programming, and your desperate attempt to create a new and better life, you begin to lose sight of the truth, of who you really are and what you are capable of accomplishing.

You begin to become, what I call, "belief driven." In other words, you get to the point where you can't even see the truth behind your situations. You don't see that your beliefs are nothing more than the sum total of all your past experiences or programming coming to the surface for evaluation. When they do arise, and you want to change, just simply observe them with silent strength, and ask yourself, "Does this feeling and belief support me in having the life I want?"

As a result of living from past programming, you will experience some of the following emotions:

- Suffering from anxiety
- Always strategizing your next victory but never accomplishing it
- Unable to relax
- Always disappointed with whatever results you produce
- Driven to always want more
- Feeling that no matter how much you have it is never enough
- Unable to enjoy peace of mind
- Always in a conflict with someone
- You are sure that *what* you have is *who* you are

These experiences produce feelings and emotions of unhappiness, stress, sadness, fear, anger, and hopelessness. These are all derived from your beliefs about how you think life should be and trying to force life to be something it's not!

On the other hand, when you begin to let go of the feelings and beliefs that no longer serve your greater good, you will find yourself:

- Never being disappointed with results
- Feeling that everything is unfolding perfectly
- Open and attracting solutions easily
- Open to new opportunities
- Living without anxiety
- Sensitive to your surroundings
- Finding unexpected solutions to seemingly unsolvable problems
- Calm and in control in any situation
- Always open-hearted
- Always at the right place at the right time.

These experiences in turn lead to feelings of confidence, inner calm, courage, balance, openness, happiness, and joy. In short, you are living from a state of resourcefulness.

It's as though the mind has been split into two parts. One part is the decisions you make that create new ideas that lead you in the direction you want to go. Then, the subconscious, based on past programming, manufactures a sort of parallel universe where the unreal, the non-supportive programming, seems more real than real itself. And it does it in an instant. In other words, you decide to create a certain thing in your life. Immediately the subconscious goes to work to offer you all the reasons, based on past experiences, why you shouldn't do it.

The subconscious is there to protect you from bad things happening, but all it has to go on is past experience. It can become a protective device or a destructive one depending on what you accept as real.

Most teachings tell us to analyze the darkness (our past programs and problems) in order to reach the light (what we want in our life). But in reality, the first step to getting what you want is simply the absence of what you don't want. When you remove what you don't want—by letting go of the feeling or belief—the solution to getting what you want will present itself.

I have had many people who were afraid to let go of a negative habit pattern or belief because they were afraid of what would fill that empty space when they did. Some had become so accustomed to living with their fears and beliefs that they were afraid they would actually die if they let it go.

What do you think fills the empty space when you let go of fear? It's filled with its opposite, which is love. When you let go of a fear, solutions appear that lead you in the direction you want to go. When the space is full of what you don't want, there is no capacity to create what you do want. When a fear arises ask yourself, "Do I need this fear, or should I let it go and leave space for something new?"

Fear or any other non-resourceful feeling is absolute proof that human beings have the ability to create. How else do you think your fears and other problems originate? We create them! Amazing! We are afraid of our own mind. We create the good and the bad; we fear both.

Do you think that each of us is simply chosen to have certain problems? Let's give this person fear, that one impatience, and someone else anger; and that one over there, let's give him anxiety! Fear is the only friction in our thought process. Anger is the fear of not being in control. Sadness is the fear of what you have lost or might lose. Anxiety is the fear of not having enough. All negative emotions and habit patterns are based in fear.

When you release the emotion connected to an old belief, solutions appear automatically. When you hang on to negative emotion, feeling, or behavior, solutions remain hidden.

To make a change, you have to see the truth behind the conflict in your life. The truth is that you created it and you can let it go. How could you possibly change something if you don't know the truth behind what you are trying to change. If you continue to attempt to change outside circumstances, you will only be creating more of the very thing you are trying to get rid of in the first place. It's essential to living the life you want. Become fully aware of the structure you have built around yourself. Even though it may be artificial or unsupportive, unless you understand it, you will continue to live from a position of fear and inner conflict. Living this way makes you cling to all sorts of self-centered judgements and beliefs, causing a great deal of personal discomfort for you and those around you.

Because we don't want to experience pain, we tend to build up a false structure in order to protect ourselves. What we don't realize is that we are building a wall around us that is designed to keep out beneficial solutions—very thing we want to experience.

Remember, all conflict is self-created conflict. True freedom is having the courage to risk being vulnerable to life as it unfolds, by letting go of the structure, letting go of your need to control outcomes, and allowing yourself to experience life as it arises, moment-to-moment and without the negative influence of old programming. When you live your life this way, you truly and fully experience who you are, without conflict or pain. Or, at the very least, you look at pain and conflict in a different way and can find solutions.

Letting go won't completely eliminate all your problems, but it will sure help you eliminate the stress and distress that comes with your problems. And of course, without stress and distress would your problems even be problems in the first place?

When you begin to let go of your fears, only then can you truly find happiness and self-acceptance and begin to experience life as it unfolds. Remember, all conflict is self-conflict. Start to observe how you create conflict in your life and the part you play. If you are feeling lonely for example, you are trapping usable energy into "I am lonely." That, instead, could be used as energy to create (i.e. "I love myself"). Until you let go of the lonely feeling, you will not have the capacity to experience its opposite, which is love. When you come from a place of loving yourself, your energy is expansive and the possibilities are endless. If you are experiencing anxiety, see that part you play in the experience. If you are a workaholic, or suffer from anxiety, notice that the more you work, the more you feel the need to work, while simultaneously getting less accomplished. If you are not self-observant, it can be difficult to recognize what is causing your conflict; you will tend to look outside yourself for answers.

There's a story about Leonardo de Vinci. He wanted to paint a portrait of Jesus Christ.

He searched and searched and finally found a young, olive-skinned man, who he thought was the perfect model for Jesus. Many years later, he wanted to paint a portrait of Judas, a man who hated Christians. Again, he searched and searched for the ideal model. Finally, he found a man evil looking enough to fit the part. As he approached the man, he discovered that he was the very same man who had modeled for Jesus years earlier.

The moral to the story is this: "A rope in the darkness can be mistaken for a snake." But does that make the rope a snake? It is not the darkness that's the real problem; it's the lack of light. You have to shed some light on your shadow side (your subconscious programming) to see if the solution it offers supports your desired outcome.

Your subconscious programs can be both your enemy and your ally, depending on how you *perceive* and utilize the messages they send you. If you use non-supportive emotions as a signal to "let go," they can become your greatest gift. If you don't understand this fact, these programs can become like a computer virus, attacking the core system. It can show you the parallel universe where it appears only pain and hardship exist. No one wants to live there, yet so many do.

These outdated programs and beliefs are real only because you make it so. In reality, all you need to do is simply empty the trash or press delete! Here's one commonly asked question about the function of these subconscious programs: "If these programs aren't real, how come they create so much stress and pain in my life?" Any old program, supportive or not, is only as real as the beliefs that support it. In other words, it is real, but only because you make it so based upon what you believe to be true. For example, stress and emotional pain exist only because you have stored the experiences that create stress and emotional pain. The solution is to no longer react to the stress and pain of past experiences.

It's often a mistaken belief, based on past programming, that you must *push* life in order to make it work properly. But pushing is what keeps you in a stressful state. Because of your beliefs, you convince yourself to struggle, to try, to change your outside circumstances, which is the real reason for your suffering in the first place. The real cause of your suffering is identifying with the past, instead of living in the present moment where the action takes place. In other words, the thing you are chasing is what's causing you to chase it.

The simple truth is this: painful experiences you endure are the *effect* of the trap, *not* the trap itself. You are causing the effect by living is the past. For example, if you feel fear, the fear is not the real problem. The real problem is that you *identify* with the fear.

You hang onto it, believing that you *are* the fear, instead of viewing it as a passenger that you can let off at the next bus stop. It's like hanging on to the tail of a wild buffalo and believing that you are the buffalo. You hang on and wonder why you are in so much pain.

Experiencing fear doesn't mean that you *are* the fear any more than hanging onto the tail of a wild buffalo makes you a buffalo, or flying in an airplane makes you an airplane. There is no stress in the moment, unless of course, you bring it in by hanging on and reliving a past experience.

Stress, fear, or any other form of non-resourceful feelings comes from two places. The first is through reliving past experiences in present time. And second, it comes from projecting a past experience into the future with the anticipation of it happening again.

Your subconscious programs are always bringing up the past, because your beliefs were developed in the past. The subconscious *is* the past…period. Some programs support you, some do not. There is no subconscious influence in the moment unless you allow it. That's why self-observation is so critical

The standard question at this point is, "Okay, what am I doing wrong?" The answer is, "You are doing nothing wrong." In fact, you are right on track. All the stresses and conflicts in your life are a sure sign that change is taking place. Here is what's really happening all the time. When you challenge your old beliefs and non-supportive programs, the subconscious goes on panic alert! Its only job is to protect you at all costs.

While the *new you* is gaining momentum, your subconscious is regrouping to prepare for another attack, making sure you have all the past info, based on past experiences, to move forward safely! The new-you says, "I want to be financially free."

The subconscious then steps in and says, "Yeah, but what about security? Remember when you lost everything ten years ago?"

The new-you says, "I'm going to start a new business." The subconscious counters with, "But what about that time you failed so miserably? Do you want to experience that again?"

The subconscious will always engage in denial in order to prove it's right. It wants to protect the programs stored on your hard drive. As long as you believe the illusion the subconscious is handing you, you have become trapped in a closed box where no light, no solutions, can enter.

You can know this for sure: every situation, every conflict, every non-resourceful feeling and emotion you experience, is an opportunity to let go and move past it. It's your opportunity to step out of your self-created prison and start living at your full potential.

Every conflict you experience, when you look for the truth behind it, allows you to more fully discover who you really are.

Your circumstances never need to change. It is your *outlook* toward your circumstances that needs to change. Instead of looking at what you are supposed to learn from a situation, you can begin looking at the "gift," what you can discover. In fact, your life is really all *about* self-discovery! Dropping emotions that support your old beliefs does not require a change at all, but more of a recognition and choice. Change is set in motion automatically when the original belief is challenged.

Remember how to challenge a belief? First, by recognizing through self-observation that it is outdated and non-supportive. And second, by letting go of the emotion that holds the belief in place. Once the energy of the feeling is released, the belief is weakened and can now be changed. Self-observation and letting go is always the entry point to changing a belief. More on self-observation later.

You could spend literally years in therapy, but until you make a choice to do life differently, nothing changes. Until you challenge your old beliefs through self-observation and letting go, there will be no real progress, only temporary patchwork solutions.

A police officer who attended one of my workshops shared his experience from twelve years earlier. He had been involved in a shoot-out that left him wounded and several innocent people killed, including a small boy, dead in his lap. He had been on a leave of absence ever since. Twelve years of twice-a-week therapy sessions had brought him no results at all. He said that his therapy sessions lasted only until he got to the elevator.

He explained that his therapist encouraged him to talk about the incident and to analyze his feelings over and over, to "get it out in the open." He said it felt good while he was in session, but the feeling of release never lasted. He said that what he had received from the two-day class and a personal fifteen-minute "letting-go" session during the program, was truly profound. He explained that not once during his twelve years of counseling had anyone ever told him he had the capacity to observe his feelings and let them go. About a month after the class, I received a note from him saying that he was no longer in therapy and was going back to work. Until you understand that your old programs and beliefs are not who you really are, you'll continue refusing to realize the games you play with yourself.

I remember many years ago I was sitting on the sofa one day with my four-year-old son, Will. I asked him what he wanted to be when he grew up. He said quite seriously that he didn't want to grow up, that he liked the little kid costume he was wearing right now. I asked if he really wanted to stay a little kid all his life, or did he want to grow up someday like dad. He said that when he was ready to grow up, he would just change his costume, but until then, he would keep the costume he had.

That about sums it up, doesn't it? We are all wearing our costumes of who we think we are, who we want others to think we are. We all have our own drama, our own story, our own costumes. Some are wearing the costume and telling a story of being the victim. Others wear the costume and tell a story of a successful businessperson suffering from stress and anxiety, or the struggling employee. Others may be wearing the always-broke costume or the lonely-heart costume or the relationship-conflict costume.

What you experience as real is simply a reflection of your belief systems, a reflection of your story. Your story is what keeps you enslaved and separate from your true potential.

We all get glimpses of real life once in a while, but we still find it difficult to experience who we really are, moment-to-moment, without our costumes. Remember, there is nothing outside of you that is a threat to you in any way. The only real threat is your internal whispers, created by your core beliefs.

A question I sometimes get is, "How can something that feels so right be so destructive?

It feels as though fear, worry, anger, and other negative emotions are in my best interest. They all seem to protect me in some way." This is because your emotions can fill you with a momentary, but false, sense of security and protection. We've all been conditioned with this approach to life for so long that we have developed a belief that it is absolutely true. We go about life and don't even question how we feel or why. I would encourage you to challenge any belief that is not leading you in the direction you want to go and let go of the emotion that keeps that belief alive.

Ask yourself, "How did I come to believe this?"

"Who taught me?"

"What if they didn't know?"

"What if it's not true?"

"Who would I be without this belief?"

For example, if I get angry with you, I feel that somehow my anger will protect me from being hurt by you. I'm using my anger to avoid the pain of not being in control or to get acceptance for being right. I could, on the other hand, let go of my anger and take responsibility for seeing the real truth behind the situation and have a discussion.

It's also important to know that how you feel has nothing to do with right or wrong, so don't get down on yourself for how you are feeling. Your feelings are just trapped energy wanting to be released. More on this later.

Right and wrong are never the issue. What you are experiencing is absolutely perfect for where you are at this point in your life. The real issue is this. Does the way you feel support your desired outcome? Does it expand your energy, leaving you open to a solution and taking you closer to your objective? Or does it restrict your energy and lead you further away? Does it add to the quality of your life? Does it make you happy and fill your life with joy? If not, let it go. If the answer is no, it's not supportive, you should simply make a choice to stop doing it; let it go and move past it! By seeing the truth, you can let it go and move on! In fact, the only way to do his is by first seeing the truth behind your situation.

All your negative feelings and emotions are always connected to past experiences in some way. They have absolutely nothing to do with what is happening right here, right now, unless of course you let them. If you allow them in, then they have everything to do with right here, right now. When you accept them as real, they become just as real as when they originally occurred. Even though these feelings may seem to have some sort of survival value, in reality they are <u>literally</u> killing you. In other words, you are choosing to die simply by not living fully in the present.

Question: How much time do you spend in a resourceful, productive state each day? To put it another way, how much do you die every day, simply by not being fully alive?

Wouldn't it be sad to reach the end of your life and discover that you had lived only ten to twenty percent of it, because you spent 80% living in the past or future?

As we have discussed, life is a self-created drama or success story. You have written each of the actors into your life's screen play, including yourself in the leading role. You have written in the co-star and even the extras.

Think about it. All the players in every drama pretend to have power, don't they? And at the same time, they are all looking to someone or something outside themselves to give them more power. However, most people don't really want power over others. What they want is to just be in charge of their own lives. They want to break free of their drama, their pain, and to experience more life the way it was meant to be experienced.

Truly successful people never seek power over others. Think about it. Why would they need to? Those who seek power over others have a dark side and are not very happy with themselves. Who you are is what you create. If you are constantly seeking power, you'll constantly find yourself with people who threaten your sense of control. And as you feel yourself losing control—somebody with more money, more success, a nicer car—you'll want to measure up, so you'll begin to seek more power in order to regain control.

It's a vicious cycle and everyone does it to one degree or another. We do it for the acceptance from others rather than for power. All we are really truly looking for is self-acceptance! Isn't it silly what we do to ourselves, when you back away and observe? When you observe with an unconditioned mind, it is absurd what we do to ourselves. If you chase life by constantly being driven to have or do more, you become the chase itself.

If you fear not having enough, you'll continually create circumstances that trigger your fear of not having enough! All any of us really want to do, deep down inside, is live our lives free from the influence of outdated beliefs and non-supportive programming. To seek to do, before you seek to know, only reinforces the outdated subconscious programs you are trying so desperately to eliminate.

Remember, you are not your drama. Your drama is not you. It is only trapped energy from experiences of how things used to be. Just like the trapped words on this page. You could choose to read them over and over again, or you could simply choose to turn the page. So, don't take your story personally; it is not you now. It's your past history. Choose not to read or live it over and over again. You can edit out all the defeat, failure, hurt, pain, and all the rest of the feelings you experience in your drama and leave the rest. Your past negative experiences don't exist in real life. They are not happening to you now unless you bring them into the present.

Stop asking the part of you that created your problems to give you the correct solutions. Those old programs will become the fault finder if you allow them to. The simple rule is this: anytime a voice inside your head speaks to you without love and compassion, you should never believe it, because it's not you! Better yet, you shouldn't even listen! Instead, just feel the emotion when it arises and see it for what it is (energy wanting to be released). Embrace it, then let it go and move on. Just observe and say, "Isn't this interesting, the things I created in the past? Isn't this fascinating, who I used to be? I'm sure glad this is not me anymore." Then, take a deep breath and let it go. The more you practice this process, the more your old subconscious programs will begin to wither away from lack of attention.

Darkness is the absence of light, just like fear is the absence of love. When you turn on the light, by letting go of your fear, you'll clearly see the way to move forward with greater ease.

TWO

The Secret to Happiness

Is there a secret to being happy? Yes, but it's no secret. It reveals itself right in front of us every day. We just can't see or hear it because of the endless chatter inside our own minds. Many of us live as though we could find true happiness if only we possessed enough security, enough money, enough love, enough education, enough respect, enough power, enough knowledge, enough something. Many literally feel imprisoned by their lack of answers to living a happy life.

Imagine walking into a room where a group of people are seated at a table with a delicious meal set before them. The table is filled with every sort of food you could imagine. It is a mouth-watering display, all perfectly prepared and right in front of their noses, easily within reach. You notice, however, that none of the people are eating. They haven't taken a single bite. Their plates are empty, and it appears that they have been seated there for a very long time; so long, in fact, they appear to be starving to death. They are starving, not because they cannot see or eat the wonderful food before them, or because eating it is forbidden or harmful. They aren't eating because they don't realize food is what they need. They don't know that those very sharp pains in their stomachs are caused by hunger. They don't see that all they need to do to stop their suffering is to eat the food that's right in front of them.

This is an example of our basic human suffering. You may sense there is something wrong, something inherently missing in your life, but you haven't a clue what the problem is or what you should do about it. We have all felt that way. It is impossible to know what you don't know. We may see faintly that what we need is somehow very close to us, but we don't connect it to the sharp pain inside. And even with time, as the pain becomes even more severe, we can't see what it is we need, because the more you focus on the pain, the more the solution stays hidden.

We all long for happiness. In fact, I would go so far as to say we are obsessed with it.

Why do you think we're all so obsessed with being happy? We seek it because it's our natural state. You might say we are homesick. What I mean by that is, happiness is a state we were all born with, and we all want to return to that state.

However, many of us seek happiness using inappropriate means. For example, pursuing happiness through bodily desires such as sex, parties, alcohol, etc. doesn't work because it is short lived and builds dependence. This is not to suggest that we should not *have* or *want* sex, go to a party, or have a drink. However, if we use it as a means to find happiness, it'll fall short every-single-time. If we attempt to find happiness as a result of gaining acceptance from others, in material possessions, or in having money, we will again be falling short of the happiness that is within our power to experience. All these methods are tied to external conditions over which we have no control whatsoever, and therefore can never lead us to true, lasting happiness.

Unfortunately, most of the emphasis these days is on learning how to more effectively get what we *think* we need to *be* happy—a new car, dress, suit of clothes, vacation, and so on. In reality, we are attempting to satisfy our addictions. Yes, we all have addictions. I'll discuss this in more detail as we make progress through the book.

What we really need to do instead of searching for happiness, is learn how to eliminate our addictions, rather than satisfy them. We will always have activities, money, relationships, and possessions, but instead of viewing them as sources of our happiness, they should be viewed as expressions of our happiness, or pleasures in life. When we begin to realize that nothing from the outside can help us find happiness, we are then free from the underlying sense of lack we all seem to have in our lives. When we lack nothing, we feel complete as we are. Feeling complete, we can then enter into a state of re-source-ful-ness. Resourceful is defined as, *"once again full of source."* The key word 'source' is defined as, *"where all things originate."*

Being resourceful simply means being present with yourself and free of all the internal chatter. Happiness is our natural state.

When we're in a state of *re-source-fulness* we can easily acquire material possessions, but we don't become dependent upon them for our happiness; we never fear losing them or our happiness. You can't lose anything that is already a part of you. All we do is cover it up in pursuit of what we already possess. What you are chasing is what's chasing you! When we fear losing what we have—our money, relationships, etc.—the fear itself will cause unhappiness.

The key to happiness is to let go of fear, to be happy with what we have, and pursue the pleasures life has to offer. When you are experiencing a fear, you are stuck in the past or future where happiness does not and cannot exist. Letting go *is* the secret to happiness. Let go of all the hurts, pains, mistakes, failures, etc. from the past and the worry about the future. Hanging on to all those things is what causes unhappiness. To be happy, simply let go of the things that cause your unhappiness.

We all believe that in order to be happy we have to resolve each of our problems in a way that completely eliminates them, or we want to deny the reality of our problems altogether. That's like ignoring the weeds in the garden and hoping they will just go away. If you do this, we all know that pretty soon you have no garden, just weeds.

By ignoring the problem, we are really trying to turn reality into something other than what's really happening.

The bottom line is this. Life involves having and dealing with problems. Name me one person who doesn't have problems, and I'll show you someone without a pulse! In fact, if you're alive and you don't have problems, you've got real problems!

Here's a good starting point to enjoying happiness: problems are a fact of life. Weeds will grow, even if you hate them and wish them gone! Why? That is the nature of weeds.

Weeds will grow even when you don't plant them. Flowers, on the other hand, will grow, wither, and die even though you love them and want them to remain. How do you feel about this reality? Maybe we should all just pretend that there are no weeds. Maybe we should all just pretend that all of what we love is not going to eventually die. Maybe we should just pretend that there are no problems and see what happens. We've all become pretty good at that one. All we need to do is look around. The whole planet is in denial. That is why so many feel so unhappy.

It's important to realize that all dissatisfaction and unhappiness originates within us.

All conflict is self-conflict. Unhappiness arises out of our own ignorance, out of being blind to reality, or out of our desire for reality to be something other than what it is.

Wanting reality to be something it's not causes unhappiness. Think about it. When we can't fit something into our belief system, we get upset.

Life is a journey. The journey should be one of getting to know ourselves once again, a journey into self-intimacy, into self-love. The real journey is to awaken to the here and now, one of being fully alive and fully present in this moment, in this reality and not in trying to make reality something it's not. You can't change reality! It is what it is. It can't be changed. But you can change how you perceive reality. How you respond to the current reality can change your reality at some point in the future—probably the very next moment. After all, this moment is all there is anyway. And how you function in this moment is the only thing you can control. The present moment is where happiness exists.

You have to come to three realizations in order to find happiness. First, you have to realize life is fleeting. It's passing you by, moment-to-moment. Second, you have to realize you are already complete as you are and worthy of happiness. And last, you have to see that you are your own refuge, your own sanctuary, and your own salvation. You need nothing from the outside to make you more or to provide you with happiness.

Remember, every conflict in your experience has a life span and that lifespan is in your control. Letting go is about shortening the lifespan of an unhappy feeling or experience from beginning to resolution. Letting go helps you break free of that spinning world in your mind and to live more fully in the moment where all action takes place and where happiness exists. By learning to let go of what disempowers you, you'll become more present in your relationship, more effective at work, and more harmonious with your family, friends and those you meet along the way.

Letting go is a choice, moment-to-moment. It's a fork in the road.

Should I let go of the old me and take the path to the new me, or do I buy into the illusion of the past and future? Letting go gives you a choice to buy into the delusion of your mind chatter, of past pains and mistakes, or live more fully in the moment.

A few years after I discovered the principles I'll be sharing throughout this book, I kept thinking about the word 'resourceful' and primarily the key word 'source.' I was looking for a deeper meaning. I was in a small town in England when I noticed a sign that read, "Antique Books." Old books have always intrigued me for some reason. As I walked into the store, I saw this huge dictionary containing several thousand pages. It looked to be really old. Not wanting to damage the book, I carefully opened it to the "S" section and looked up the word 'source.'

There were multiple definitions, but one that really caught my eye. 'Source' had one definition, "love." That really made sense to me. Re-source-ful, *"once again full of source."* Webster defined 'source' as *"where all things originate."* Re-source-ful, in my new definition, is *"once again full of love."* What does that mean? Love is *"where all things originate."* Your only other option is fear. When you fall in love with what you want in life— your goals, dreams, happiness, peace of mind, or whatever—that's when you start to create it. Love is not a word or simply a feeling; it is a power source. It is an energy! You can call on it, turn it off and on at will. You can send it out and focus it for all sorts of uses. It will never fail you and is always available within. Love is the common thread that connects all things.

To have happiness, or anything you want in life, it is not necessary to discover the universal workings of things. You don't need to study meta-physics or black holes. It comes from your effort to remain *re-source-ful,* connected to or in a state of love, loving yourself, loving what you want in life. Love is simply being connected to source, where all things originate.

I've heard people say that to let go is to give up. Letting go is not about giving up your skills or control of anything. Instead, you simply give up using your skills to manipulate the world out of fear of not getting your part. When you die to the old, you create a vacuum for the new. Nothing can be added to a space that is full. When a non-resourceful belief or emotion is surrendered, the vacuum that is created can be filled with something you love.

Happiness is whatever is happening right now. It is what's taking place at this very moment. There is no place else it could be. It's not in the future, is it? It's not in the past, is it? Happiness is here and now. Where is here and now? As you sit having your dinner tonight with the family, where is the upset you experienced this morning at the office? If you are still reliving it, you will not be in the moment where happiness exists. If the past doesn't exist, then there can no longer be an upset, can there? Unless you are reliving the upset or thinking about how you're going to fix the upset tomorrow. But where is tomorrow? It doesn't yet exist.

So, let me ask you. What is real? What does exist? There's just your upset about this morning and tomorrow that you are bringing back into your reality. Those *were* reality. But there is only now. Your story about what happened this morning is not happening now unless you bring it in to now. It is only your story. What's real is the stress headache and unhappiness you've created for yourself out of something that doesn't even exist any longer. Of course, you may have to deal with the problem tomorrow. But dealing with it over and over now will not solve what happened this morning.

While the mind can be in the past or the future, the body always remains in the present moment because of its feeling nature. Feelings are always in the moment. Being in the moment is a condition that we all strive to attain, because deep inside we know happiness is happening in the moment. At this very moment, there is just what's happening. There is nothing you have to gain in order to be happy. You can never avoid this moment. You may not be awake to it at this moment, but it is always right here and now. You can only avoid seeing it. When you are avoiding this moment, you are avoiding your own happiness. You are avoiding life itself.

If something in your life is not working, and you are miserable about it, that's it, that's life! Let go and be with the misery, observe it, and watch it disappear. When you let go of the misery, that is where you'll find happiness. Don't worry about the future. No one can make wrong decisions about the future, because a present decision does not create a future event. Present decisions only create present events. On the other hand, a present experience that you hang onto, can and will create an event in a present moment somewhere in the future. This is why it so vitally important to deal with feelings and emotions as they arise, instead of putting them off to deal with in the future.

A decision does not make the future turn out a certain way, it is how you continue to think, feel and the actions you take after you make a decision that makes the future turn out the way it does. When you learn to observe your unhappy state and let go of how things *used* to be, and any expectation of how the future *should* be, you can live life as it is right now, which is the only life you have anyway. When you let go, moment-to-moment, of how you think things *should* be, you will soon discover happiness.

There's a story about fishermen from many years ago. Every morning they would go out early and fish until mid-afternoon. They would then come in and unload their catch on the dock, spending the rest of the afternoon preparing their boat for the next day's fishing. While the men were getting the boat ready, their wives would put the day's catch in their baskets, place the baskets on their heads, and go to the market.

One day, they had to go to a market that was further away, requiring an overnight stay.

As it began to get dark, the women started looking for a comfortable place to bed down for the night. One woman spotted a beautiful meadow full of wildflowers and suggested they sleep there. They laid their baskets of fish at the edge of the meadow and walked out among the beautiful flowers and bedded down for the night amidst the wonderful fragrance. However, they tossed and turned for hours; they just couldn't go to sleep. Finally, one woman picked up her blanket and walked to the edge of the field where the other baskets of fish were sitting. She laid her head down beside the basket of stinking fish, and within seconds, she fell fast asleep.

The moral to the story is this: sometimes we get so attached to our stinking circumstances and old beliefs, we can't feel comfortable amongst the beauty that surrounds us. Another way of saying it is, we become so attached to our self-imposed limitations that we can't see a better way. We have literally become hypnotized by our own inner dialog.

You create a beautiful vision of how you want your life to be, then hear those familiar whispers, *"Don't forget your self-judgement report card."*

"You don't deserve to have that."

"You can't be happy without this or that."

We have literally become hypnotized by our subconscious programs and internal voices.

So, how do we break this hypnotic spell? The very first step is to get clear about what it is you really want in your life. If you don't know what you want, how will you know if the action you are taking is going to get you there? If you want your circumstances to change, you have to make a conscious choice to change the rules you are playing by, because your circumstances won't change until you do.

Here are four important points to consider:

1. If you want to achieve a different result in your life, you must *do* something different.

2. In order to do something different, you must first *know* something different to do.

3. In order to know something different to do, you have to at least *suspect* that if the key to being happy was in the places you've been looking, you would have found it by now.

4. You must be *open* to trying a new way. If you want to make a change, you must be open to changing the rules of your game. We don't have to continue playing by the same old rules that got us where we are today.

Let's say that you and I sat down to play a game of Checkers. We each have 12 pieces; 12 are red and 12 are black.

We both know that the objective is to jump and remove all our opponent's pieces as we move across the board in one direction. When either of us reaches the other side safely, we are crowned. Now, we have a new advantage. We can move freely in either direction. The game continues until one of us has lost all our pieces.

Now, what if I step in and change the rules. What if I crowned all my pieces up front, so that I could move either direction from the start? I would have an unfair advantage over you, wouldn't I?

Or maybe, I went a little further in changing the rules and took my hand and just wiped all of your pieces off the board and said, "I won!"

Now, you might say, "You can't do that, there are rules."

And I say, "Well, I changed the rules."

And you say, "You can't change the rules."

And I say, "Why not? Who wrote the rules? Why can't I change them? Who says I can't?"

You probably wouldn't want to play checkers with me anymore. It wouldn't be a lot of fun for either of us, would it? What about the game of life? What about your happiness? Who wrote the rules? Why can't we change them? Who says we can't?

Let's look at the game of Chess. We have the same board as Checkers. How many moves can we make? How many choices do we have? Unlimited! Same playing field and the exact same number of pieces as checkers. The only difference is that we have unlimited choices.

The very same principle applies to the game of life. We all play on the same playing field, and we have unlimited choices. Every single choice we make creates a different future. The question is, are you making intelligent choices or choices from convenience?

Are you simply going along with the rules that someone else may have set up for you or on what you believe to be right for you? Until we make the intelligent choice to do life differently, we'll continue to play within our old rules with a limited amount of choices, and with a limited amount of happiness.

First, we have to determine just what happiness is. Just what is happiness anyway?

When I first looked at what I thought happiness wasn't, these thoughts crossed my mind.

Happiness is not being broke. I grew up broke and didn't find happiness, so that wouldn't be happiness, would it?

Happiness is not having a broken relationship. I had that and it didn't make me happy.

Happiness is not being lonely. And my list went on:

Happiness is not driving a junk car.

Happiness is not living where you don't want to live.

Happiness is not being sick.

Happiness is not working in a profession you hate.

None of these things would be happiness, would they?

I set out to find ultimate happiness. So, I took the same questions and turned them around.

If I just had money, would that do it, would that be the ultimate happiness?

If I just had the perfect relationship? Would that do it for me?

If I could just get that new car I really wanted? Would that really make me happy?

What about the perfect profession?

If I could just get my life organized, would that do it?

If I could just get away for a while?

Then, it really hit me like a ton of bricks! If having those things—money, cars, etc.—was not happiness, and not having those things was not happiness, then what or where would I ever find happiness?

Then I thought, 'Happiness couldn't happen yesterday, nor could it happen tomorrow. Could it?'

I finally concluded that if happiness was not in things, the past or the future, then it must be happening in the moment—that *all* these things had to be happiness, or not, depending on your view. Happiness is whatever's happening right here, right now! What else could it be?

You might be thinking that I'm saying happiness is being lonely.

Happiness is having a fulfilling relationship.

Happiness is being sick.

Happiness is being healthy.

Happiness is being broke.

Happiness is having money.

Yes. That is what I'm saying. Happiness has to be whatever you are experiencing right now! You are not your past or your future. The only time is now. There is no past or future.

Many people believe they are living in the moment, when in reality, they are fearfully running from one moment to the next trying to find happiness. And as soon as you begin the chase, leaving this moment—which is all that exists—you are leaving happiness behind.

We very often fear what we don't truly understand. By living in the present, we begin to realize that our fears are simply 'mental mistakes.' As you truly observe them in the present, you'll begin to see that your fears are a gift presented to you as a perfectly planned opportunity to let go and find happiness.

It's interesting how the words *'happiness'* and *'happening'* are so similar. *Happiness* is whatever's *happening* at any given moment. Here is my point. At any moment, there is just what's happening. That's it! Nothing more!

If you tie your happiness to some external condition somewhere in the future, it becomes impossible to ever find happiness. Why? Because there is no future, just like there is no past. The only reality is what's happening right here, right now, in this moment. Now *is* reality. Trying to find happiness out there in the future somewhere is just as much of an impossibility as trying to find happiness by reliving your past.

So often we become caught up in the illusion of it all, and say, "Forget reality. I want more. More is what would make me happy. I can't be happy with what I have. I need more to really be happy."

Having more is great. I believe we should all have more of the finer things in life. But, having more should be the result of your happiness, not the cause of it.

You may be asking yourself, "How can I be in the moment, when I have bills to pay, or have an important meeting next week?" Here is the real question. Which would be more effective, to be focused in the present, on the here and now, or on the future that doesn't yet exist? I'm not saying do not plan for the future. What I am saying is you should make plans for the future, and then stay focused in the present where the real action is—where reality exist.

Every moment, if you're truly in it, offers a wealth of opportunities. When you are truly in the moment, you'll start to see the conflict between what you want, how you think things should be, and what is really happening.

Logic tells us to look at life this way:

When I get through all these problems…

Right after the first of the year…

As soon as my money problems get better…

As soon as the kids are older…

Then I'll relax and be happy and live in the present. Well it ain't gonna happen! Why? Because all your stuff, all your problems, the house payment, the kids, etc., that's your life. That's everyone's life.

The problem is, I'm not happy.

The problem is, I need to make more money.

The problem is, I am lonely.

The problem list goes on and on.

I heard a great line in a movie a while back. The man was lying on his deathbed as he said to his friend at his bedside, "All I ever wanted to do was live a normal life."

His friend responded by saying, "There is no normal life, there's only life."

There are always going to be problems to deal with: family problems, relationship problems, business problems, money problems, and personal problems. That's what life is all about, solving problems and being happy doing it. When we get through all that we're dealing with right now, we'll simply be through all that we're dealing with, and that's it! Then there will be more to follow. We'll have a whole new set of reasons to not be happy.

We don't have to look out there to figure anything about who we are. There's nothing to figure out. There's nothing to acquire in order to be happy. You don't have to go off to a retreat or anywhere else to find happiness.

Now on the other hand, if going to a retreat, attending a seminar, reading book, or whatever, can help you in learning how to *see* the truth, it can be a *very* beneficial tool.

A seminar cannot teach truth, only you can discover the truth. There is no path to the truth except your own. However, any aid is good aid. If reading a book can help you in some way to discover *your* truth, then read it; if not, then why waste the time.

The stresses we face today will always seem insurmountable if we continue to look at them through the eyes of the past or future. There is no stress in the moment. Why? This is because stress is created from fear. Fear is where the past and the future meet with the here and now.

Emotional stress is the net effect of a condition you are resisting or trying to escape from.

But the condition has no power in itself. Nothing outside us has the power to create stress. For example, going through the loss of a job may be a painful experience if it is not wanted, while for another it may mean freedom.

We are exactly where we need to be. The feast is spread before us. All we need to do is eat! Whether you see your life as an opportunity or a burden depends on your point of view, not your circumstances. We would all *like* to believe, as many do, that our external circumstances are the cause of what we're experiencing. We attempt to avoid our unpleasant feelings by staying focused on past mistakes, blaming the past for how we feel and worrying about future events. We don't even realize that our focus on the past and future is what's causing us to feel the way we do in the present.

The objective should be to simply *see* what the problem is and deal with it. The faster you deal with it, the sooner it will go away. It's called living consciously, not for the sake of a belief or idea, but for the sake of living in the present where the action is, where happiness exists.

My point is, we spend most of our creativity, imagination, and vital energy, living in the past or future so we can avoid the present, which consists of real life. Anytime you are out of the moment, you are avoiding those things that matter the most. Truly living in the present is a condition worth striving for. Why? Because your life is taking place in the present.

You will never grow or experience any degree of happiness by daydreaming about future perceived wonderful events, or by remembering and getting caught up in your past accomplishments.

The process of setting goals simply for the purpose of having more things becomes like a rollercoaster ride. You anticipate the ride and the thrill of it all. You get on board and enjoy the ride. Up, down, around, and upside down. It is definitely thrilling. But, after the ride is over, you get off at the same place you began, ready for a new ride, which will eventually bring you back to the same place again.

I'm not by any means saying that we shouldn't achieve things or have goals. Being achievement oriented is part of being human. Growth comes from your experiences—experiences of anger, sadness, fear, and anxiety. In fact, your challenges can be your best teachers—your only teachers when it comes to growth.

Your fears, anger, etc. offer you an opportunity to let them go and move past them.

Without them you would have no idea what it is you even need to move past in the first place.

There are various levels of being unhappy, but ignorance is number one! We *"ig-nor"* our happiness.

If you focus attention on the present, you can always make it better. And when you improve upon the present, what comes later will also improve. Happiness comes from you, not at you. The key is to treat results, good or not so good, with indifference. An outcome is an outcome, not good or bad, just simply an outcome. It is the result of your own life level. It is where you are. It happened. And you can't escape it no matter how hard you try.

You may be wondering, *'Why can't we just be good, as opposed to bad, then we'll be happy?* The reason is, it is impossible to establish *good* or *bad*. They aren't absolutes.

Good or bad are only judgements or beliefs. They are both just perceptions based on our ignorance of what's really happening. We see a man steal a loaf of bread and say he was bad for doing so. We then discover he took the bread to feed his starving children. Was the act *good* or *bad?* It depends on your perspective, doesn't it? What you *believe* to be good. What you *believe* to be bad. A belief is just your opinion.

During a war, both sides claim to have the support of God on their side. It is very clear to each side they are doing *good*. Both claim to be good, both claim the other to be *bad*. Again, good or bad is not the issue. It's only through seeing reality that you can even hope to find what lies beyond your ideas of good and bad.

Emotional excitement is not being happy either. It is artificial and will eventually let you crash. Again, nothing wrong with getting excited. True happiness is having total freedom from anything that makes you unhappy.

We all have an attachment to the past in some way. This is a characteristic of being human. We see the past as somehow sacred. We fantasize about events gone by long ago. We remember all our mistakes. We hang on to the memories of our failings. But, how could you possibly remain connected to or experience the present when we are preoccupied with feelings and memories from the past? Just remember, the past is gone, the future doesn't exist, and happiness is our natural state; and it only happens in this moment.

I called a friend of mine one day, and his assistant said that he had gone to his mountain cabin to get away for a few days. The next day, I called him at his cabin. I asked if he was enjoying his time away? He said he was spending all his time thinking about problems at the office. I asked him to do himself a favor and take a walk on his property.

During his walk, I asked him to think about nothing else for the next 30 minutes or so, to just observe his surroundings. He called back a while later and shared with me what he had experienced. He said he saw things that he never knew were there. He said, among other things, he saw a beaver, an elk, a bald eagle, and several springs bubbling up out of the ground. He was amazed by his experience, simply by being in that moment.

Take 15 minutes, right now if possible, and take a walk; put all your attention on experiencing the moment and see what happens. Do that every day and you'll be pleasantly surprised by the results—not only what you experience during your walk, but what you will experience as a residual effect the rest of the day.

Just stop and notice once in a while how you spend your whole life trying to "arrive" at some destination. Where is it you think you are going anyway? What is it you feel needs to be accomplished? It is your perception of who you think we are that believes there must be something missing? In reality, everything is perfect just the way it is.

Your pain and suffering come from one source, your resistance to happiness. That's amazing isn't it? We seek happiness at every moment, and at the same time resist happiness, which causes us to seek it even more. In other words, we resist what comes naturally. And when we resist, we actually push it away.

Pain and suffering are what results when you don't allow life to flow without resistance as it should. Stress and hardship occur when you don't accept your fear as a gift that adds to your growth and happiness when you let it go. All your pain comes from the lack of being present with yourself and believing you need something more in order to be happy.

Now, you may think this approach to life is a bit different, or even strange. Most people don't want to believe that life, or happiness, can be that simple. They want to believe that it has to be more difficult, that there needs to be some kind of system, or guru to follow, in order to become happy…someday. By following a system, you only become limited by the system. We've been conditioned to complicate everything, to look for answers outside ourselves, to find someone to offer us a system to follow. We want someone to "feed" us the answers to living a happy life.

Personal development is not what we need. What we need instead is to wake up. If you wake up to the fact that every moment of your life is your teacher, you cannot avoid growing; you cannot avoid happiness.

So, what is happiness? It is living fully in the moment with no attachments to yesterday or tomorrow. We already do this to one degree or another. Think about it. All that you've accomplished in life is a result of the time you've spent living in the moment. All the good memories you have, all the things you have, and all that you have learned, happened in a moment sometime in the past.

It takes courage to let go of the past and give your full attention to the task at hand. When you are eating, simply be with your meal—concentrate on eating. When you are working, concentrate on work. If you are exercising, be with the experience of exercising. If you are with your family or those you love, why not concentrate on being right there with them. Your life is happening right now! Everything else is just a thought about the past or the future. If you are in a conversation with someone, concentrate on being right there with the person instead of letting your thoughts or imagination carry you away to someplace else. Wouldn't that be a more effective way to live your life?

Most of us have been taught we have to figure something out in order for our lives to work, and *that* conditioning is exactly why our lives aren't working the way we wish they would.

Having feelings of unhappiness is not a requirement. Letting go of non-supportive feelings and emotions is not a requirement. Living in the moment is not a requirement. It is simply a method of ending unhappiness in your life.

So, what does it really mean to stay focused on the present? It means becoming more intimately and consciously aware of the input from your senses, to become more fully observant of what is really going on in your world, inside as well as outside. Begin to pay attention to how you think and feel. Begin to observe the words you speak and the actions you take.

When you can "be" happiness, you can "find" happiness. Forget the left-brain programming you've learned from society. Shut out the logic and reason that tells you to keep bringing up the past in order to protect you from being hurt again. Instead hook yourself up to your intuition, hook yourself up to this moment. Use all your senses. Begin today to be happy. Smell happiness, taste it, see it, feel it, and think it. If you begin to pay close attention to the present, you can always improve upon it. If you improve upon the present, what comes later will also be better. Yes, by all means plan for your future, take action, achieve great things, get wealthy, but let go of the past and live in the present where the action takes place.

When you can be happy, you can find happiness. Do not pursue happiness, it cannot be caught. What you become is what you'll experience.

THREE

Letting Go

Letting go of whatever is wrong in your life must always precede creating what is right.

What if you owned a factory where you manufactured beautiful dining room furniture? What would you need to produce the product? You would probably need a clear vision of the product you wanted to produce. You would need a set of plans or a blueprint to follow showing how to build the furniture. You would also need raw materials: wood, paint, sandpaper, pegs, brackets, castors, shipping crates, and all the other materials needed to build furniture. You would need to know how many pieces you were going to be able to manufacture in a given period of time within the space you occupy. And of course, you would need a designated workplace where you assembled the furniture. You would also need a place where you discarded all the waste materials: the paint cans, wood shavings, pieces of wood, saw dust, worn out sandpaper, etc.

What would happen if you didn't toss the waste out of your manufacturing area for a day? You might still be able to function by stepping over the waste. What about waiting for two days? How about three, a week, or a month? At some point it would be very difficult to get around and work efficiently, wouldn't it? And eventually, if you didn't clean the waste out of your workplace, you'd be out of business.

Now let's consider the human body. Your body is like a factory as well. In your factory, you have a vision to stay healthy and productive. You might even have a place where you exercise, a garden to grow fresh vegetables, sort of a blueprint of how you would keep yourself healthy. You attempt to take care of your health as best you can. You stock your kitchen with the best raw materials:

food, drink, vitamins, etc. You consume all these raw materials in hopes of achieving your vision of health and vitality.

Your body then digest and assimilates the food, water, and other nutrients from your chosen sources in order to keep your organs healthy and vibrant. And of course, just like the furniture factory, our bodies give off waste. What do you think would happen to your body if you didn't get rid of the waste? After a day or two you'd probably get a little uncomfortable, and unable to perform at your optimum—similar to working in the factory with waste piled high. Next, you might start feeling a little tired, and you can't think clearly because your body is working harder than it should. Then, sickness would set in. Eventually, if we never eliminated the waste, you would be out of business. In other words, your body would die.

What about your mental and emotional factory? Do you think you have waste you need to get rid of? Yes. We all do, and lots of it! You have a vision of how you would like your life to be. We all basically want some of the same things. We want to be happy, healthy, successful, to be well balanced, have satisfying work, some fun, and peace of mind.

Our mental factory also utilizes raw materials. However, the whole world becomes our warehouse of raw materials, as well as our workshop. We get our raw materials from many sources: our work environment, family, the books we read, the people with whom we associate, the news, television, mail, traffic, personal experiences, relaxation, noise, fun time, nature, etc. Within the time span of scrolling through Facebook, we can hear about the latest weight loss craze—lose 29 pounds in 30 days, someone famous commits suicide, aliens spotted over New Jersey, top 10 investments to attain financial freedom, mass shootings, tainted foods, vaccines, genetic engineering, and more!

We have a hundred decisions to make in our business. We have to decide what the best use is of our money. We have to think about the family, our relationships, and our health. We hear about wars, riots, murders, etc., all of which are attempting to create an emotional response within us, to get us to pay attention.

We also have a lot of good material from which to make our choices as well. But a lot of the input, or raw material, we receive every day is designed to create a negative emotional response. When was the last time you saw "good news" on a television station? That is because good news doesn't sell.

Anyway, here we are with all this raw material to choose from to produce a happy, joyful life.

We gather it, process it, decide what we want to utilize, and we eliminate the rest. Right? Wrong!

We leave a lot more than we need just lying around, just in case we need it for later. What about all those past mistakes, pains, hurts, and failures? Well, we just never know when we might need one of those to protect us from the same thing happening again. What about that time when you got fired from your job? You don't want to let that anger toward your former boss go, do you? You might need that one for the next boss. What about that failed marriage or relationship? You don't want to repeat that one again, do you? Better hang onto that for sure, just for protection and to remind you of how bad a marriage can be! We want to remember all the sad details so we don't find ourselves in another situation like that one.

We all have more information coming through our mental factory needing processing in a day's time than we could effectively handle in a week. What happens over time if we don't eliminate the waste from our mental and emotional factory? Here's what happens: stress, loneliness, anxiety, worry, depression, fear, exhaustion, time pressure, doubt, feelings of being victimized, overwhelmed, feelings of being out of control, not sure about your future. Could the excess emotional waste we don't let go of cause these kinds of responses? Could they take their toll on your happiness and peace of mind? Could hanging on to these things affect you physically, causing responses such as high blood pressure, stress, anxiety, cancer, heart attacks, and the like? You bet they can, and they do!

Here's the problem we all face. Our lives have become much too complicated. Compared to a couple of thousand years ago, or even 50 years ago, when we received an hour of input, we had a week to process it. Today, it's a little more intense. We receive a week's worth of input in a single day, and we have only an hour to process it.

So, what is the solution? The solution is to learn to quickly recognize and let go of those thoughts, feelings, emotions, and behaviors that no longer support your vision of how you want your life to be.

If watching or reading the news or reading the newspaper in the morning supports you, then you should read or watch it. I have personally never read a newspaper, and I don't watch the news; and I don't think I've missed anything. I get all my news through rumors. All I am saying is that if it is not supportive to your life, then you should let it go and find something more productive to do with your time. Maybe a half hour of meditation, or a long walk might do you more good.

If the upset you had at the office this morning, yesterday, or last week supports your life and makes it better, hang on to it. If not, why not let it go and move on? Maybe you have to deal with the upset tomorrow, but don't let it consume you today. We all want to have our lives work better, yet we continue to hang on to those things that keep us in a non-resourceful, upset and unhappy state.

Here's a question for you. Which is more productive, the action you take from a position of upset, or the action you take from being clear about what you want? In other words, is it more productive to take action from a clear mind and open heart, or through the filters of yesterday's upset? We should all stand back and observe our behaviors, what we are hanging onto, and see what's working and what we need to let go of.

If you were creating an arrangement of roses, at some point you would probably step back and observe, maybe move a flower or two, until you got it just the way you wanted it. Our lives should be treated in a similar manner. We observe ourselves combing our hair, getting dressed, etc., but do we truly look at ourselves and how we function on a day-to-day basis? Begin to look at yourself as you hang onto your drama. Watch yourself as you hang onto feeling sorry for yourself, or when you are stressed with anxiety. Observe yourself as you latch onto and play a role in someone else's drama. Watch yourself as you cling to all those personal problems, as you feel stressed as a result of your need to be right or to control how someone else is acting. Watch yourself when you feel you have to be in control of every outcome. Observe yourself as you hang onto that state of anger as a form of protection in order to avoid some pain or in order to prove you are right.

That is what I mean by hanging onto your drama. We say we want to be free of our problems, but the real truth is we don't! In fact, we love our problems, and we love our drama. Why? Because we are addicted to them, that's why! We want to complain about how awful things are, what other people did to us, how broke we are, and how life is not fair. We unconsciously want to feel the way we do in order to justify not taking responsibility for where we are in life, and to avoid the pain associated with changing. It is so much easier to just blame someone else, or an outside circumstance, for where you are in life. "I can't because" is what we say in order to keep pretending we are not in control of our lives.

Happiness or unhappiness, success or failure, stress or peace of mind, healthy or unhealthy all boil down to a question of what you honor. Ask yourself this question: "Which do I honor the most, the life I really want to live, or my circumstances, my drama?" With mathematical accuracy, we will always create exactly what we *honor* the most. Remember, the *Law of Cause and Effect* is always working whether you acknowledge it or not. It works the same for everyone. We all cause the effect in our lives.

I recently had a call from an acquaintance, telling me that he was thinking of getting involved in a new home-based business. He knew that I taught a course for entrepreneurs, and he wanted to know if I thought it would be a viable business. After he filled me in on the details, I told him I believed it could be a great business and that I thought he would be very good at it. He shared with me how excited he was about all he planned to accomplish once he got his new business under way. I asked him when he planned to get started? He said he was going to just as soon as he tied up some loose ends. He explained that the IRS was after him for back taxes, so he had to take care of that first. He said he was going through a divorce, and there was a possibility that his job may not last much longer, among several other things. It was a depressing list of reasons, or rather excuses. He said he was going to get started in his new business and create the new life he wanted just as soon as he took care of all those things.

I asked him, "Which do you honor the most, the vision of the new life you want to create, or your circumstances?"

His answer was, "I honor my vision the most, of course."

So, I said, "Then why are you going to wait to get started with your new business until all your problems are resolved?"

He said, "I just told you why I can't," and proceeded to go back through his list of excuses.

I said, "So, what you're telling me is, you honor your *stuff* more than your new life plan. What you're telling me is, you honor the IRS, the divorce you are going through, and the possibility of losing your job, more than your vision. That's your choice."

We always act upon and create what we honor the most in our lives. What you have in the future will always be based upon what you honor the most in the present. And what you have in the present, is totally based upon what you have honored in the past, nothing more, nothing less. The more you let go of and cease to honor your distresses, the less you will need to complain about how things are and the more productive you become.

Here's the thing about problems. When you finally get through with your problems, you'll be finished with those, but there will be a whole new set of problems that appear in their place. There will always be things we're dealing with that we use as an excuse for not doing well, not following our dreams, or not getting started today. If we wait until all our problems are resolved before taking action, we will always be waiting, because all of our problems will never be resolved. Problems are a part of life. Just don't make them your focus. Handle them, yes. But don't let them consume you.

Letting go of the feelings, behaviors, and emotions that keep us stuck is the answer. Letting go is simple and easy. For example, if I am holding a book in my hand, that doesn't mean I have to hold it in my hand for the rest of my life. I can lay it down. And if I want, I can choose to never pick it up again. Letting go is about making the right choice and not letting old subconscious programs keep you stuck.

If you find yourself needing acceptance from others, that means you haven't let go of your need for acceptance. It means you are honoring your need for acceptance more than your peace of mind. If you find yourself needing to control others, or outside circumstances over which you have no control, you haven't let go. The more you make a conscious effort to let go of those things that no longer serve your greater good, the more you'll begin to discover who you really are and what you're really capable of doing in life. Letting go of what's wrong in your life must always precede creating what's right. Letting go is always a choice. We justify hanging on in order to keep pretending we are not responsible for how we feel or that our situation is caused by some outside circumstance.

Your life is not about the lessons you may think you are here to learn, as most people believe.

Your life is about discovering who you really are and the gifts you have to offer to the world. It is about uncovering the real you. Waking up to who you are requires letting go of who you imagine yourself to be. When you begin to let go of what is false, you automatically exist in what is true. The real you does not have to hang onto anything, or learn anything, because you already *are* everything.

There will always be incompetent and irresponsible people around you. At times, there may be a lack of money, good jobs, vacations, and opportunities. There will always be all sorts of unexpected circumstances. The traffic will always be too heavy when you are in a hurry. There will always be rainy days and Mondays. There will sometimes not be a parking space. There will always be stupid people. You may not have a choice about what sometimes gets handed to you in life, but here's what you do have a choice about. You have a choice about how you handle what is handed to you. What you do about what is handed to you is a choice.

Most of us keep our minds in a state of being immobile. Our minds are on hold, like a telephone with 10 lines, all blinking at once, all waiting for us to answer! There is so much going on that we don't know what to do or which line to answer first. So, what do we do? We avoid the ones we don't want to handle right now, and we keep them on hold until later—but at the high cost of taking up space in your mental factory. Just like a multiple line telephone system, our brain is holding all those unresolved experiences, all taking up space, all creating certain kinds of emotional responses, and giving us the same messages over and over. We put off, or suppress, the messages we don't want to deal with and dodge the ones that might cause us pain or discomfort.

There's a line holding for every person you haven't forgiven. There's one holding for every emotional hurt you've encountered and haven't resolved. There's a line holding for literally every unresolved experience you've had in your life. Because of all the pressure created by all the lines you have on hold and haven't resolved, you begin to take an "automatic" position on some of the current issues you have to deal with. In other words, we deal with them based upon past programming, which is not necessarily the truth of the situation.

Let's say you're in sales. You're making a sales call, but you're still hanging onto the "no" that you received from your past four calls. What's happening is that you are now making your new sales call looking through the filters of a past experience. The real question is this, does hanging on support your vision of making an effective sales call and a new sale? No, of course not! Why? It is because you are taking action from a place of fear, and that is what you'll create more of in return. Cause and effect.

Another example might be that you are entering into a new relationship, hoping it will be better than the last one. At the same time, you are still holding onto the hurt from the last relationship.

You are hanging onto and remembering your past experience, so that you won't make the same mistake again. You are going into the new relationship looking through your filters from your last experience, your past programming of failure or hurt. So, you enter this new relationship with a closed heart. The chances of making the new relationship work with this approach is roughly zero percent. Why?

It's because we always get that which we honor the most. We create what we're projecting out to the world. And what we are projecting, or honoring, is fear! Cause and effect.

So, the questions are: How do you resolve the issue? How do you reduce the number of lines on hold? How do you let go? How do you stop the pain? How do you let go of the fear? How do you experience more love in your life? How do you accept others? How do you let go of the past without losing control of your life in the present?

Let me ask you a question. How did you learn to walk, to ride a bicycle, to swim, or to drive a car? For that matter, how did you learn to interpret the words you are reading right now? Did someone tell you what takes place in your brain in order to learn to listen and interpret? Did someone tell you what takes place in your body in order to take a single step? Did someone explain to you how each muscle and tendon had to work in concert, and how messages have to come from your brain in order to start the process?

Or one day, perhaps you just up and said, "I've had it with all this crawling around on my knees. I'm going to learn to walk!" One day, you just decided you were going to learn to ride a bicycle, read a book, or drive a car. You instinctively knew that the only way to do these things was to simply do it.

Letting go is just like learning to do any of these things. It takes basically four things to let go: self-observation, intention, willingness, and commitment. However, if you choose to hang on to your old programs, it also requires the same four things: lack of self-observation, intention, willingness, and commitment.

You let go of things every day. All you really need to do is become more conscious of the process and not complicate it. Being more conscious means becoming more self-observant. You are in charge. You are the CEO, the observer of your brain and what it tells you to do.

I suppose you could live with unwanted emotions and behaviors for a while longer. That's your choice. But I don't think you'll really want to hang onto them for the rest of your life, do you? The very fact that you are reading this book tells me you are tired of how you are feeling and the results you are producing. Is that not true?

To begin the letting go process, you must be willing to "tune in," and observe your feelings and behaviors; determine which feels painful and which feels pleasant. Then, you must make an effort to consciously let go of the painful ones. This requires self-observation, intention, willingness, and commitment. You have to observe what you are feeling and the actions you are about to take. Then, you have to have the intention to let the feeling go or take a different course of action, or both. Next, you have to be willing to let it go; then you must commit to letting it go. And, the most important thing of all is to become more self-observant of your feelings and behaviors by asking yourself, "Is this feeling or behavior moving me in the direction I want to go?"

Let's say for example, you find yourself in an abusive or unfulfilling relationship, stuck financially, or anything else that may be holding you back in life. In fact, think of something right now that you feel is holding you back from the life you want. Get in touch with how that makes you feel. Then, ask yourself these questions:

"Do I like feeling this way?" If the answer is "No" move to the next question.

"Do I want to let it go?" If the answer is "Yes" move to the next question.

"Am I willing to let it go?" If the answer is "Yes" move to the last and most important question of all.

"When? When are you willing to let it go?" The correct answer is "Now."

There's really nothing mysterious about feelings or behaviors, or about letting them go, once you truly understand what they are in the first place—simply trapped energy created from past experiences and attached to old subconscious programming that no longer serves your greater good. This fear, anger, sadness, doubt, etc., are nothing more than trapped energy patterns that have been developed through your past experiences. Think about it. If you didn't have a past, would you have doubts, fears, anger, etc.? No, of course not. If you had no past, you would have no emotions, because emotions are created from feelings trapped in place as a result of your past experiences.

Most of the time we think of events as having a starting and ending point. But do they really?

What about the words you are reading right now? Stop reading for a minute. Where are the words you just read? They really don't exist anymore once you look away, do they? When you've finished reading the whole book, where is it? Where are the words? There are no words anymore. All that's left are the memory patterns that were put there by the spell that was cast by the sound of the words as you read them and how you experienced them. All that is left are the memory patterns and feelings created by the impact, or your experience, of the words you just read. And the memory patterns are at best, incomplete. We remember only the words and concepts that *impact* us in some way, and thus create an attached feeling.

When we organize a group of letters in a certain sequence, it creates a word, doesn't it? We call that *spelling*. Think about the word *'spelling.'* What do you think it means? Spelling is *"The organization and structuring of letters into a word."* But here is another definition that is more powerful, *"To cast a spell."* When we organize a group of letters into a certain sequence and speak the word to someone else, like I am speaking to you right now. As you read, I am actually casting a *spell* on you, the receiver. I am also casting a spell on me, the one transmitting the words.

Even when you think a thought about someone else, that word in your thought casts a spell on both of you, the sender as well as the receiver. That's right. Even if you think a thought toward another, it has an effect on both of you. It casts a spell on both of you.

What about the word *'sentence?'* A sentence is the organization of a series of *spelling* words. A series of words that cast spells. The power of a sentence is much stronger than a single word by itself. It doesn't just cast a *spell*, it pronounces a *sentence* on the sender and receiver. As an example, yelling at a child in a state of emotional rage, *sentences* that child to a life of emotional scars that may never heal.

And at the same time, it further suppresses the anger of the sender. That is how we got many of our programs, the dramas we're all dealing with today. And until we make a choice to do it differently, to let go and move past them, we will remain as prisoners of our own programming. Our *sentence* will keep us locked up in our self-created prison, until we make a conscious choice to take a different approach.

The question should always be, "Is the language I'm using, the spell I'm casting, empowering to both the sender and receiver? Is the feeling I'm hanging onto, or the emotion I'm experiencing, moving me closer to or further away from what I would love to have in my life?"

Try this exercise: recall a past upset. Maybe a conflict, or an argument you had with someone.

Next, remember when the tension or upset first began. Now, recall when you felt the most intense about the issue. Let's call that the middle. And last, recall when it was over and you were relaxed once again (if it is actually over). How long has it been from the first upset to the ending, or until now if it is not yet over.

You may have experienced an upset this morning at the office, and by now it is gone. You have let it go. On the other hand, I've had people in my workshops that have been hanging onto an upset for 30 to 40 years and more! They have refused to let it go all those years. They have had the intention, willingness, and commitment to hang on, not knowing they can let it go. Think of the damage done and the time lost hanging on for that many years.

And in some cases, they say they *want* to let it go, but they aren't *willing* to do so. They want to hang on, thinking it provides them some sort of protection from it never happening again, or they are somehow punishing the other person by hanging on. Some are actually afraid to let go. They believe that letting go is being passive, that they'll get walked on again if they do. Letting go is not being passive at all. Letting go is about high action and low attachment. It's about taking action from a resourceful place rather than a place of fear.

It's impossible to experience self-love when we're hanging onto self-hate or hating someone else. It always comes down to the question of what you honor. Which is more peaceful and productive? Taking action from upset or action from a peaceful place? By letting go of the upset, you can then see more clearly the real situation and what needs to be done to resolve it. Not what would make you feel good, or help avoid some temporary pain, but what the right solution is for all involved.

In other words, without first letting go of upset, we can't *see* reality, we can't see the truth, and we aren't open for the right solution. And maybe the right solution is to simply let go and do nothing.

But, without first seeing the truth, you wouldn't know the right solution if it hit you in the face!

Hanging on to an upset creates a connection between you and that event or person. It creates what I call a *"chain of pain."* When you hang on to an old upset you've had with another, you create a chain of pain between the two of you. What's really happening when you hang on, is you create a "vibrational harmony" with that person or condition, which in turn creates more of the same. Until the chain is broken, you will continue to respond again and again in the same way. This will continue until you take responsibility and break the chain. Letting go breaks the chain of pain.

Anything you cling to will eventually cause you pain. Let's say you are in the habit of having a couple cups of coffee every morning when you first get up. What if one morning you didn't get to have your two cups of coffee? What happens around 10:00 AM? Right, a headache, a withdrawal symptom. Anything we cling to will eventually cause us pain.

A few years ago, a woman in my workshop shared with the group that she had had a bitter argument with her mother, which resulted in her mother not speaking to her for the past 20 years. She tried numerous times to make amends, but her mother wouldn't respond. She would call, leave messages, and write letters, but her mother would never answer. The daughter shared how upset she was with her mother, how much she loved her, and at the same time, how angry she was toward her for not responding. She was deeply hurt.

I worked with the woman for about 15 minutes, helping her to let go of the feelings and emotions she had toward her mother. She wanted acceptance from her mother, and she also wanted to control her mother's actions. This was on Saturday, the first day of the seminar around three o'clock in the afternoon.

The next day, when she arrived at class, she was overwhelmed with joy! She shared with the group that upon arriving at home around six o'clock, she checked her messages, and to her surprise, she had one from her mother after 20 years of no contact. Her mother said, "I was just thinking that this anger has gone on between us long enough. Could we get together and resolve the issue?" And guess what time the message came in from her mother? It was shortly after 3:00 PM Saturday—within minutes after she had let go of her resentment toward her mother in the class.

You could call it a coincidence, I suppose. What really happened was that she finally took responsibility for her own feelings toward her mother, and when she did, the chain of pain, the energetic connection, between her and her mother was broken. It takes two to keep the chain connected. Or, you could call it a coincidence. All she really needed to do was take responsibility for how *she* felt, not how her mother felt. She needed to let go of her resentment and anger toward her mother. And with that, she was no longer in "vibrational harmony" with the conflict. We are the problem, and at the same time, we are the solution.

To let go is defined as, "To be open to other possibilities. To let alone. To lose one's hold of. To behave in an unrestrained way." Letting go sets your emotional counter back to zero.

E-motion: *"Energy in motion."* When you let go, you are taking the non-resourceful energy out-of-motion. Why would you want to get back to zero? At zero point, you can just *"be,"* with no attachments to outcomes. You can connect with people without the filters of past experiences or fears of future anticipated ones.

You get hurt by others, not because of what they say or do, but because you demand they should say and do what you expect. When you let go of your demands, people can then act as they wish, and at the same time, you can remain at peace. Doesn't that make more sense than hanging on and destroying your own happiness and peace of mind? These old "pop-ups" or "inner dialog" prevent you from truly being in the present and really connecting with yourself or the other person.

In most of our relationships in life, we connect with others through our "roles," our filters within our dramas, created from our core beliefs. In other words, we connect based on who we want others to think we are vs. who we really are. The main reason we sometimes feel disconnected from others is because of all our "stuff" gets in the way of being who we really are. Letting go and getting to point zero allows you to truly connect on a deeper level, heart-to-heart.

Instead of just living our lives as they are, the reality is that we spend most of our time, and most of our energy, keeping our "stuff" alive by trying to control everything so our drama keeps making sense. That is probably why so many are so tired all the time. When we feel a need to control a situation, we don't realize that we remain out of control. However, when we let go of our need to be in control, we are now in complete control. More on this later.

When you detach yourself from a non-resourceful feeling, you also detach yourself from the stress it causes in your life. One moment of letting go is worth more to your growth than a thousand hours of intellectual information and stimulation.

Many believe that letting go is an anxious pursuit to find new solutions to their problems. On the contrary, letting go is not a pursuit at all. What letting go does is create a space for new solutions to come to you. When you're in hot pursuit to find answers, you are in a non-resourceful state, in a state of chasing solutions, or should I say, pushing solutions away while stifling your imagination and creativity.

Letting go lets you live in the present, where the action is, and where solutions appear!

Letting go is living in a state of love.

Letting go lets you do what you do with love.

Letting go lets you raise more empowered children.

Letting go lets you enjoy a more fulfilling relationship.

Letting go lets you be more productive at work.

Letting go lets you live a healthier life.

Letting go lets you live free of anxiety and stress.

Letting go lets you be the true person that you are.

Your inner emotional world is really no different than your outer physical world. As an example, if you severely cut our hand, you wouldn't just sit around trying to figure out why you caused this to happen, what your "lesson" was in all this, or what the real meaning was behind it. You wouldn't just let it bleed and do nothing about it, so that you would clearly remember your lesson. No! You would go to the doctor, get some stitches, stop the bleeding; and you'd probably go there as fast as you could. The first message is very clear, "My hand is severely cut." And the second message is, "Take action right now to stop the bleeding!"

The very same thing should apply to an inner hurt. Heal the pain first by letting go, then if you want to analyze it, go ahead. Of course, once you let go and it's healed, you'll have no reason at all to analyze it. Why? Because the problem will probably be gone, and if it's not, you can now take resourceful action to solve it. The only reason you feel compelled to analyze it in the first place is because it hurts. And it hurts only because you're hanging on and analyzing it! Letting go is a choice to break free of an addiction. Of course, *not* letting go is also a choice. "I can't let go, or I don't have time to let go," is how we justify or pretend that we're not responsible or in control of how we feel or the choices we make. It takes no effort at all to let go. It's simple and natural. It's like a tree shedding its leaves in the fall. They drop what they no longer need in order to make room for the new in the spring.

Right now, think of something that you're hanging onto, an old hurt, resentment, anger because of an argument, a fear, or a worry. Get in touch with how that makes you feel. Notice where you feel the feeling in your body. Let it grow in strength. Let the emotion come up to the surface.

Now consider the following questions:

1. Does feeling this help you to move in the direction you want?
2. Do you like feeling that way? That's self-observation.
3. Do you want to let it go? That's intention.
4. Are you willing to let it go? That's willingness.
5. When are you willing to let it go? That's a commitment.

If you hesitated on any of these questions, you need to go back, observe the feeling once again, and reconsider until you are sure you don't like feeling that way. Some do. They feel it provides them with some sort of protection that will keep the event from happening again or as a means of staying in control. You also have to be sure that you want to let it go. I've talked with people before that absolutely refuse to want to let it go. You have to *want to*. Otherwise, there is no way to let go.

Are you *willing* to let it go? This step becomes a little tougher. Being willing says you are willing to take responsibility for what's happening in your life. That you will no longer be able to use this as an excuse for being unhappy or whatever.

And the final one is, when? That's the really hard one. *When* are you willing to let it go? That's making a commitment to do it right now.

First, it's self-observation, then the key words are, *want to, willing to,* and *when!* Self-observation, intention, willingness, and commitment. In fact, to do anything requires intention, willingness, and commitment. Doing nothing requires intention, willingness, and commitment. Hanging on requires intention, willingness, and commitment.

As I have mentioned before, there's only one major difference between hanging on or letting go. Letting go requires *no* energy at all, only a choice. Whereas hanging on requires a lot of energy! That is also a choice.

FOUR

Self-Observation

Self-observation allows you to clearly understand what you are seeing rather than being controlled by it. You could call it self-management.

A number of years, ago a woman approached me following a seminar I was presenting.

She said she had heard about this letting go stuff and was experiencing some conflicts in her life that she hadn't been able to resolve.

She asked me, "If attended your two-day seminar, can you give me a system that I can use to transform my life?"

My immediate response was, "No, my seminar will not transform your life. And my answer to the second part of your question is, there is no system that I know of that can transform your life."

She asked, "But I thought you offered a system for people to follow that will lead to personal transformation?"

"No," I said, "I only present ideas that have worked in my own life. As far as transformation," I said, "That is your choice. It's up to you what you do with the information. It's up to you what direction you take and what information you choose to utilize."

Transformation is a choice that begins with self-awareness. The definition of self-awareness is, *"Having knowledge or realization of oneself."* In other words, in order to experience transformation, you must first become aware of the fact that transformation is needed in the first place.

There's a story about a successful entrepreneur. One morning, he was out for a drive along a deserted country road when his attention was drawn toward some sort of activity out in the middle of a field. As he got closer, he noticed a man running around under a huge tree. As he got even closer, he saw that it was a farmer running around under a huge apple tree chasing about 200 tiny little pigs. The man observed the situation for about an hour. The farmer would run around this apple tree and finally catch a baby piglet. He would then hold it up to the tree and let the pig eat an apple off the tree. Then he put the pig down and would begin chasing another. And again, as he caught a pig, he would hold it up to the tree and let it eat an apple. He continued the same process over and over.

Finally, the entrepreneur thought, there must surely be a better, more efficient method. So, he decided to walk out into the field and have a chat with the man.

He approached the farmer and said, "Excuse me, sir. I've been watching you for about an hour now, and would you mind telling me what you are doing?"

The farmer responded by saying, "Well I'm feeding these apples to my pigs." He said, "They like apples."

The man said, "I'm a bit confused. Why don't you just pick all the apples off the tree, throw them on the ground, and let the pigs run around and eat the apples? Wouldn't that save a lot of time?"

And the farmer responded back with, "Well, what's time to a pig?"

Do you think there might be a better way? Of course, at least from your perspective as an observer, but how about from the farmer's perspective? Probably not, otherwise he would be using it. In so many ways, so many of us are like the farmer. We are locked into our core beliefs and habits so firmly that we don't even stop to think there could be a better way.

If we are doing something a certain way, and we've always done it that way—and we don't even suspect there could be a better way—then chances are we'll continue doing it the way we've always done it.

My point… in order to *attain* a different result, what has to happen? You have to *do* something different. In order to *do* something different, you must first *know* something different to do. And in order to *know* something different to do, you have to first *suspect* that your present method needs improving. That is called awareness.

There is no system that I or anyone else could offer to change anyone's perceptions unless they thought they needed improving and were open to a new and better way. I may offer you some ideas, but you have to take the initiative and observe your own methods, your own actions and beliefs, then only you can make the choice to change your methods, or to self-transform. As an example, if I believe a certain thing to be true, or if I believe that my way is the only way or the best way, then I will be heavily invested in protecting what I believe. Some will go to any extreme to prove to themselves and the outside world that what they believe is true. On the other hand, if something or someone wakes them up to the truth or to a better way, and they discover they do have a choice, they then free themselves to look with a new perspective and begin the process of transformation.

Your core beliefs are what hold you back. For example, you may be experiencing financial struggle; therefore, you say, *"I am broke!"* Or you may possess a certain degree from college, let's say in psychology; therefore, you say, *"I am a psychologist."* Or you may say, *"I resent successful people;"* therefore *"I am resentful."* These are all beliefs we develop from which we live our lives and form our circumstances. Our beliefs have become so imprinted on our self-identity that we have built powerful support systems to reassure one another that what we do, what we believe, and what we have is who we are.

Here is a truth you may find hard to believe. All beliefs are false! That's right. Just think of any belief you have and prove it to be true. A belief is something you decide is true. It may not be true at all. It may be only true for you. I may believe that it's cold outside and you may believe it is comfortable. Which is true? Neither and both. But your belief is only true for you and mine for me.

So how do you change a belief? Intention is the starting point for changing beliefs. In order to make a permanent change, you must first have the intention to understand yourself and see the truth. For example, let's say a person says they are broke. They say that the reason they are broke is because of high taxes, inflation, the economy, education, or whatever. The question is, "Is that true?" And the answer is, "Yes." It is true for that person. But is it true for all?

The questions are: "How did I come to believe this? Who taught me to believe this way? What if they didn't know the truth? What if it's not true?" And more importantly, "Who would I be without this belief?"

Self-knowledge—seeing the truth—is the beginning of wisdom. Self-knowledge cannot be given to you by learning a system or from someone else. No one can ever see the truth inside you. You have to see it within. If your intention to know yourself is weak, then just a casual wish or hope to change is of very little significance.

We seem to always want to change outside circumstances, other people, the government, our relationships, our job, and so on, in an attempt to change our lives. Change outside circumstances and surroundings, and eventually you will be right back in the same situation. *All* transformation begins with self-knowledge, from knowing who you are and your beliefs about life. Because, without knowing who we are, there is no foundation for correct thinking. There is no reality. And without a foundation for correct thinking based upon self-knowledge, there can be no transformation. Seeing the truth is the only starting point.

Have you ever heard the statement, *"The truth will set you free?"* The truth begins with an understanding of that which you are without distortion. That's what the statement means. It is not referring to merely telling the truth, although that's a good place to start, but rather understanding or *seeing* the truth about yourself and how you arrived where you are today. That's where transformation begins. In fact, that's the only place it can begin. Reality is essential. Reality gives you true freedom, the freedom to change your circumstances. Reality comes from the understanding of what is, not what you believe it to be, or think it should be. When you're working toward reality through some system that someone else has created for you to follow, that's called *postponement*. Following someone else's system is called the cover-up of what is, with what we would like it to be.

Letting go is not a system. It is a way of life. In order to create a new life and let go of the old one, you must want to know reality. You must want to know the truth. All the goal setting, vision boards, lie on the floor exercises, are all temporary patchwork solutions.

Without knowing the truth, there is no freedom. Without freedom, there can be no transformation. Difficulty and conflict arise because we are unwilling to look at the truth.

We want a system to avoid the pain of seeing the truth, but knowing the truth is where all transformation starts. By following a system of any kind, you will merely produce a result that is created by the system itself, which will always be limited. The result of a system will obviously not be self-understanding. Without self-understanding there can be no basis for truth, or change, in your life. How could there possibly be? All systems are, by their very nature, limited and not based in reality for each individual, because we are each different.

For example, let's say you decide to follow a system of using affirmations as a method of transforming your life. While affirmations may change your mind temporarily, or even in some cases permanently, they will certainly not provide you a method for *seeing* truth. Only you can know the truth when *you* see it. No one can teach it to you. A system, on the other hand, may provide you with some sort of tool or method that may help you *see* your truth. Letting go is a tool not a system. For example, following a discipline of meditation one hour everyday will not show you the truth, but it may provide you with the quiet time you need to slow down your mind long enough to see the truth.

By living your life according to some preset pattern, it can't be reality based because a set pattern does not lead to self-understanding. If God had meant for us to follow a set system, he would not have created everyone as unique individuals. He would have cut only one pattern for the entire human race or given us a set system to follow.

Someone once asked me, "Well what about the Bible? Isn't that a system designed for everyone to follow?" Yes, it is a system, but each individual must experience and interpret it for themselves in order to know it to be true. I once heard The Dalai Lama speak and someone asked which religion was the correct one to the exclusion of all others. His answer, "There should be as many religions on the planet as there are people." You will never find two people who interpret the Bible exactly the same. Just look at the number and variations of religions that are all based on the Bible, but slightly different in their beliefs. Believing in a certain religion is only an opinion, a belief, that you see as the right thing to do for you. And as I mentioned earlier, all beliefs are false until you decide it is true. And then, it is only true for you. Any system that does not cause you to look at yourself is at best, incomplete.

Everyone is searching for the correct path to the truth, but the real truth is that there is no correct path, except the one you create for yourself. The only method I know for gaining truth is through self-observation. It means being in touch with what's going on around you, as opposed to having your view clouded by feelings, emotions, beliefs, and thoughts, or the beliefs and thoughts of those around you.

Don't try this at home, but I heard that if you drop a frog into boiling water, it will immediately jump out. On the other hand, it is said that if you place a frog into lukewarm water and gradually raise the temperature to a boil, he will stay there until he dies.

By the way, that's just a system I heard about, I don't know it to be true! ☺

Unlike a frog, you have the capacity to *see* when you are slipping too far into hot water—into an unhealthy situation. You can stop, observe the situation, and decide if you want to proceed or take a different, more productive course of action. This can only be done, however, if you are willing to see the reality of the situation, then act on what you know to be truth. "This discussion is turning into a heated argument. Should I let go of my need to control or be right?" Remember, it takes two to argue.

Let's say you are driving your car down the road at high speed, and suddenly you see another car in your lane coming directly at you. A head-on collision is about to happen in about three seconds if you don't act fast. So, what do you do? Are you going to take the time and weigh the pros and cons of continuing on your collision course? "Let's see, he is traveling at 60 mph and I'm going 60. That means this is going to be like hitting a brick wall at 120. The odds of surviving are 1 in 50. Now, if my air bags deploy, it might be 1 in 25. And it will be his fault because he's in my lane." No, of course you wouldn't do that! If you are faced with a head–on collision, you are not going to contemplate the situation, you are going to act! You have no other choice, do you? You see the truth. You see reality! You can see that on your current course it could be disastrous, even deadly.

Beliefs are what limit us in the first place. Seeing truth is observing what is actually happening at that moment and making a choice to proceed or take another path.

You can *want* transformation. You can *want* to know the truth. You can *want* to gain greater wisdom. You can have the intention for having all these things, but none of them are possible without self-observation, seeing the truth of the situation and choosing the correct course of action for your greatest good.

Courage is the entry point. Because it takes courage to observe yourself in a situation, or what happened to you in the past, and choose to let go and no longer react to the pain. It takes courage to challenge an old belief and choose to no longer believe that way.

You will always suffer unconsciously what you do not face consciously. So, when a problem or pain arises, ask not, "What do I do now," but rather, "What do I need to understand before taking action?"

Whether you see life as a hardship or an opportunity depends on your view, not your circumstances. And your view will always depend on your core beliefs about life.

Self-observation is where you remain conscious of what you're thinking, feeling, speaking, and of course, your actions. For example, if you observe yourself feeling fearful, if you really step back and observe, you'll begin to see the reasons for your fear.

You'll begin to see the belief behind the fear. You'll begin to see the truth and immediately know which action to take.

Through self-observation you'll see that your fears are simply a series of recurring thoughts, feelings, emotions, reflected in a mirror of how we *believe* life should or shouldn't be. This is all based on our subconscious programming from the past. Some useful, some not. Your fears can also come from how you believe others should or shouldn't be, or how it used to be in the past, or how you expect the future to be, or how you can manipulate people and your circumstances to get what you want. None of which have anything at all to do with what is really happening right now, this moment. And that's the only thing that truly matters, because this moment is the only thing that's truly real.

If someone hurt you in the past, is that real today? Of course not. But if you bring the past into the present, it feels as though it is happening now. If you bring the past or future into the present, it is happening now. Does that mean that it is really happening now? Is that the truth of your situation? The only thing truly holding your fears in place are your beliefs about how things should be.

Self-observation is the key to releasing those fears and changing a belief. Fear exists only in our thoughts and feelings. Amazing, isn't it, to be afraid of our own thoughts and feelings! Self-observation means, "The gathering of information about yourself for analysis." Without gathering data, you don't even know what needs to change. If you don't first gather data and look for the truth in your situation, how would you ever know what you need to change in the first place? Self-observation is about making your fears, feelings, beliefs, and emotions conscious, instead of going round and round on your mental merry-go-round trying so desperately to look and feel better. While at the same time, we continue to avoid the real issues and end up right back in the place we started.

Avoiding these feelings only causes them to become escaping behaviors which create further suppression. When you suppress a feeling it only strengthens the corresponding belief, allowing it to surface at a later time even stronger. We attempt to avoid our feelings so we can escape the pain of change. Feeling guilty or depressed about who you believe you've become, is an escape. When you feel guilty, you begin to create situations that make you feel even more guilty. And again, you don't attract these situations as most believe; you create them based on your view of life. When your focus is on the problem you want to get rid of, you simply create more of the same. Only when you begin to observe and experience yourself as you truly are, do these beliefs, feelings, and behaviors begin to dissolve. When you see the truth behind your situation, that feeling loses its hold on you. Or rather, I should say, you lose your hold on it.

When you truly back away, investigate, and become more self-observant—when you begin to peel off those painful emotional layers—only then do you truly begin to discover who you really are and the power you have to change. When you begin to observe yourself, you begin to see clearly what "is," and you'll also realize that what "was" can't be changed. Remember this: you can learn more from looking inward for a moment, than you can by looking outward for a lifetime.

Some believe that being self-observant is a difficult thing, when in reality, there is nothing simpler. If you can walk across the room and observe yourself doing so, at that moment you are in a state of observation. If you can observe yourself feeling lonely, then you can be free from loneliness. If you cannot bring up your fear, observe it, and let it go, then you are not free and can never be free. If you can observe your fear and allow yourself to experience it, you have let it go. On the other hand, if you observe your fear, then attempt to disassociate yourself from it through some sort of positive thinking, or other mental or evasive maneuver, you are only burying it deeper, leaving it to rear its ugly head again at a later time.

If you truly want transformation, you must start today to observe your every thought, feeling, belief, and emotion, even your language and behaviors. If you discover yourself speaking and acting in a certain way that you don't like, then you must realize that you also have some underlying belief that is causing you to speak and act in that way.

A woman in one of my workshops believed that letting go wouldn't help her solve her problem. She had two things to deal with. The first was to change her belief that letting go wouldn't help. So, I went to work to find her real issue, which was a fear of the unknown. This fear was planted in her subconscious when she lost both her parents in an auto accident when she was eight. She then spent years in an orphanage. She was afraid of letting go of the fear because she was so vested in it. She had identified so strongly with her fear that she thought her story was real forty years later.

She discovered she was using her fear as a form of protection to justify being stuck in many areas of her life. She made choices in all areas of life based on her feeling of abandonment. She couldn't keep her finances in order. She never had a relationship that lasted more than a few months. She would sabotage her relationships and initiate the breakup so she didn't have to experience someone leaving her. Pretty much everything in her life wasn't working because of her fear of abandonment. When she finally let go of the fear, that burden she had been carrying for so many years, she looked about ten years younger.

If you want to change, you must be willing to step out of your comfort zone, endure some pain, and let go even when you don't know what will be there when you do.

In order to make permanent change you must become self-observant, look for, and accept the real truth behind your issue.

Observe how you are when you are alone.

Observe how you are in an uncomfortable situation.

Observe how you are in your relationships.

Observe how you are when you make love.

Observe how you are around in a crowded situation.

Observe how you are when you communicate with a person.

Observe how you are in your work environment.

If you want to make a change, there is nothing about yourself that should not be observed. You don't have to stop everything you're doing just to observe yourself. In fact, when you're being active is the only logical time to be self-observant. If you happen to be doing nothing, you can simply observe yourself doing nothing. You may be surprised at your discoveries. You may find that when you thought you were doing nothing you were still doing something so that you didn't have to confront the real issue. You may discover that you have a problem just being with yourself. Any aspect about yourself that you don't observe remains unclear. And without self-observation and clarity, everything will always seem to be outside your control.

Self-observation lets you figure out your own nonproductive beliefs, feelings, and behaviors and make conscious that which has been unconscious. Self-observation means developing the habit of checking in with yourself before taking action, or when you are feeling stuck or uncomfortable. There is no reality in the absence of observation. Observation creates reality.

I remember when I was on my way to the airport and running late. Of course, the traffic was at a standstill. It seemed to me that the traffic was there to hold me up and create some stress. I got totally caught up in the traffic and truly felt it was all there just to slow me down. You've been there I'm sure.

What I really needed to do was observe my problem from a higher perspective. First, to let go of my impatience. Second, to stop trying to control something that was beyond my control. And when I really looked at it, I was part of the problem. I was part of the traffic. As soon as I let go of my impatient feelings and accepted that I was stuck in traffic and there was nothing I could do about it, the traffic began to move right along. I'm not saying that letting go moved the traffic. All I'm saying is, when faced with a situation over which you have no control, let go of your need to control it.

Often, I get asked what the difference between self-awareness and self-observation is.

Imagine for a moment you are standing in the middle of the freeway, in between two lanes of traffic. There is traffic about a foot on either side of you, traveling at 70 miles per hour. Got the picture? How would you feel? You probably wouldn't feel very comfortable, would you? In fact, you would more than likely feel immobilized and afraid to move at all. You are aware of where you are, and you don't like it. That's called self-awareness.

What if you were on the side of the freeway, observing the traffic from there? You are still close to the traffic, aren't you? But it wouldn't feel quite so intimidating. You would still be aware of the traffic, but you could observe it from a little higher viewpoint.

What if you backed off a little further and observed the traffic from, let's say, 500 feet in the air in a helicopter. It would not appear threatening at all. What if you were in an airplane at 5000 feet and observed the traffic from there? It might look like a beautiful rainbow-colored ribbon woven through the landscape. That's called observation.

Self-awareness is knowing you are aware of the issue, like *"I am angry."* Whereas self-observation is separating yourself from the issue and observing your experience of anger. You can now discover the real issue, the part you play, and the correct action to make a change. When you observe with a panoramic view, you start to see that the traffic is just traffic and not out to get you at all. By observing your life from a higher perspective, you begin to see places where you feel challenged as just a part of your life—not good or bad, just part of life.

When you feel anxious, you can be aware that you are anxious. You can even feel that you *are* the anxiety itself. But when you back away and observe the situation, you'll discover that you are in a great big hurry going nowhere. When you stop and observe yourself feeling anxious, you will also discover what you really need to do; instead of going faster, is to stop and regroup, get refocused, then move forward. Being more self-observant and learning to let go, you will eventually reach a place where you accept all that is happening as the gift it really is. You can begin to enjoy your life and not feel trapped. When you accept life as it is, instead of spending all your time trying to make it something it's not, life becomes more enjoyable. When you become more self-observant, you'll begin to see that your fears are gifts telling you there's some feeling or belief you need to let go. The less attention you give to anxiety, or any other negative emotion, the more it weakens its hold on you—or your hold on it.

Whatever you focus your attention on is what gets created in your life. Where your attention goes, the energy flows; and where energy flows, manifestation takes place.

Intention to change is the starting point. You have to want change. Your circumstances won't change until you do.

I remember in one of my classes a few years ago, there was a couple attending together.

They were apparently having some sort of major conflict in their relationship. She was really holding some resentment toward her husband for something he had done. In one of the exercises, she shared her anger toward him.

I asked her if she liked feeling this way, and she answered, "No, I don't." Then, I asked if she would like to let that feeling go? She answered very hesitantly, "Yes." I asked if she was willing to let it go? She answered very quickly, "No! I'm not willing to let it go at all, not now, not ever!"

And I said, "Fine, let's move to the next person."

You see, without willingness, there's no need to proceed any further. A few months later I heard that the couple had unfortunately filed for a divorce. When a person holds onto that kind of resentment, there's no room left for a resourceful solution to come forth. There's no room for healing to take place. It takes a lot of courage to observe what is really happening, to observe it from a higher place and be willing to let it go. But it takes a lot more energy to hang on and say, "No, I'm not willing to take a closer look."

One person said to me that they didn't have the time to practice letting go. It doesn't take any time at all to observe yourself and let go. However, hanging on to a non-resourceful emotion can be a HUGE time and energy waster.

Anyone can learn to let go. We all learned to walk, to talk, to put on clothes, to tie our shoes, to drive a car, etc. I remember observing my dad driving the car when I was about twelve. It seemed so easy. I couldn't wait until I was sixteen to get behind the wheel. However, when I started learning to drive, it seemed scary. The steering wheel seemed so big and the road so narrow. I couldn't get the brake, clutch, and gas petals to work just right. I knew what the gas, brake, clutch and gearshift were for, but they didn't seem to work as easily for me as they did for my dad. However, over time, I got more and more comfortable until one day, without even noticing, driving a car became second nature.

The same goes for self-observation and letting go. After you do it for a while, it becomes second nature just like hanging on has become second nature.

Which do you think would be more productive walking 200 miles or driving your car 200 miles? Which do you think might be more productive, letting go or continuing to hang on, burning up your energy, creativity, and productivity? We have all done all sorts of things that seemed impossible in the beginning. The reality is we all let go all the time.

I remember when my brother was teaching me to swim. Every time I tried to swim, I sank like a rock. I couldn't quite figure out how it all worked. I couldn't make my hands and feet move together and keep my head above water and breath at the same time.

I thought I would never get it! I must have swallowed 200 gallons of water in the process; but finally, with a lot of practice, I learned to swim. Why did I do it? It's simple. I had the intention, willingness, and courage to commit myself to the process of learning no matter what. Sure, it was scary, but I wanted to swim more than I was willing to stand on the side of the pool and watch others having all the fun. You've got to want your emotional freedom more than you want to continue with the way that's familiar to you. You've got to want peace of mind more than you want conflict.

Look at it this way. Let's say you wanted to be a snow skier. You could just call yourself a skier and never go to the slopes. Or you could borrow some skies, go out, and give it a try. However, if you were truly serious about being a skier, you could buy your own skis, take a few lessons, and ski when you had the time. If you wanted to get even better, you could take a few lessons and go skiing regularly. If you wanted to become a master skier, what would you do? You would hire the best instructor you could find, commit your life to learning, practice every moment you could, and ski at every opportunity. That is the way you become a master skier.

If you want to master letting go, you've got to practice it at every moment. You already practice hanging on. We all do. All you really have to do is quit practicing hanging on. Realize that what is not working in your life is due to what you are hanging onto.

You may say, "I don't have time to observe, to become aware, or to let go." Not letting go and not being self-observant is what consumes the majority of your time in the first place. Practicing letting go will actually give you more time. It's alright to hang on and stay where you are, if that's what you want. But it's really good to know that you're the one in charge of making changes, if you decide to. Just make a conscious choice to become more self-observant and let go because you want to, not out of a sense of obligation. On the other hand, if you believe that life is difficult and you choose not to observe your actions and let go, then your own point of reference regarding life will always be, *"Life is difficult."* Also realize that this belief has become your filtering system for all incoming data about how life is and all outgoing data and perceptions that are projected out to others. Most importantly, know that only *you* have the power to challenge and change your beliefs, to put an end to your outdated filtering system.

FIVE

The Addictive Cycle

Let's start by discussing our thoughts. As human beings, we think altogether too much and about altogether too many things. Within a single moment, our minds can contemplate a vast number of unrelated conceptions and half-formed ideas—more thoughts than could be found on the pages of a dictionary. One second, we're looking out over a beautiful meadow, the mountains in the distance, and a sunset. The next thing we know, we're suffering with anxiety over problems in our business. A split second later, our thoughts are at home with the family. We jump around haphazardly from one thought to another totally unguided, unguarded, and unfocused. We buy into whatever happens to be presented to us across our mental movie screen and determine that it must be *real* or *true*.

Look around you. Everything you see in your life is a tool for your advancement. Your hands are tools to make your life easier and more productive. Imagine what it would be like trying to type on the keyboard without any fingers or to drink a glass of water with no hands. Your lungs, heart, and other vital organs are tools to keep you alive. And the better you take care of those tools, the longer you live. The vehicle you drive is a tool to get you from point "A" to point "B." The computer is a tool to make you more efficient and to send messages from one point to another. Your eyes are tools to help you to see your way. Look around you. You have many tools at your disposal, all designed to enhance your life in some way. Even a negative emotion is a tool to let you know that there is something you need to let go of in order to experience more of what you want in life. Your mind is a tool to help you gather data, reason, and make decisions.

Let me let you in on a secret. You are not a tool. You are the CEO and user of those tools.

You are not your mind, your negative emotions, your automobile, your eyes, or any of these things I mentioned. You are the CEO, the observer and user of those tools. And it is up to you how efficient you become with the tools at your disposal.

The human mind, which is a tool, is a multi-dimensional machine that processes thoughts. And to make better use of that tool, it's good to know some of your thoughts are in the development stage, while others are on their way to completion. Your thoughts go out in a continuing series. An example of this would be that while you are engaged in some activity, you may also be eating, driving your car, walking, or thinking about that new car you are going to buy or the vacation you want to take. In other words, you are thinking on a multi-dimensional basis.

The subconscious part of your brain proceeds to bring your desires into fruition by seeking out ways it could occur based on past experiences. You decide to buy a new automobile, and right away your mind starts a brain scan looking for information that might relate to where to purchase that new car. You want a new BMW, and your brain is searching your subconscious for knowledge of a BMW dealership near you.

This is the multi-dimensional aspect of the human mind and its activity. We can do one thing and be thinking about several other things at the same time. We could have hundreds of activities going on at the same time. Scary huh? The mind never stops. And without even realizing it, with each thought, we are planting a seed. You only passed by that BMW dealer a couple times, but it is stored for later retrieval. And who knows, even when we are asleep the brain is probably creating some sort of back up program so you don't lose your data.

We start the mind moving in one direction, stop it, start it off again in another direction, recall it, send it off again, and we do it thousands of times every hour. We have developed habits of totally and absolutely undisciplined thinking, wouldn't you agree? And we do this without even considering the possible outcome of such random thinking.

We are thinking about some project we are working on at the office, then suddenly a thought about some personal issue pops into our mind and we are off in another direction.

Without stopping to complete either thought, we are now on to thinking about going fishing over the weekend. What we are actually doing is sending a half-finished message off to the universe for answers. What do you think you'll receive back? Right! A half-finished answer. What kind of harvest should you expect from your planting?

If you want to grow corn you plow, plant the seed, cover it with dirt, water it, and keep the weeds out. Most people are plowing the field, planting the seeds, and forgetting the rest while they move on to something else. Then, they wonder why the corn crop didn't produce.

One moment you feel happy and entertain happy thoughts, and then you receive a telephone call that didn't go the way you wanted, and now you feel unhappy and entertain unhappy thoughts. A friend pays you a compliment, "That is a beautiful outfit you are wearing," and you feel great. An acquaintance criticizes you, "That outfit, while it is very nice, makes you look too thin," and you now feel resentful. And very often, where any discipline whatsoever exists, it is aimed at non-resourceful thinking such as worry, anxiety, fear, doubt and such. Those things seem to be easy to stay focused on.

We always seem to be waiting for input from the outside to determine what thoughts we will reject and which ones we will accept. We even become victims of other people's thoughts and belief systems. Our lives become a never-ending chain of circumstances over which we feel we have no control.

There's a story about a bricklayer who was working three stories up on a scaffold. When he finished the job, he had a scaffold full of bricks left over at the top. He didn't want to throw them down and break all the bricks, so he tied a rope to a large bucket and ran the rope over a pulley. He then filled the bucket with bricks and climbed down. He grabbed the rope and gave it a hard tug, allowing the bucket full of bricks to swing out so he could lower it to the ground. To his surprise, the buckets of bricks were heavier than was he, and down they came. Startled, he hung onto the rope, and up he went. He and the bricks met halfway, banging into each other. When he hit the top, his fingers got caught in the pulley. At the same time, the bucket of bricks hit the ground, spilling some of them. Of course, he's now heavier than the bucket of bricks. Still holding on to the rope, he goes down and the bucket of bricks come back up. Again, they meet in the middle, banging him around. He then hits the ground and finally lets go of the rope. Now, the bucket of bricks is certainly heavier than the rope, so the bucket of bricks comes down, hitting him on the head. That is called a chain of circumstances! He got the job done, but he sure got beat up in the process, wouldn't you agree? Do you think he might want to consider a little different approach next time? Without even stopping to consider the potential outcome, many of us approach our thinking and daily challenges in much the same way.

You have a vast intelligence at work for you. Your conscious and subconscious mind is like a sensory organ that keeps this intelligence informed as to the circumstances you want to create in any given situation. So, whatever conclusions you arrive at on a conscious and subconscious level get forwarded to this higher intelligence to assist you in creation, which gets returned to us in physical reality.

Our thoughts, when they become conclusive, and are backed up by emotions, positive or negative, are turned into reality; we can't stop the process. The process is automatic.

The only reason all of our thoughts are not turned into physical reality is, one: they are not convictions of the heart; and two: we change our thoughts so rapidly, therefore, canceling out the original ones. This may be difficult to comprehend, but every thought backed up with a conviction is manifested. Once the conscious and subconscious are convinced, it becomes a reality. The ones that you don't manifest are the ones that you have simply lost your conviction toward.

For example, let's say you decide to earn a certain amount of money within a given time frame. Your mind now goes to work. Because of past programming, it may offer conflicting thoughts. It tells you why you don't deserve it, or how hard it will be, or brings up the last time you tried and failed, etc. This data, if you listen to it, will in turn take you off in a whole new direction. These opposing thoughts are triggered by your core beliefs. Your beliefs are kept alive by suppressed energy patterns known as feelings, which are the result of some past experience we have not yet resolved. And the bad news is, you can become literally addicted to these patterns.

You have tried your utmost to get what you want in life by working longer hours, going to seminars, and putting out sheer effort. You have crawled, pushed, and shoved your way through the growing piles of emotional waste that clutters your mind to keep cranking out results at all cost. Is this not true? It is exhausting, isn't it?

Why not simply let go of whatever is keeping you from what you want? Success and happiness have very little to do with effort and struggle and very much to do with cleansing yourself of outdated beliefs, habits, and emotions. Trying to be happy and successful without this cleansing process is like trying to drive your car while standing on the brake. It literally becomes an addiction. Any difficulty you are having in getting and keeping what you want in life is a direct result of your addiction to your current counter-productive patterns.

Drugs like heroin and meth are not their users. And the pattern you are addicted to is not "YOU" but the remnants of past experiences. Let me explain how the addictive cycle works. From birth to the present, every experience you've had has an attached feeling to it, positive or negative.

Let's say, for example, you grew up with a verbally abusive parent and were repeatedly told that you would never amount to anything and could never measure up to your siblings. Every time you experienced this verbal abuse, you attached a feeling to it. Then, before long, you began to think you would never amount to anything. As you were growing up, you watched your siblings excel at everything, but you struggled at everything. Pretty soon you started to believe that your parent was right. After all, they must know better because they were your authority figure, and you were supposed to look up to them.

Next, your behaviors start to match your beliefs. And believing you will never amount to anything, then acting on that belief, means you will go to any extreme to prove to yourself and the outside world that what you believe is true.

Your behaviors create the result, "I failed again," which reinforces the original experience of, "I will never amount to anything."

So, it's an endless cycle: Experience–Thinking–Belief–Behavior–Result–Emotion–Experience.

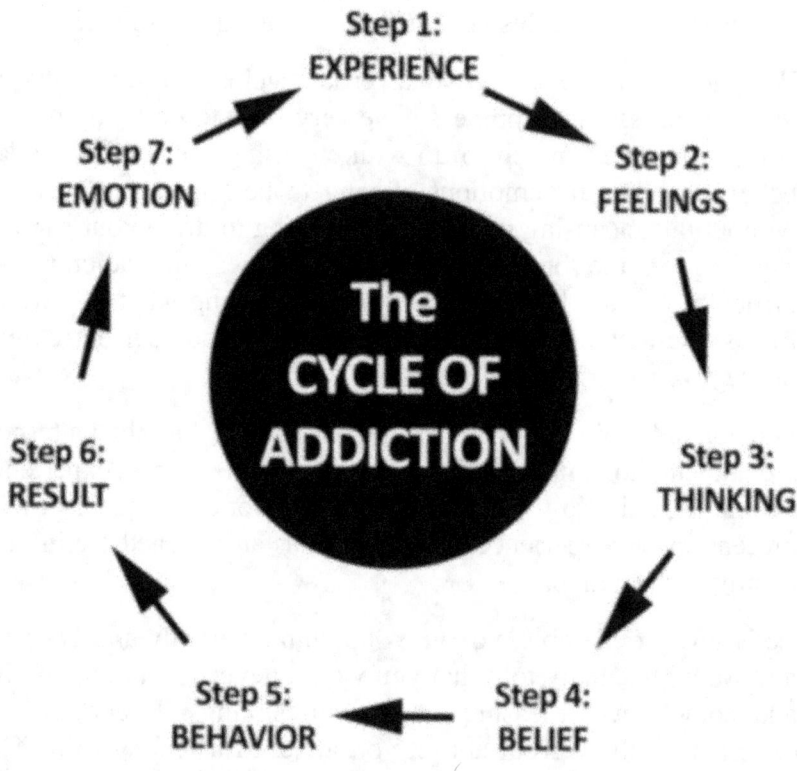

Each of our inner obstacles is layered and interconnected with every other obstacle experienced in past created addictions. For example, you may be conditioned to believe that life is hard, and even during easy times, you make things hard for yourself.

Until you break the addiction, you will always approach life like you are never good enough. You try harder and harder to crack and change this belief by brute force, which only further feeds your belief that life is hard and you are not good enough.

Then when you do achieve some goal, you may feel temporarily satisfied, but deep down it is the worst thing that could happen because you feel unworthy! So, you sabotage your next attempt so you have a reason to feel unworthy. The fact that something came easy took you out of your comfort zone, and now your subconscious will do anything it can to keep you addicted, even if that means sabotaging your success. This supports both your unworthiness addiction and your struggle addiction, and the cycle begins again with yet another set of buried feelings to its credit, that strengthens the original experience.

This example may or may not specifically describe your situation, but I think you get the general idea. We are ALL addicted in one way or another. Negative addictive cycles are crazymaking! The sooner you can start breaking any negative addictions you have, the better. Because they are all interconnected. When you break one addiction, another pops up. Or you might break one and weaken another at the same time.

Here is a look at some of the most common negative emotional patterns people tend to be addicted to. I labeled them according to common feelings because that is the quickest and easiest way for you to decide whether one or more of these patterns describe your own life.

Read through this list and see how many of them you can relate to. It doesn't matter how many or how few of these patterns you have in your life. What matters is the effect they have on you, how much life energy they force you to burn up, and how they keep you from getting what you want in life.

Constant Fear and Anxiety

Many of us are slaves to our fears and worries. We spend so much time worried that something might happen, we actually go out of our way to make it happen. The reality is that focusing a lot of attention on something that frightens us is a great way to make it happen. For example, if you are scared of dogs, then dogs are more likely to bark at you or even attack you, because dogs can literally smell the chemicals produced by your fear.

Another example: Have you ever worried about going deeper into debt and found yourself there in a matter of months?

Have you ever feared that the pile of money you just earned would soon vanish, then watched your bank account dwindle?

Have you ever gone home hoping that another heated argument with your spouse or partner would not happen and it did the moment you got there?

I once suggested to a friend that he let go of the idea that his co-worker was manipulative and hard to get along with. After some hesitation, he said, "I'll give it a try." And for the first time ever, his coworker was pleasant all day!

This is not the Law of Attraction at work. More on this later, but the Law of Attraction is not real. It can't and doesn't work the way it is portrayed. This is simply your addiction filtering how you interpret events. The man with the manipulative coworker interpreted everything that person did as manipulative, whether or not they intended it that way. Replacing that filter with one that saw the worker as a decent person made him interpret his coworker's actions as pleasant. As a result, he also acted more pleasant toward his co-worker, which made him more pleasant. Changing yourself changes people around you. When you change, your view of the world and your circumstances change.

Anytime you try to control how someone acts, you will face stiff resistance. That need to be in control is simply an addiction brought on at some point in your life when you felt out of control. Letting go of the need to control something over which you have no control, puts you in total control. When you let go of the need to control the other person, there will be nothing to resist. The only person you can control is you. I'll discuss this in a lot more detail later.

Interpreting what your spouse or partner says as an attack is a great way to get into a fight. Choosing to be peaceful lets you sidestep any attack or even see that what you thought was an attack as really a plea for attention or love.

Learning to understand the addiction that triggers the need for control or approval, fear, anxiety, worry, or doubt helps you break that addiction. Understanding lets you release the associated emotions and interpret the exact same events in a completely new way.

The event may still happen, but it will not trigger your addiction, and you'll view it differently. With practice, you will learn that all conflict is really self-conflict. Understanding this alone has made miraculous changes in the lives of tens of thousands of people around the world.

Frustration, Anger, and Resentment

Life can be frustrating. We all know that. People sometimes do things that really tick you off or even hurt you. It's only natural to let anger and frustration get the better of you sometimes, or even to hold a grudge because of what someone did or how they acted. The only problem with holding a grudge and anger is that you are the one who gets hurt.

A woman at one of my seminars told me that she could never be successful because her father had verbally abused her as a child. He repeatedly told her that she would never be successful at anything.

I asked, "Where is your father now?

She said, "He has been dead for over 10 years."

I then asked, "So who is abusing you now?"

She said, "I don't understand the question."

I said, "Well, if your father died 10 years ago, who is abusing you now?"

She said, "I still don't understand the question?"

I said, "You think about it for a while and I'll be back to you."

I returned about 20 minutes later and asked, "Well, did you come up with the answer to who's abusing you now?"

She said, "Oh my God! I am abusing me! I am carrying on his abuse."

This realization helped her let go of her negative core belief that she would never be successful and replace it with an empowering one that supported her success.

The word 'happened' is the key. It happened. Whatever the event, its not happening to you now, unless you bring it into now. All of the woman's anger and resentment cannot possibly hurt her dead father. She was the one being hurt.

What about you? What past events are you still angry about? What old frustrations do you carry with you? Who do you resent? Do you really think any of this is affecting the other person, whether they are dead or alive? Do you really think a person's frustration over being unable to have the money they want is helping them actually make that money? Do you think that someone hanging onto resentment from a past broken relationship will help them to find new loving relationship?

This logic works in the present moment as well. Say you are in a heated argument with someone. Your first question should be, "Who wins in an argument?" The merits of the argument don't matter at all. Nobody ever wins any argument. We argue because we want to be right and force our beliefs on someone else. The fact that our beliefs form our truth says nothing about how someone else views them. Remember all beliefs are false until you decide it is true. Then, it is only true for you.

What about your anger, frustration, and resentment? Is it leading you toward or away from what you want? What are these negative emotions helping to make real? Any feeling or belief you have is either moving you toward or away from what you want. That's what's real. I absolutely guarantee that your frustration, anger, or resentment is not getting you what you want.

Reliving the Past

Have you experienced any or all of the following?

- A bad business deal or lost money
- Being hurt by someone you love
- Something you said or did that you wish had gone differently
- Or maybe even experiencing fraud or deception

Bad things happen to good people. Everyone goes through things like this sometimes.

The difference is that some of us let these incidents pass over us like water off a duck's back, while others hang on and keep reliving them over and over like watching an old movie—but at such a HUGE cost.

For example, you may not trust your current partner because your last partner cheated on you. Does hanging onto the past experience with your partner help or hurt your current relationship? Are you opening yourself up to a loving relationship by treating your partner like a cheater, or are you creating unnecessary conflict?

The same questions apply to every event you keep reliving even if that event was positive. Hanging onto a negative event taints every new opportunity. Hanging onto a positive event makes it impossible to enjoy the present on its own merits because you will compare it to the past. And, you'll probably find ways in which your current experience is not as good or satisfying as the past one. Either way, you can't possibly get ahead if you keep thinking about and reliving the past.

It's fine, and even necessary, to learn from past experiences. Just don't bring that past into the present unless it is a useful experience

SIX

Releasing Emotional Addictions

What does everyone want in life? Each of us is a unique being with equally unique goals and dreams. We all tend to follow a very common pattern because everyone alive today wants pretty much the same things. We just seek them in different ways.

Some of these things you may already have, and some may be missing. Let's review:

Work

We all seek to be productive in our own way and want our efforts to be a source of joy and fulfillment. We want to know that we are creating something positive and leaving a lasting legacy. The problem comes when we start defining "work" as the effort itself and losing focus on the desired result, which is fulfillment. This leads to struggle. Struggle causes stress. Stress can cause many physical and emotional ailments up to and including premature death. Embracing the idea that work is measured not in effort or struggle, but in output or results, can free you from much of your daily stress. Combine this with finding and living your life mission and you will be well on the path to the success and happiness you want and deserve.

Money

We all seek to have enough money to never have to worry about how we live our lives. Money itself is nothing more than a tool for facilitating exchanges. It also gives you options as to how you live your life. There is nothing good or evil about money or any other tool you may have. You can use a hammer to build a home or to destroy it. You can use a pen or the computer to spread messages of love or hate. The tool itself is not the issue. Our perceptions and emotions surrounding the tool are what matter.

Too many self-help programs equate wealth with a huge bank account and the luxuries that come with it. I define wealth as the freedom to fulfil one's life mission. If you were born to live a life of financial poverty in a spiritual outpost, and you do that, then you are rich. If you were born to live a life of extraordinary material abundance, and you do that, then you are rich. If you were born to live in a monastery, but are living a lavish lifestyle, then you are truly poor.

Health

We all seek to be able to count on our bodies to respond when asked and to be free from pain. Anyone who suffers from health problems knows that health good enough to take for granted is something we all desire.

Obtaining and maintaining this sought-after health can be challenging because we face many stresses and temptations each day. I believe that many of our real and imagined ills may stem from not accepting or following one's individual path or from reliving the past and future in the present. So, to begin, let go of the past that no longer serves you and stop worrying about the future.

Love

The greatest of all human needs is the need to be wanted, cared for, or loved. We all seek to build and maintain loving supportive bonds with others. Unfortunately, we often seek this love because of some sense of emptiness or longing to satisfy some unfilled need. This leads to codependency, divorce, infidelity, and many other problems, when we realize that the person we love cannot satisfy those needs.

Love should never be the symptom of other's needs or a source of pleasure. Pleasure is temporary where love, like happiness, is a state of being. It's who you are. Love comes from you not at you from an outside experience.

This very subtle difference is not always easy to discern, yet the results are tremendous when you understand that love is an energy that travels so fast it is everywhere all at once.

Fun

We all seek to have at least some fun in our lives. Truly happy people look for the fun in everything they do and at every moment of every day. They don't chase fun and never segregate their lives into "drudgery" and "fun." Every waking moment of every day is fun for someone who is living the life he or she was meant to live.

Longevity

We all seek to postpone death as long as possible under normal circumstances. The best reason to avoid death as long as possible is to have enough life to gain the wisdom to truly appreciate all of your accomplishments. The path to this is built around having a satisfying life's work.

Freedom

We all seek to be free. However, freedom may mean something totally different to each individual. There is one word that is inseparable with freedom, and that is responsibility. If you want to be free, whatever that means for you, you must be the one to take total responsibility for defining and living that freedom.

Happiness

It's the most sought-after commodity in the world. Everyone is looking for it. From a princess trying to find a second chance at real love, to a celebrity on drugs trying to escape their personal pain. People try to find it through their families and significant relationships, their careers, their religious or spiritual affiliations, sex, vacations, hobbies, cars, money, and addictions; the list goes on and on.

What seems to get in the way of experiencing happiness consistently is our dramas in life.

Relationship drama. Work drama. Health drama. Money drama. Family drama. Spiritual drama. We all have it, from the president of the United States, to the abuse victim, to the single mom on welfare sitting home watching TV. The dramas are all around us. It is all we see in the news, on TV talk shows, in newspapers and magazines, in movies, in our lives, in our friend's lives; we see drama everywhere. Yet, everyone from the president to the single mom on welfare is trying to figure out the same thing—how to let go and move past their drama to find real happiness and peace of mind.

How do you achieve *real* happiness? How do you break free of your drama successfully? How can you let go of the emotions and pain from the past, the fear of the future, and the anxieties of daily life that are always a part of the drama?

Try a little exercise: Recall a time in your life when you felt worried about money, anxious about success, depressed, concerned about a relationship or family problem, that there wasn't enough time, or out of control. How does that make you feel now? Does it negatively affect you? Are these negative feelings associated with experiences from the past hurting you in the present? The correct answer is "Yes!"

We literally feel like we are being pulled in two directions at the same time. Our desire for success and happiness inspires us to move forward, and at the same time those negative feelings, emotions, and behaviors pull us back down. It's like driving a car with one foot on the gas and the other on the brake wondering why we're not getting anywhere! Sound familiar at all?

In an attempt to avoid these feelings or push them away, we have programmed our minds, made lists, learned while we slept, followed a guru, thought positively, attended recovery support groups, pulled our own strings, walked on fire, and more looking for the answers. But the startling truth is, after all this, most are still searching. Why? It is the lack of clear understanding about how our unhappiness originated in the first place.

Self-improvement is not what any of us needs. I'm not saying not to improve yourself. I'm saying that self-improvement will not make you happy. What we need is to wake up. Wake up to the fact that the feelings and underlying beliefs locked away in our subconscious programs are what restrict us from living the lives we want. We've all become so accustomed to our unhappy feelings that we don't even see *we* are hanging onto them. Instead, we feel *they* are hanging onto us! We create an exciting new vision of something we want, then like a thief in the night, these deeply buried feelings and beliefs hidden away in our subconscious programming sneak in and take over. They push us around, offering confusing, conflicting messages, dictating what we can and cannot do.

Most people today are wandering around on auto pilot, but their plane (or life) isn't going where they want it to go! I am going to show you how to turn off your auto pilot, let go, and break free of your drama to go in the direction *you* want to go.

When you begin to let go of the emotional waste, you will begin to enjoy abundance in every area of your life. Your financial status, health, relationships, family, and personal happiness will become more than you ever thought they could be.

Throughout this book you will discover what causes your pain, failures and other blocks in life. You'll learn how to let go of the fears and emotions that cause your unhappiness and lack of success. You'll find methods to de-activate your internal failure mechanism before it's engaged. You'll learn to forgive the past, and yourself, and break free from the "chain of pain."

There are five critical elements that come to mind as necessary for self-healing and growth.

You'll need all five in order for the principles throughout this book to work for you.

1. ***Concern:*** concern means caring enough about yourself to be interested in taking the time to explore, with an open mind, what might be done to facilitate emotional self- healing and growth in a whole new way.

2. ***Willingness:*** the willingness to be self-observant, to put into practice the principles throughout this book. You must be willing to give them a try before making any judgements as to whether they will work for you or not.

3. ***Patience:*** patience is required for the necessary clearing and re-balancing of your system. We've been emotionally abusing ourselves for a long time by hanging onto and

suppressing our negative experiences, feelings, and emotions.

4. ***Nurturing:*** nurturing is the first step toward loving yourself. It will activate your heart and let you feel your real true happy self once again. As you begin to open your heart, the real you will step forward and take center stage. Remember, the "You" reading this book is the most important person on the planet. At least, you should be to you.

5. ***Courage:*** courage is required to face and own your circumstances instead of blaming external conditions. When you have courage, you'll begin to feel your warrior spirit emerge as you face and let go of your fears. Without courage, fear will take over and run your life. Courage is the antidote to fear. Once you've let go of your fears, you'll find you no longer have a need for courage. Courage is only needed when fear is present. Without fear, courage simply becomes a natural act, like breathing.

Happiness is our natural state. Unhappiness is a learned behavior. In other words, we were born happy, and we learn to be unhappy through our experiences and programming in life. Happiness only exists when you see that the unhappiness you are experiencing is not connected to the event itself, but rather to how you perceive the event based on past programming.

Here's the bottom line. All the pain and suffering we experience is of our own making.

It develops out of our hearts and minds. It comes out of our own confusion and misconceptions about what causes our suffering. In addition, if we don't begin to see where the problems originate, or what they really are, we will only increase their strength for a later attack. And because it's all we know we will teach our children the same confusion. It will continue generation after generation, just more of the same.

We (you and I) are the pivotal generation. For things to change in our lives, our children's lives, and in the world, WE must make a change! If you want something different in your life, in the world—

and I assume you do or you wouldn't be reading this book—you have to be willing to do something different, because circumstances won't change until you do.

We all want to be free of our problems, but folks, here's the real truth. No person's life ever is, was, or will be free from difficulty. What I'm offering is a new way of observing the true nature of your problems—what they are, where they originated, and how to deal with them in a stress-free way. It's not a *sit-back-and-let it-happen* philosophy. It's simply about getting to the basics. It's about getting to the root cause of your pain, failures, or difficulties, then acting on it from a different point of view.

There's a story I heard once about a man who went to a spiritual master hoping to get rid of all his problems. He explained for hours the long list of problems he faced. He explained that even though his children were good, they sometimes just didn't respect him enough. He explained that even though he dearly loved his wife, she nagged too much. He explained that sales in his business were declining, and he barely had enough money to pay the bills. The list of problems went on and on.

The master sat in silence listening to every word the man had to say. Finally, the man wound down and waited for the master's response; he waited for the master to give him the secret to handling all his problems.

When the all-knowing master finally responded, he said, "I can't help you."

"What do you mean you can't help me?" the man cried!

The master said, "Well, we each have fifty-one problems, and there's nothing I or anyone else can do about it." He said, "If you work really hard on one of them, you just might fix it, but as soon as you do, there'll be another to take its place."

"What do you mean?" asked the man.

The master said, "Well, for example, you are going to die someday, and so is your wife and children. Now that's a problem, and there's absolutely nothing you, me or anyone else can do about it."

The man became very angry and shouted, "I thought you were a great master. I thought you could help me solve my problems! What good are your teachings anyway?"

"Well," the master said, "Maybe I can help you with your fifty-second problem, your greatest problem of all."

"My fifty-second problem?" the man shouted! "What's my fifty-second problem?"

"Your fifty-second problem," the master said, "is that you want to not have any problems."

Most of us continue to choose the way that causes us pain or unhappiness because we're good at doing it. We're familiar, comfortable with it even. And instead of taking action to change, we retreat into familiarity. It's what we know, and it's who we *believe* we are. We've all literally become addicted to our pain and problems. It feels safe and comfortable. We know exactly how to do it. After all, we've been doing it all our lives.

The reason we continue with our old methods is because there's no risk. Things would have to get pretty stressful before most of us would risk moving out of our comfort zone.

Reading this book, and applying it, is pretty risky. You are going to be asked to step out of your comfort zone and do it differently. I'm not saying I will show you how to eliminate your problems. However, I will show you how to deal with them in a sane and stress-free way.

You are going to be asked to face the pain, yes. You're going to have to challenge yourself and let go of beliefs about what you thought would bring you happiness.

The only reason you have unhappiness is because you continue to hang on to what you believe happiness *should* be. Most refuse to let go of our belief systems. Their willingness to let go of the old only happens when the pain of hanging on becomes more than they can handle.

There are basically five reasons for your unhappiness.

1. Not getting what you want in life.
2. Getting what you want, but not being satisfied with it.
3. Suffering the absence of something or someone you love.
4. Enduring the presence of something or someone you do not want in your life.
5. Living in the past or in the future—not being here, now.

How do you respond to the above five reasons? Either they lead you toward happiness or further away.

Throughout this book, you'll be encouraged to observe yourself in order to discover why you do what you do and why you continue to make the choices you make. You'll be encouraged to see whether your thoughts, beliefs, feelings, language, behaviors, and perceptions cause you to experience happiness or move away from it.

There are four important ingredients needed to create change in your life.

1. ***Desire:*** This is where it starts. You have to want to change. If you don't want to change, then I suggest you close the book and go back to what you were doing. Without a desire to change, nothing will.

2. ***Intention:*** This is simply making an irrevocable decision to do life differently.

3. ***Willingness:*** Being willing to take the necessary action and follow through even if it means challenging some life-long beliefs and feeling some discomfort.

4. ***Self-observation:*** Self-observation is being willing to observe yourself and your problems from a whole new perspective—to look for the *truth* behind what you *believe* to be true.

5. ***Commitment***: It's that extra resource you call upon when things get tough.

If you want change, you must *know* that change is needed. You must have a desire to change. You must *intend* to change. You must be *willing* to change. And, you must *commit* to change, otherwise nothing will change for you.

SEVEN

Look for the Truth

Let's begin this chapter by exploring in more detail your thoughts, beliefs, language, feelings, and behaviors. Observing these areas will allow you the opportunity to see yourself and your behaviors a little more clearly. You'll begin to see how you approach life, how you think, and how powerful your words are. You'll learn how you choose your values, why you have certain behaviors, and how your language can have a tremendous effect on the outcome of your life.

You should not concern yourself if what you are doing is "right" or "wrong," because neither will apply. It is not my objective to persuade you to do anything about how you think, believe, feel, your language, or your behavior. However, what I would like for you to do is have an open mind, explore the whole process, and see how these things are affecting your life. Then, you can decide what to do with the information.

As the process unfolds, I'd like you to focus upon *you* and not the content of your life.

Changing what you think, believe, feel, speak, or your behaviors will not be the point.

Why you do it is the point. However, once you learn why you do a certain thing, you are likely going to make a change.

You may, for example, hold a belief that life is very difficult. That's a very simple statement; one that is heard often. Here's what I would like to encourage you to do. I want you to observe yourself when you say, "Life is very difficult," and explore how it is you came to believe that life is difficult. Who taught you to believe that? What sequence of events supported that belief? And more importantly, how has having that belief affected your life? Does it add to your happiness? Does it help ease your pain? Or does it cause you to suffer more? What would happen to your life if you suddenly challenged that belief? How would your life be different? That is the real issue. That's what I want you to explore.

My purpose is to get you to ask yourself why you have certain beliefs, and for you to ask yourself, "What if it's not true?" I want you to ask yourself, "Is this belief really necessary?" I want to encourage you to back off and observe how you are living your life. That is the real purpose of this book in its entirety.

This book isn't about motivation. We've had enough motivation to last a lifetime. Motivation is self-addition and a form of suppression. What's needed is awakening and self-correction! I want you to discover what de-motivates you, not how to get re-motivated every time you feel down or when things aren't going your way. I want you to discover what may have turned you off and left you feeling like you need motivation in the first place. Getting turned on is easy. We can do that at the drop of a hat. Staying turned on is the problem we are all face with every waking moment. Finding out what keeps turning you off is the key to happiness and success.

Only when you discover what is holding you back and causing you to suffer, will you find the success you are looking for.

Here is how the mind works:

- An experience creates a feeling.
- Feelings influence how you think.
- Thoughts form beliefs and choose your direction.
- Beliefs motivate language and behavior.
- Language and behavior influences results.
- Results create a new experience.

A mutually supporting cycle is created. Remember the addictive cycle we discussed in an earlier chapter?

Experiences–feelings–thinking–belief–behavior–results–support the initial experience

So, what is a belief anyway? The definition of belief is, "Something accepted as real or true." Does this then make all beliefs true? No. As the definition states, "Something accepted as real or true." A belief is something you *decide* is true. It may not be.

For example, you may believe that life is tough, while someone else believes that life is a joyful experience. Someone else might believe that life is good only under certain circumstances. So, which one is true? Answer: All three. And none of them. What it really depends upon is your view of life. A belief is something you *decide* is true based upon your perceptions of life and on the filters of your programming.

A belief is simply a belief; nothing more, nothing less. It is your opinion of how you think things should be. And, know this for certain, whatever your belief may be, you can rest assured that it has total control over your life. Your life is a reflection of what you believe to be true, whether it is or not. Restated, your life today is a result of your past and present beliefs.

Attempting to change a belief and replace it with a new one can be like hitting your head against a brick wall if you don't know how to do it. The brick wall can come down, but not by continually hitting it with your head. Ouch! Banging your head against it will only cause you more pain, as most have already discovered. What many have not yet discovered is a less painful way to stop. First, you have to *see* the brick wall before you can stop hitting it. Makes sense, right?

I'm sure you've heard the expression, 'Seeing is believing.' What we need to realize however, is that believing is not true seeing, or 'seeing truth.' In fact, they are quite the opposite. What you believe is what you will see. Your belief about how something should be is nothing more than an educated, partially informed, guess about reality. On the other hand, a direct experience is the direct perception of reality itself.

As an example, let's say I hold two closed fists in front of you. I tell you one holds a hundred-dollar bill, and if you guess the correct hand, the money is yours. Now, I may be lying, or I may be telling the truth. Only I know the truth, only I can see reality. Either way, you do not really know as long as I keep my hand closed. The most you can do is speculate, believe, or have an opinion about which hand the money is in. As I open my hands, the usefulness of your belief completely vanishes, does it not? Why is this? Because now, you know the reality. You now know the truth.

So it is with any question, situation, or problem you may face. Your belief may serve as a useful tool in the absence of actual experience, but once you see reality through observation, belief becomes unnecessary. The fact is that, often times, your beliefs stand in the way of actually seeing reality, of seeing the truth behind your situation or problem.

The first step to changing a belief is to *know* that you cannot rely on it if you wish to see truth or reality. You can only rely on actual perception or direct experience. You don't have to go to someone, whether it is a teacher, master, priest, your parents, a shaman, or any other authority, in order to change a belief and see reality. Truth comes from direct experience. To see or experience is to know.

Some spend their lives trying to find happiness by saying they get their answers channeled to them by communicating with life forms on other planets. You might even believe there are beings on other planets that hold the answers to your happiness.

My question is, even if life does exist on other planets—and no one really knows for sure—what do they know about finding happiness on this planet where you already know life exists. Life is about here and now. Happiness is about here and now.

Happiness is about seeing life the way it *is* versus the way you *wish* it would be. Happiness comes from seeing truth. Truth comes from seeing the reality of your current situation. Not from your past situation or some future event, but from what is actually happening now. The past is not the truth. The past is the past. The future is not the truth, it's only a projection. Any attempt to avoid seeing your experience for what it is, in order to avoid pain, is what is causing your pain in the first place.

Let's say, for example, you had a previous painful relationship. You now feel you are ready for a new relationship. And of course, you don't want to get hurt again, so you are going to proceed with a lot of caution, with your heart closed, in order to protect yourself until you know for sure this is the right one; then you will open your heart. Think about this: with a closed heart, you will experience the new person through the eyes of the old you who is still seeing and experiencing pain from the past. You want to overlook truth in order to avoid the pain, not knowing that what you are really attracting is more pain. In your desperate attempt to avoid pain, you will very likely repeat the same mistake by attracting the same type of person you are trying so desperately to avoid. And the addictive cycle will continue until you let go of your fears and approach the relationship with an open heart.

How do you create your beliefs? One way is through repetition. If you experience something often enough, or long enough, it can become a belief. For example, if as a child you observed your parents fighting all the time, you might grow up believing that this is the way all relationships function. And because of this belief, you repeat the same pattern in your own relationships.

Another example: let's say you grew up with a dominating father and a submissive mother. Usually in this case, later in life, a child takes on one or the other of those traits in their relationship. It might be a reversed role. The son observes the dominating father and becomes a submissive adult.

A child may hear repeated statements from his or her parents such as, "You'll never amount to anything" or "We're poor," and "When you grow up, you'll be just like your father." You grow up believing that your father was the cause of the family being poor and that you are just like your father. Then, as an adult you take on the same role as your father. Or you might be determined to reverse the role to prove everyone wrong about you, so you spend your life trying to be rich and unconsciously seeking approval from others. This sort of upbringing may also cause the child to grow up with a lot of self-doubt and to feel unworthy of having success or money.

The opposite may also happen. A person could grow up in a wealthy family and observe what having money can do to people if not handled properly. The child decides that money is bad and consequently struggles with money as an adult.

Parents may have frequently yelled at their child. Then, as the child grows older, this results in his/her holding onto a lot of built-up anger. Since the child is afraid of expressing himself, he holds it all inside. And over time, it becomes a belief that you should not express yourself, or it may become a belief that when you do express yourself, it should be with a lot of anger.

It's as if we are all walking around with an invisible computer keyboard strapped to us.

The only problem is, it's turned outward, ready and waiting for anyone and everyone to give us input on how we should or should not live our lives before metaphorically pressing "enter."

"I told you not to do that!" Enter!

"When will you ever learn?" Enter.

"Why don't you ever listen?" Enter.

"I'll give you something to cry about!" Enter.

"You should be ashamed of yourself." Enter.

"Don't touch that, you'll go blind!" Enter.

"Just once, why don't you do something right!" Enter.

"You little brat, it's all your fault!" Enter.

"Money doesn't grow on trees." Enter. And on and on.

Somewhere along the way, we may develop the belief, "There must be something wrong with me." What else could we think? "There must be something wrong with me, otherwise I would be happy, and

I wouldn't have so much pain. If something wasn't wrong with me, my life would be working."

Well-meaning parents often teach wrong behaviors. There is no one to blame for how you turned out. Your parents did their best based upon what they knew. We all adopt certain beliefs and behaviors into our lives that we feel we need in order to survive. The same well-meaning parents may have even taught us to hate those behavioral traits and to see them as "bad." For example, let's say you were told repeatedly not to speak unless spoken to, or that kids should be seen and not heard. Later in life, let's say in high school, you now have a tremendous fear of speaking in front of others. Then, when you bring home your report card reflecting this problem you are having in speech class, your parents now tell you to have courage, to stand up and be heard!

Here is the trap created: "I believe I must be this way in order to survive." The result of past programming. And, "I hate myself for feeling the way I do." The end result:

Self-judgement equals, "I have to be this way in order to survive."

"I have to be this way in order to survive," equals self-judgement.

A self-supporting addictive cycle is born.

If you could just observe your life for a moment with an unconditioned mind, you would see that not only is this not true, but it is absolutely ridiculous what we do to ourselves as the result of past programming! Then, to top it off, we create a self-judgement report card. You look at what you have accomplished compared to everyone else. You look at all the things you have compared to everyone else. You look at who you think you have become, and you compare yourself to everyone else. You create a report card.

What you've accomplished compared to our neighbor: C-

What you have compared to your friends and peers: B+

Who you've become compared to others with the same education: D

Then, those silent whispers kick in, supporting the beliefs you have about yourself.

"I shouldn't feel this way."

"Won't I ever learn?

"I should have known better."

"I am so stupid for doing that"

"That was really a dumb thing to do! I can't believe I did it again."

There you have it, your very own self-judgement accounting system! Always clinging to what should have been, or what you should have done, or the way you think things should be. Then, you think that your beliefs and ideas, your accounting system, can be relied upon to guide you and give you satisfaction. But, if you examine the effect it is having on you, you'll see that, at best, it only brings temporary satisfaction. In fact, when you see the truth, you'll see that your accounting system is actually your primary source of anxiety and fear, because it always places doubt in your mind and doubt creates uncertainty, which is based in fear.

Doubt is the flip side of belief. As soon as you look at belief, doubt arises with it. Doubt is your past programs surfacing. Doubt and belief are inseparable. The moment you buy into a false idea about yourself from a past program, rather than relying on direct perception of what's really happening, it will inevitably give rise to anxiety or fear. As soon as you see the truth, doubt vanishes.

You create your own suffering through the repetition of your confusion. If you buy into counter-productive programming, your life can become like driving a car with a flat tire. It moves along, but the ride is rough and slow. You're thinking that something is wrong, but you're not exactly sure what's causing the bumping. This becomes a mutually self-supporting system for your outdated beliefs. It keeps them alive while the bumping continues. The wanting and craving something outside you becomes the trap. Your job is to see what does not make sense when things are not working. In other words, seeing the truth about what's causing the bumping. Your confusion and "head bashing" against that brick wall comes from your illusionary belief that you are separate from what's really going on. In other words, you are separate from the bumping. You believe something or someone out there is doing it *to* you.

The second way your beliefs are created is through emotional impact. Let's say that as a four-year-old child you loved to pick flowers and give them to your mother. While picking flowers from your neighbor's yard one day, not aware you were doing anything wrong, the neighbor, a very tall and big man, confronted you. "You little brat! You're the one who's been picking my flowers! Wait till I get my hands on you! You're going to be in a lot of trouble!" You may then grow up thinking that, tall people are mean. You feel as though you can't trust tall people or are afraid of tall people because they may hurt you. As an adult, you may show up as a person who just can't seem to get along with tall men, and you don't even know why.

I remember one young woman in one of my seminars. We were discussing relationships and marriage when the woman said that even though she really wanted to have a loving marriage, she would never get married. With some further questioning, she said that her reason was due to her parents. She said she would never forget the day her parents told her they were getting a divorce and that she should never get married. She developed a belief, due to the emotional impact of that moment, that marriage would end in pain—a pain that she didn't want to experience again.

If you have a false belief, it becomes difficult to see the truth, because you are blinded by your perceptions of what you believe to be truth based on past programming. I urge you to stop for a moment, sit back, relax, and observe your beliefs in any area of your life that are not working.

What do you *believe* about relationships? How's that belief working for you? What are your money beliefs? What have you experienced around money? I encourage you to examine your beliefs about relationships, money, career, family, health, and spiritually, and how those beliefs are working for you. Stop and reflect for a moment. How did this particular belief originate? Who says it is true? Is it true? Who would you be without that belief?

Are all relationships difficult? No!

Do all relationships end in divorce? No!

Are all teenagers difficult to raise? No!

Does everyone live with lack? No!

Remember that a belief is something you *decide* is true, yet it may not be true at all.

EIGHT

How to Change a Belief

So how do you change a belief? We do it all the time. Think about some of the things you believed to be true in high school. Do you still believe those things to be true? For the most part, probably not. As an example, a girl that I was in love with in the ninth grade broke up with me. I was devastated! I wasn't sure I could go on living without her. I was miserable for at least a week. Now, what was her name? I really can't remember.

You may have something you believed last month even, but now no longer believe to be true. As I have said before, a belief is something you have decided is true. It may not be at all. All beliefs are false, at least until you decide they are true; and then, they are only true for you.

Pick a belief you have. Now ask yourself:

"How did I come to believe this?"

"Who taught me to believe this way?"

"What if they didn't know?"

"Who taught them?"

"Does believing this add to the value of my life?"

"Who would I be without this belief?"

In other words, challenge your beliefs, unravel them until you see the real truth behind them. Only then will you be free to change them. If you believe something to be true you will literally fight to the death to prove to yourself and the outside world that what you believe is true. If you don't believe this, just take a look at the wars happening all over the world today. All this conflict is based on someone or some group's belief, and some fight to the death to protect it.

Take a moment and try this exercise. Close your eyes and relax for a moment. Now recall a time in your past, an incident that upset you. Maybe you missed your plane, you were really late for an important appointment, or you had an argument with someone. Visualize yourself again right in the middle of the incident. Recreate it with all the same feelings and emotions. As you are re-experiencing the incident, begin to observe yourself in the situation.

In other words, there is the "You" in the situation, and there is the "You" observing the situation. Observe all your thoughts, feelings, emotions, and behaviors relating to the experience. Begin to notice if there's any difference in the two situations—being in the experience versus being the observer of the experience.

Now, let's take it a step further and look for the truth behind the situation. What really caused the problem or conflict? What part did you play? What belief were you trying to protect by experiencing the internal conflict? Try this the next time you get upset about something, or at someone, and notice how you feel. What belief are you trying to protect?

Once you stop and observe your feelings, determining the belief you are protecting, you'll see the truth behind the internal conflict. You will notice an immediate improvement in how you feel and in your circumstances. You'll also see the truth that you are the one in control of how you feel, not someone else and certainly not your situation.

A few years ago entered into a business agreement with a close friend. About a year later, she realized there was a point in the agreement that needed to be better clarified regarding how she was to get paid. She asked if I would be willing to make the revision, and I agreed to do so. As the agreement was passed back and forth several times to make sure everything was correct regarding the issue, she began to want to change other things within the agreement. Before long, it became something totally different from how it started.

She began to knit pick everything, wanting more than we had originally agreed upon in several areas. Each time a revision was made to satisfy her, she became even more knit-picky, even angry because I didn't agree with her around other changes.

As the correspondence grew, I found myself getting a bit angry. The next thing I knew, she had hired an attorney to represent her, claiming that if I didn't agree with everything she wanted, he was going to take legal action to gain total control of the project. What started as a friendly business arrangement, where she was commissioned to do a certain job for a certain amount of royalties for ongoing sales, was now looking like it could turn into a legal battle.

I suddenly found myself feeling a bit, or rather a lot, taken advantage of on the whole deal. I began to get angry and even hurt about the situation. The more I thought about it, the angrier I became. I explained the situation to my wife. She asked me how I felt about it? I said that I felt hurt, betrayed, and angry. Right away, I saw what I was doing. I was buying into my business partner's control drama, instead of being resourceful and finding a solution to the problem. Stepping back and observing, I realized it was her problem, not mine. I already had a signed agreement. I didn't have to make any changes if I chose not to.

Once you identify with a feeling such as anger, for example, you lose your ability to see a resourceful solution to the situation. In other words, you remain stuck in the problem, or even become part of the problem. But once you look for the truth behind the problem, you can then be open to a solution. As you begin to catch yourself in a non-resourceful situation, observing your own part in the drama—which, in my case, was my need to control her—you'll realize you are simply in transition between behavior patterns and can now find a solution.

A person who is angry usually doesn't see himself as an angry person; in fact, he probably doesn't see himself at all. But, as he catches himself, even once, he has made the first step in changing the belief or habit pattern that caused his anger. When you make an emotional mistake and discover the part you play in it, the end result is real growth.

A word of caution. Beating yourself up for making a mistake is not the answer. In other words, you shouldn't use self-observation for self-punishment. Self-observation is simply a method for seeing the truth behind a conflict. Don't blame yourself or anyone else for how you feel. It isn't anyone's fault, it's just what's happening—not good or bad, just what is.

Non-resourceful feelings, emotions, and events in your life show up in order to facilitate your growth. You develop the capacity to improve yourself only by developing a greater understanding of who you are. Those non-resourceful feelings open up possibilities for a new future by presenting new options.

Most people believe themselves to be victims, victims of some sort of cruel fate. They think their misery is caused by their unhappiness, when in reality, their unhappiness is caused by complaints about their misery. On the other hand, their complaints are actually caused by some underlying belief about what they think happiness should be.

And, because of the fear of finding out that they may have been blaming someone else for something they controlled all those years, they just avoid the issue altogether.

We put off facing our fears, as well as our difficult tasks, because we are always bouncing back and forth between *conformity* and *non-conformity*. Let's say you arrive at work in the morning, and you know you have a difficult issue with an employee that you need to confront—one you really don't want to deal with. Later in the afternoon, you suddenly realize you still haven't dealt with it. You've found fifty things to do, none of which were confronting the issue. Your initial response upon arriving at work was that you should do it right now. You're the boss and it's your job; you have to do it. That's called 'conformity.' Your next response is, "I'm the boss, and I don't have to do it" or, "I can do it later." That's called 'non-conformity.' The instant you step back, observe both sides, and begin to see what you're doing, you confront the issue. However, if you never take the time to observe, you may put off taking any action at all. You won't even realize you're putting it off in the first place. You'll find some way to justify why you aren't confronting the issue; it makes you feel better and avoids the pain of the confrontation.

Self-observation lets you see through and understand the maze you are caught up in.

By being self-observant, the first thing you will see is what you are doing. The second thing you will see is a resourceful solution. You'll begin to see how you swing between conformity and non-conformity, caught between a resourceful and non-resourceful state. By becoming more self-observant, you'll begin to realize you are the one pushing your own swing. So, what's the solution? The solution is to resolve the problem by experiencing that which you don't want to experience. Simply feel the fear and surrender to the experience. When you do, you have weakened its hold on you, or rather your hold on it. When you surrender to the experience, everything will begin to shift, allowing you to see clearly what needs to be done.

We always want to cling to the familiar which, in the moment, seems to be the less painful way out. But, if you want to become a serious observer, you'll need to open yourself to the experience and become more aware of when you get on the "swing"— and even more importantly, that you're the one pushing the swing.

Try this self-observation exercise. It will help you gain a new perspective. Recall a non-resourceful situation in your life. Now imagine what you look like in that situation.

Next, imagine that a mirror is right in front of you. Observe your movements, your posture, gestures, and the expression on your face.

Now, ask yourself, "Why have I created this obstacle in my life? Observe it as if you are seeing it for the very first time. Look for the real truth. Now, write down what you see.

Next, write down how you *feel* about what you see. How you feel is much more important than what you think or see, but seeing starts the process. How do you feel right now? What message are you receiving regarding how you feel? What do you need to *let go* of? What action do you need to take? If you don't stop to see the truth, you'll avoid, or should I say suppress, how you feel and miss an opportunity to grow.

One of the most common emotions people experience when they begin to confront their own issues is fear. When you say or think, *"I'm afraid,"* you literally become consumed by your fear, consumed by an endless cycle of thoughts, beliefs, and feelings feeding one another. Your feelings of fear feed your belief. When you say, *"I am afraid,"* you see yourself as the fear itself and you believe it to be true. As the fear feeds the belief, the belief feeds the feeling of fear in return, which ends up causing an endless loop of fearful reactions to the situation.

"I'm afraid I'm going to lose my job." This may trigger…

"I'm afraid I won't have enough money to live." This may trigger…

"I'm afraid I won't be able to get another job." Which may trigger…

"I'm afraid that losing my job will affect my relationship." Which may trigger…

"I'm afraid if that happens, he/she will leave me, and I'll be all alone."

So, you can see in this example that the real fear is not of losing your job, but rather loneliness.

Here's the solution. When you observe the first fearful feeling as it arises, such as *"I'm afraid I'll lose my job,"* ask yourself this question, *"From where does this thought or feeling originate?"* When you do, you'll disconnect from the fear and you'll be open to seeing the truth behind your fear. Once you understand that you are not your thoughts, beliefs, feelings, emotions or fears, but rather the observer of these things, a greater sense of clarity will come over you, and the right solution will always appear.

Some ask, "How do I know if I'm observing or not?" If you were identical to your feelings or thoughts, you couldn't observe them, or even know they existed. Observation and knowing suggests a separation between it and the real you. You might be riding a horse.

You can observe yourself riding the horse, but that certainly doesn't make you a horse, does it?

There is no reality in the absence of self-observation. Observation creates reality. In other words, you create your reality through what you observe through the filters of past programming. If you continue to observe from the false reality of your outdated beliefs and programs, you'll continue living within that maze of false beliefs, going around that circle eight, with no beginning and no end.

You can be aware that you are lonely, but that does very little, if anything, to change the situation. On the other hand, self-observation lets you see the reason for your loneliness.

Self-observation is the capacity to go beyond your mind, where you can observe your thoughts, emotions, and behaviors as they are happening. Both awareness and observation are intellectual functions of the mind. The mind does not connect to your feelings.

If you feel anxious, for example, you can consciously choose to use your awareness to think good thoughts. Observation is separating yourself from the experience and looking at it from a higher viewpoint. You can think good, clear thoughts all you want, but if you don't stop, observe how you feel and let go of your anxiety or whatever, before very long you will be entertaining unclear, fearful thoughts once again.

Your conscious mind is the part of you that is aware of internal and external input from your memories, intuition, thinking, the flow of ideas, etc. It is also aware of all your senses such as sight, sound, touch, smell, taste, movement, etc. The conscious mind sort of sits on the fence between the inner and outer world. Its primary function is decision making through the use of intuition, feelings, attention, experience, beliefs, interpreting what it sees externally, and what it receives from your data bank of past programs. Of course, the main decision the conscious mind has to make, out of literally thousands of things it is also aware of, is where to focus its attention. If you want 100% self-awareness, this requires that the conscious mind be in a state of total inaction. In other words, doing nothing, as in a meditative state. You cannot watch television, drive a car, and read a book while being 100% aware at the same time.

Taking action, on the other hand, requires excluding other things. If you want to do a specific thing, you have to exclude other things. This is why making clear decisions is so critical. Do you intend to push on the brake or push on the gas? One stops you and one moves you forward. One or the other has to be excluded. You cannot act on everything at once. If you feel as though you are traveling down the road of life with one foot on the gas and the other on the brake, getting nowhere, you might want to stop and re-clarify your decision. Is it clear? To increase your awareness of one thing requires decreasing your awareness of another. It's like success and failure. It is one choice or the other. One choice eliminates the other.

One of the functions of your conscious mind is to make decisions in order to improve your skills, knowledge. and effectiveness. This is why it is critical to decide what is important to you, and then make a clear decision to have it. You must decide what feelings, beliefs, behaviors, etc., no longer serve you and let them go in order to stay on course with your decision. Your clear conscious mind keeps your intention on target and directs your awareness and your activities, so you know what to focus your attention upon. If your mind is unclear as to what you want, your conscious mind will simply direct you to the circle eight for another ride.

You don't attract what you want as the Law of Attraction claims, you create it. As an example, let's say I decide I want to purchase a new 760 BMW. I can see and feel myself driving it. My intent is strong. I have made a firm decision. Next, I noticed my awareness kicking in. I start to become aware of all the 760 BMW's on the road similar to the one I want. Next, I have to decide how I will pay the $120K. Check. Next comes action. I have to go to a dealer to purchase the car. Which dealer do I go to? A Honda dealer? No, a BMW dealer, of course. What color will I settle for? Nothing less than black! Why? That is my decision. On the other hand, if I have made a weak decision, and they have no black 760s, I might be convinced to settle for a 540 model.

Self-observation is a function of the conscious mind. Does this thought, feeling, emotion, or behavior support my intention, or is it moving me further away? That is a conscious choice. You can think positive all you want, but if your intention is weak, and you fail to observe reality, nothing happens—except maybe going around in your circle eight a bit faster. Your thinking process is only the mechanism that chooses the direction you want to take. Your passion for what you want will keep you taking action in the right direction. Using positive thinking as a means to stay focused only further suppresses the non-supportive feeling that keep your old beliefs alive. You cannot replace a negative emotion with a positive thought. Eventually, the emotion will win out.

The key to staying on purpose is self-observation. This means observing your thoughts, your language, your feelings, and behaviors—observing the soap opera going on in your head. You know the one I'm talking about. Everyone has one. It's going on right now.

Stop for a moment and observe your own drama. Some are *'Searching for Tomorrow.'* They are anxious or fearful about the future. For some it's *'General Hospital.'* They are always living their health drama. For others it's *"The Young and the Restless."* Or maybe *"Guiding Light."* Some love to watch old reruns, playing the same story over and over again. Some are into silent movies. Others watch the news looking for some exciting rumor to broadcast to others. You know the one I'm talking about! The soap opera! The one going on right now in your head. Just sit back on occasion and observe your own drama. You will see it.

Look at all the players you have assembled to assist you in playing out your drama.

Who is the main star? Is it you? Who is the co-star or the victim. Who's the villain? Look at the whole cast of characters—even the extras walking across the street. The emails coming in and the posts you pay attention to on social media, are all a part of the drama you've created for yourself! Understanding the part that others play in your drama can only be understood to the degree that you understand your part in your own drama.

Here's the really good news! *You* are the scriptwriter! You can write a new screen play, change the characters, get rid of the victim, get new players, change the extras, and even change the scenery. You can change a story of loneliness into a love story. You can write a story of financial success and happiness. You can create a whole new set, a new location shoot, hire new extras, and create new back drops. You can create anything your heart desires. Anything you can imagine, you can create. After all, you are the script writer.

How do you think your drama got created in the first place? Did it just happen? No. We each created our own story, and the cast of characters are simply a projection of our story.

But here's the key. For things to change, you have to make a change. If you continue to do what you've always done, even if you change the players, location and script, you'll create the same story all over again. When you change, your story will change. The question is, what does your heart desire? What do you want to create? What is your intention? What story do you want to live? Everyone has to have a story, and you can choose the one you want to live. Even if you choose not to choose one, you have chosen a story. Does that make sense? What I mean is, you have a choice. You can live consciously or unconsciously.

I encourage you to step out of the box for a moment. Look inside. Observe what's really going on. Rewrite your story if you don't like what you see. Realize that you are not your story; you are only a player in the story, and also the script writer. Take a moment right now and seriously consider your story, your role, your character. Now label it. Is it one of love, happiness, and joy or is it one of fear, loneliness, or depression?

Or maybe it's anxiety! That's a good one! Anxiety is when we mix fear, depression, and anger. The fear tenses your body and holds you back. The depression tenses your body and pulls you inward. The anger tenses your body and pushes you forward. So, you end up going in three directions all at the same time. What a great story that will make!!

You are *angry* about not getting what you want fast enough. You become *depressed* that you don't have it now, but someone else does. You are *fearful* to take a step forward because you might lose again or make the wrong move. Wow! That's the role of a split personality!! But what a great story!! If this is you, I would suggest you take some time to re-group, evaluate, and decide what screen play best suits you.

Stop, regroup, and get focused. Let go of the need to be in control of every outcome and move forward taking action from a place of resourcefulness.

Here's the underlying issue. It's not your drama that's the problem. It's your outdated programs. Your past experiences, being fed by your subconscious, don't want to resolve the issue! You have to consciously choose to resolve it. The subconscious doesn't want to stop and observe! Why? It's trying to protect you based on past data—some good and some not so good for you. When you begin to step back, observe, and let go of the old data, you'll slowly begin to enter a new dimension in which you'll know exactly what to do, what action to take on the spot, in any situation. Not only what actions to take for yourself, but for the benefit of others as well. You will also begin to see that your subconscious is truly your ally, showing you exactly what you need to deal with or let go of in order to further your growth.

Try this simple exercise. Pick a day. All day long, observe your thoughts, feelings, and behaviors. Observe your own drama. Don't judge it, just observe it. Observe the characters in your story. Notice the roll you play. Begin to notice your beliefs about certain issues. You'll be absolutely amazed!

Then, pick another day and observe the stories of the people around you. Notice what role you are playing in other people's drama as well as your own. This will shock you! Watch other people's drama at work, at home, on the freeway. Where do you fit in? Are you the controller or the one being controlled? Do you seek to gain acceptance from others? Are you the victim? Do you like the role you have allowed them to create for you in their drama? If not, what could you do to change your role? You could simply say, "I quit! I am not playing this role anymore."

Someone once asked me which was more important, self-observation or letting go?

The answer is that you can't have one without the other. In order to let go, it requires you first be in a state of self-observation. And when you're in a state of self-observation you are automatically letting go because you are detaching from the emotion and seeing it for what it is, past programming. As soon as you observe a non-resourceful feeling, you separate yourself from it, and in turn peel off a layer of that feeling, decreasing its power over you. In fact, it is impossible to observe yourself in a state of anger, for example, and remain angry. Try it. The act of observation in itself will defuse the anger.

The way to increase your effectiveness at letting go is to increase your effectiveness at self-observation. If you find yourself getting upset, know that you have lost your effectiveness at self-observation.

You have heard the saying, "You can't see the forest for the trees." In other words, you get so caught up in your problems, that you aren't open to, or can't see, the solution. On the other hand, you can't be upset about a situation if you are in a state of self-observation. Why? Because you, the observer, the real you behind the subconscious, never gets upset. As an observer, you can watch your own drama with interest and curiosity, but without getting the least bit upset. Becoming a consistent and persistent observer is the only answer I know of for remaining resourceful. If you observe, you will one day see life as it truly is, not how you think it should be.

We've all had those moments. We look at a sunset, and for those brief moments, we have no barriers, no drama. All there is, is just you and the sunset; and for that moment, you experience the real you. That's the way life is supposed to be.

Self-defeat in any endeavor doesn't mean victory doesn't exist; it simply means you approached it incorrectly. On the other hand, through self-observation, you become open to solutions. As you begin to observe, all your fears and drama can be put into proper perspective. Through persistent self-observation, the clouds covering the beautiful landscape and sunset eventually begin to disappear, the pain begins to subside, and your fears will go away.

You may be asking yourself a question or two at this point. "If I'm always trying to live in the moment, how do I plan for tomorrow? Do I still set goals and plan for my future?

How can I live for today and still plan for tomorrow?" We humans always want to try to figure everything out, don't we? We want to know all the minor details about how tomorrow will be. We want to predict the outcome of that all-important meeting next week.

The truth is, there is no way in the world to know how tomorrow is going to turn out! I'm not saying, even for a minute, that we should refrain from making plans for the future if that's what you want to do. You certainly want to plan for tomorrow, and you want to plan for that important meeting. But here is the solution to staying resourceful. Don't try to live tomorrow, today! Don't attempt to figure out or control an outcome over which you have no control. If you do, you'll miss today. You'll miss what's really going on in your life. Anytime you are not living this moment, you are out of this moment, and this moment is where your life is taking place. It's where the real action takes place!

Einstein said that the average person only uses 10% of their brain. That is because the average person is only in the moment, where he/she can use their brain, only 10% of the time. If you are only in the moment 10% of the time, that means you are out of the moment, where life takes place, 90% of the time! If that's true, that means in reality you are missing 90% of your life! Wow! What a concept!

We always seem to want to drift off into what's going-to-happen next week or even next year. We start to think about our money problems, our fears, and worries about tomorrow. This places you into a non-resourceful state where there's nothing, I mean nothing, going on that is productive in any way. There is nothing wrong with planning for your future, but you should avoid getting lost in it. When you are lost in your thoughts about the future or the past, you *are* lost, and you *have* lost! And before you know it, you are at the end of the day, or even worse, the end of your life, and you discover you have only lived one-tenth of it. But this is what most people do. We don't do it just part of the time, we do it a lot of the time. Look around you and you will see what I mean. All you do is waste your precious time stuck in a non-resourceful state where there's nothing going on, except your confusion about what's going on and what might happen.

Try this for just thirty days. When unwanted feelings arise, step back and observe. Label your feeling, not just fear, but be more specific. "I'm feeling fearful about losing my job," or whatever. If you find things happening too fast to deal with them, try stopping for a moment and labeling your feelings. "I'm feeling anxious." Stop, observe yourself, take a deep breath, and let it go. If the same feeling keeps popping up again and again, this is a sign that progress in taking place.

If you resist, instead of observing an unwanted feeling, three things happen. One—you suppress the feeling, allowing it to grow in strength and surface again later. Two—you miss the gift that it offers in your growth. Three—you completely miss the moment.

Self-observation and letting go is not being passive, as many people believe. It's about living a life of high action and low attachment. When you let go prior to taking action, your action will be reality based, not action created and motivated by conditioning, fears, or non-supporting programs and beliefs. Resourceful actions will always produce resourceful results.

It is also important to know that through self-observation and letting go, you are freeing yourself from all programming, rather than attempting to re-program. Attempting to re-program without first letting go of the old one is like jumping out of the pot into the fire.

You may think you have discovered a better program, a better system, but the whole point is to not let your life be run by a program or system in the first place. By following a system or program, you become limited by that system or program.

Let's say for example a young man went to work as a salesperson in telemarketing and it was the worst experience of his working career. He made hundreds of calls a day, received enormous rejection from prospects, and made no sales—no money. Later in life, he was offered a very good job as a national sales director for a large company.

The job paid very well, but he was afraid he couldn't handle it based on his past sales experience. Even though he was fully qualified and perfect in the eyes of the interviewer, the word 'sales,' frightened him to no end. He was still carrying around his past experience in selling. He was allowing it to affect him even though it had absolutely nothing to do with the present situation.

You will always suffer unconsciously what you do not face consciously. You can learn more and make more progress in your development in one day through self-observation than you could learn from external input or motivation in a lifetime. Look at it this way. Looking outside is only dreaming, while looking inside is waking up.

We have all developed our automatic patterns. Some are very helpful—like driving a car, putting on your clothes, walking, talking, etc.—but what you want to do is interrupt the non-supportive ones. How? By observing them and seeing the truth behind why they are there! I would like to challenge you to discover just *one* non-resourceful pattern each week, to observe it, let it go, and see what happens. Look for the truth behind your actions and results produced. Look for the truth behind how that habit pattern was created and how it may be negatively influencing your life.

Another important component of observation is to be honest with yourself, to admit you're being judgmental or whatever. I realize it is hard to have that kind of honesty with yourself, but you don't have to share it with anyone. No one has to know but you. If you want to truly experience growth, you'll eventually have to admit to yourself that you are chasing perfection, rather than letting go of your imperfections.

Don't attempt to go too fast. Speed is not the answer. You may increase your speed, but at the same time, lessen your results. By being a patient observer, you'll begin to discover that most of your deadlines, if you truly admit it to yourself, are deadlines that have been imposed upon you by others, not deadlines you've set for yourself.

It's also important to take some time for yourself, where you have nothing to do at all.

Observe yourself not being busy. Then observe yourself being busy and let go of the need to be busy all the time. When you do, you'll be surprised at how your level of creativity, productivity, and peace of mind increases.

If you find yourself feeling overwhelmed, the old you may say, "My loneliness overwhelms me." Instead, say to yourself, "Sometimes I decide to be lonely or feel overwhelmed." It is your choice, you know. The non-observer says, "I feel stuck. What do I do now?" Whereas the observer says, "What do I need to understand about myself that makes me feel stuck?" One approach is problem-oriented, and the other is solution-oriented.

Observation works in many ways. If you begin to observe any given thing on the face of the planet, it can reveal a solution for you. A blade of grass, a tree, an animal, anything!

I once saw a small piece of bread that seemed to be moving on its own across the floor.

At closer look, I discovered about six ants all working together to carry the bread back to their anthill. I saw discipline, teamwork, intention, action, and consistency. The message I got from that act of observation was something I really needed at the time, "You can't do everything for yourself, you need a team." Again, any given thing on the face of the earth can reveal to you the solution to your problems if you just observe and listen to your own inner voice.

Try opening a magazine to any page, and see if you can find the solution to a problem? You'll be shocked by the experience. Look at a person's hand, turn over a card, or watch a bird in flight and find a solution. Whatever you observe, you can find a connection to your own experience, if you are truly open to receiving it.

Begin today to take responsibility, but not for *how* or *why* your programs and patterns got developed, or what you are experiencing as a result. None of that matters in the least. It only creates guilt and more self-conflict. Instead, observe and ask yourself if the feeling you are experiencing is supportive or non-supportive. If it's not supportive, let it go and move on!

What I'm talking about is taking responsibility for observing your thoughts, feelings, emotions, beliefs, language, and behaviors. Then let go of those things that disempower you.

Instead of asking yourself, "Why does this always happen to me?" Why not take the resourceful approach and ask, "What feeling and belief am I hanging onto that is causing this painful situation?"

Instead of asking yourself, "How do I relieve my anxiety?" Why not ask, "What belief am I hanging onto that's causing me to feel anxious?"

Instead of asking yourself, "Why is this person acting this way?" Why not ask, "Why should I suffer over how someone is acting?" How they are acting is their problem, not yours anyway. If you suffer over how someone else is acting, you are taking on their problems. You become a player in their drama. We all have enough problems of our own without taking on someone else's.

Instead of asking yourself, "If god really exists, why doesn't he help me?" Well, god is really busy these days. Why not try a resourceful solution.

Observe yourself feeling sorry for yourself, and ask, "How come I have created such a stupid drama for myself, and what do I need to do to make a change?"

Self-knowledge is the *only* starting point for transformation. The intention to know yourself is the starting point to being happy and to having all you want in life. You must have the intent to know why you do what you do in order to gain true understanding and make changes.

Self-understanding requires self-observation, and self-observation must be followed by the discipline to let go of the old and allow the new you, the real you, to step forward and take center stage.

Remember, what you see and experience, is simply a projection of who you are, a projection of your story, and that is the end of the story!

NINE

The Frequency of Emotions

Emotions are the energy of the feeling you are hanging onto because of some past experience surfacing and being put into motion...e-motion. Emotions are the result of feelings being filtered through your beliefs.

Let's say you are feeling tired. That is a pure feeling. However, you may believe that you should not be tired. That's a belief. Because of the fact that you *believe* you should not be tired, you now may get depressed. When you get depressed, you feel even more tired, and now you feel like doing nothing at all, feeling hopeless. Do you see how one thing can lead to the next? There you are feeling tired, and the next minute you are feeling hopeless and you don't even know how you got there. All you know is that you are tired, even though you believe you shouldn't, and so it goes...around that addictive cycle feeding itself.

Emotions are like energy frequencies. You can sense another person's energy frequency when you are in their presence. Anger, for example, carries a different frequency than sadness; and I'm sure you have felt those frequencies in someone else, or yourself. It feels different to experience or to be around someone who is experiencing sadness versus anger.

Let's take a look at some of the emotional frequencies and how they may affect you.

Hopelessness: This is almost a non-feeling emotion. You feel stuck, not knowing where to turn or what to do. We've all felt it at times for a moment or longer. The emotion is held deep inside. When you are experiencing hopelessness, you feel restricted and immobilized. You lose your creativity and ambition. Often times, you may see this state with someone living on the street. Even though they may be broke and there may be jobs all around, they can't see them because of how they feel about themselves.

I remember a while back I was exiting a shopping center parking lot and stopped at the light. I looked over to my left at a young man, maybe in his twenties, holding a sign: "Need help-will work for food." Right behind him was a Carl's JR fast food restaurant with a sign in the window: "Help Wanted." When I looked at this young man's face, he looked hopeless. I'm sure he had seen the Help Wanted sign, but most likely thought, *'Why would they hire someone like me living on the street.'* He could have had a sign: "I need help to get some clean cloths, a room for a few days to clean up and apply for the job behind me." However, when you are feeling hopeless, you lose your ability to think creatively. Your view of the world creates the world in which you live. When you are locked in hopelessness, it becomes almost impossible to *see* the truth of your own situation or the opportunities around you.

Bottom line—hopelessness does not feel good. In fact, you don't feel at all…except stuck. Often times, in order to pull out of this emotional state, it requires being acted upon by an outside force that almost shocks you into looking at yourself and taking action to change. We've all felt this emotion at times, but because we have a higher purpose we don't remain there for long. The cure for hopelessness is having a purpose to work toward.

Next up the frequency scale is **Sadness**.

As we increase the frequency to a higher level, we find sadness. Being sad does not feel very good either, but it is still a higher-level frequency than hopelessness. Sadness is an emotion that leads to loneliness and depression. It tenses your body and holds you inward. In this state, your energy begins to move, but you still feel a restricted energy flow. The energy is moving, but mostly you are holding it all inside.

Fear is the next level.

Fear is an emotion that tenses your body and holds you back. It's a state of re-living the past or projecting into the future with the anticipation of something happening again, then re-experiencing it in the present. Worry is a good example. You worry about something that might happen, trying to control something that is not within your control.

When you are experiencing fear, you want to move, but the anticipation of pain holds you back. An example is a salesperson not wanting to make the next call for fear of rejection.

Anger is the next frequency level.

Anger is an emotion that tenses your body and pushes you forward. Anger is usually brought on by an extreme need for approval, even though it appears to be a need for control. The angry person has a need to be 'right' therefor they have a need to control their surroundings. They believe that by being perceived as 'right,' they receive the approval of others, or more accurately approval of themselves.

Anxiety is the next frequency level.

This is a combination of fear that holds you back, anger that pushes you forward, and depression that holds you inward. You experience all at the same time. You can probably see why you don't really get anywhere in a state of anxiety. You seem to be really busy, getting very little accomplished, and burning vital energy. It never really occurs to you because you are in such a panic with so much to do that what you really need to do is simply stop and re-group! To cure anxiety, you need to take a breather and stop believing that your maze of important things to do is actually leading you somewhere. I'm sure some are important, but if you are going off in different directions, burning vital energy, you will accomplish very little. Just remember, multi-tasking is multi getting nothing done.

Ask yourself these two questions. First, "How do I feel when I attempt to slow down, try to relax, or when I take a day or two off?" The next question is, "How do I keep myself from relaxing, slowing down, or taking time off?" Might as well relax a bit. Being the fastest person in a maze doesn't get you anywhere any faster anyway. Besides, there is really nothing to prove, or win, or achieve anyway.

Look at it this way. We are all entered in the race of life, and in the end, we will discover that we were just racing against ourselves anyway. When you truly look at it, you'll see there is really no destination at all! So why not just relax now and allow life to happen.

Let's look at one of the emotional states, or vibrations; let's say, anger. Think of a time when you were in a playful or peaceful mood, and suddenly you came in contact with someone who was angry. They might have been angry with you, or it might not have been about you at all. Either way, how did you feel being around that person? You could feel that downward pull, couldn't you? The reason is that their frequency doesn't resonate with yours, and therefore you feel uncomfortable and want to get away.

It's like two channels coming in on the same radio station. Either one signal is stronger than the other, pushing the other out, or there is a feeling of static and confusion. This holds true with any emotional state. When you're around people who aren't on your frequency, or are on a lower frequency, you feel like you want to get away from or change them. It's like mixing happiness and sadness. One or the other will always dominate. Both are stories, and one will always dominate.

You are not born with emotions. All emotions come from past experiences and feelings generated from those experiences. Emotions are simply a surfacing of buried feelings that are tied to past experiences.

Emotions come and go like the tone scale on a stereo. One minute, you might be in a state of hopelessness, and the next moment, you might be in a state of anger, depending on what triggers that emotion to surface. Then, the next person you come in contact with reminds you of someone who hurt you years ago and upsets you again. Then the next moment, you might find yourself looking at a sunset and feeling nostalgic. Then, you find yourself in a peaceful state because of a song you just heard. You can go in and out of various emotions based upon what you are experiencing at a given time.

Let's go through the language you might use, or self-talk you listen to, that represents an emotional state. Notice if any of the following words or phrases resonate with you.

I can't.

Failure.

I give up.

What's the use?

I can't win.

I am confused.

I feel stuck.

I feel worthless.

Nobody loves me.

Nobody cares about me.

I feel helpless.

These are emotions of hopelessness. If you are in this state, that is exactly how you will perceive the world around you. If you feel hopelessness, your world seems hopeless and you create more hopelessness for yourself.

Say the word 'hopeless.' Say it again. Hopeless. How does it make you feel to say it? Hopeless. It doesn't feel very good does it? Remember words carry power. They are hypnotic.

How does a person get into a hopeless state? We all do it. It's just that some stay there longer than others. A person can get there a little at a time, or it can happen all at once.

In a small town where I lived for a while, there was a man who lived inside a drainpipe at the edge of town. He never bothered anyone. He would hang around one of the restaurants at closing because the owner gave him food. Everyone seemed to know him. One day, I asked someone where he came from and who he was.

What I discovered was startling. He was once a stockbroker, with a seat on the New York stock exchange and living in a high-rise plush penthouse. One day, he lost it all. He lost millions of dollars. He went from a seat on the stock exchange and living the good life, to living in a drainpipe. He went from having it all, to hopelessness, and there he stayed until he died a few years later. He was killed by his own belief that his life was hopeless. In other words, he died from a disease called 'hopelessness.'

The human body is very loyal. It will even die for you if you tell it to do so. The real truth is, we kill ourselves everyday by what we are hanging onto that keeps us from living fully. It is not what happens to us that matters, it's how we handle what happens to us that makes the difference.

Let's move up the emotional frequency scale a bit to a higher frequency. Notice how you feel as you read the following words or phrases:

>It's not fair.

>I feel lost.

>Why does this always happen to me?

>I feel unhappy.

>I feel hurt.

>I am disappointed.

>I feel guilty.

How do these emotions make you feel? Maybe a little better than hopelessness, but still not very good. These feelings produce an emotional state of *sadness*, which is actually a higher frequency than hopelessness. Sadness has more movement, more feeling than hopelessness. You feel less 'stuck.' Say the word *'sadness.'* How does that make you feel? Say the word *'disappointed.'* Does that make you feel sad? See how the words you speak make you feel a certain way? Words are truly hypnotic.

Moving up the emotional frequency scale even more, listen as you say these words out loud. Notice how they make you feel. Notice the energy they produce inside you.

>I am worried.

I feel afraid.

I feel immobilized.

I am frustrated.

I feel insecure.

What emotion do you feel? It is fear! The emotional frequency of fear. In fact, all negative emotions are really based in fear, they are just disguised as something else.

Take hopelessness, for example. It is really the ultimate state of fear. In hopelessness we fear even moving. We've been beaten down so many times that we just don't have the will to try again. We fear taking any action at all. Hopelessness is the ultimate fear of failing, as well as the fear of living. We are so fear-'full' that we become immobilized. Our energy is 'stuck.'

Moving up the emotional frequency scale again, see if you can identify with any of these emotions.

I want it done now!

Why don't you ever listen?

It's my way or no way.

I am jealous.

You are wrong!

What do you think? Anger! We've probably all experienced this one at one time or another. Take a look at the word 'impatient.' Feel yourself feeling impatient. Can you see the anger behind the feeling of impatience? Can you see how the feeling of impatience creates the emotional frequency of anger? Anger is one of the ultimate control dramas. And the more you experience it, the more out of control you become.

Now let's move on up to the top of the non-resourceful emotional frequency scale. This is where we find a great deal of those we believe to be 'high achievers.' See if you can identify with any of these?

Always busy

Being selfish

No time

Being snobbish

Being a know it all

Being rigid

Being narrow-minded

Being opinionated

Being resistant to input

Being vain

This is the emotional frequency of anxiety.

"Look at me!"

"Look what I did!

"Look what I accomplished!"

"I need no help from a higher power or anyone else!"

"I can do it myself!"

"Who needs resourcefulness, love etc.? I can accomplish anything all by myself. I'm a multi-tasker. I can do it all myself."

This frequency creates a lot of movement, a lot of anxiety, and burns *a lot* of energy. It also creates a lot of undue stress, heart attacks, and other major illnesses! The person in this emotional state is always *in* pursuit, and never satisfied with the results he/she produces, or what they have. No matter how much they have, they always want more. They want life to be more. They want to have more fun. The problem is, when you are in this emotional state, you never get enough, because enough is never enough.

So, up the emotional frequency scale: hopelessness, sadness, fear, anger, anxiety. Begin to notice when you are in any of these states.

Begin to notice what it feels like to feel sad or angry, when fear is holding you back, or when anxiety has you running in circles.

Begin to notice how you can observe yourself in any emotional state. Begin to notice how these emotional frequencies keep you away from happiness, success and self-fulfillment.

Letting go of an emotion state, such as anger, is far more effective than just letting go of a single feeling. You can let go of your inpatient feeling, but when you let go of the anger that's causing your impatience, you not only release your anger, but your impatience will be weakened as well.

Not only that, but all the other feelings that are connected to your impatience will be weakened as well. When you let go of an emotional state like anger, you are literally dumping, or unraveling and disconnecting, a tremendous amount of feelings that are keeping that emotion alive—as well as the belief that fuels the emotion.

Can you now begin to see why just changing your thinking, or thinking positively, won't do it? Correct thinking by looking for the truth is the starting point, but positive thinking will not change a belief or release a feeling or emotion. There's a lot more involved than just positive thinking. If you want permanent change, you have to let go of the feeling or emotion that holds the belief in place. Also understand that the emotion is not the problem as some might think. The emotion is the result of the problem! The emotion is also the solution to the problem. The emotion is a perfect opportunity to let go and grow.

Look at it this way, the emotion is just the tip of the iceberg; 90% is still under the water in the form of core beliefs, trapped energy, or feelings, that need to be released. As you begin to observe and let go of the emotion, the submerged portion begins to move into the light of observation and melt away.

Each emotion is connected to an experience and connecting feelings, and at the same time, feelings are connected to each other because experiences are connected to each other. So, when you let go of one feeling, you will also be releasing many connecting feelings at the same time, or at least bringing them to the surface for observation and release.

A few years ago, a man in one of my workshops was having a problem getting in touch with his feelings. I tried several approaches and exercises to break through and get him in touch with his feelings. Nothing worked. I had promised that he would experience a breakthrough before the two days ended. Finally, thirty minutes before the workshop ended, during a final exercise, he got a glimpse of a feeling connected to something he had experienced from some time in his past.

Three days later, I received a panicked call from him claiming that his whole life had been in shambles since the workshop. He said he was having some problems in his relationship. He was upset about the fact that someone had taken him for a large sum of money, among other things. I asked how he felt. He said he felt hurt, angry, and betrayed. I said, "But you are feeling, right?" I went on to explain what was happening. By letting go of one feeling, a multitude of connecting feelings began to surface as well, and he was going to need to deal with them.

As I worked with him on the phone, helping him to let go, he explained that the first release felt like a small hole being poked in a huge dam. Later, he said he felt like the whole dam had broken. A week or so later, he called and told me he had never felt so empowered.

Can you see the incredible value of letting go of an emotion such as fear, anger, etc? Each feeling is connected to and supporting other feelings, holding them in place. And it is holding you in place as well! Breaking the dam of feelings and emotions is absolutely the best thing that could happen to you. That is, as long as you understand the nature of the feelings and how to deal with them at a core level—as just energy, nothing to fear, just something that needs to be released. Again, all emotions are derived from past experiences and attached feelings. The sum total of your experiences are within your subconscious.

Someone asked me one day what the purpose of the subconscious was anyway.

I said, "Its real purpose is to protect you. It also creates problems by offering you outdated data so you will pay attention to what you need to let go of in order to move forward." Actually, if you understand it fully, your subconscious is your greatest ally. It's like the hard drive in a computer. It stores your experiences and knowledge. It is also a problem solver. It provides an awesome opportunity for growth! Look at your subconscious as your assistant. It is really an *impartial* assistant. It stores everything as permanent record for later retrieval.

You create a new vision for your life. At the same time, it draws upon past experience, looking for supporting or conflicting data and beliefs to help you. When it brings up supporting data, you become inspired to move ahead. When it brings up data like, "That flame is hot, so don't put your hand in it," that can be very helpful. However, it can also bring up conflicting data that tells you not to do something because of a past experience that may not have any bearing on what you are doing now. On the other hand, if you recognize this fact, it is offering you a perfectly planned opportunity to let go, resolve an old issue, and grow or move past the outdated belief. You just have to be careful what information you act upon. Observe and ask yourself, 'Is this information based on a past experience, and does it have any bearing on the issue at hand? Should I press detete?'

It also may be bringing up information that, at first impression, is telling you not to move forward when in reality the opposite may be true. That's why it's so important to consider the information and determine if it contributes to what you want to accomplish or not. Your greatest power will come with the understanding that you do not have to respond to any voices, suggestions, data, or disturbances within. You simply observe the data and act upon the part that serves you, letting the rest go.

When you feel any emotion, fear, anger, etc., just know that the proper use of that emotion is simply to first, get the message, then turn off the alarm clock by observing it and letting it go. When you feel an emotion, such as fear, it is there to get you to realize exactly what it is you are frightened of in the first place. Once you *see* the truth, see exactly what it is you are frightened of, you can resign yourself to it… should it really happen. This will also turn off your fear alarm allowing you to move forward with greater ease. It is also really important to not take any steps to resolve your fear until you've turned off the fear alarm. Taking any steps without first turning off the alarm—in other words, observing it first—will actually strengthen and feed the fear, allowing it to return at a later time with more strength. When you feel anger, it will allow you to realize what you are attached to and afraid of losing. The first step is to turn off your anger alarm by observing it and letting it go. If you take steps before turning off your alarm, you will be taking action from a place of anger and producing more of the very thing you are trying so hard to get rid of in the first place.

There is a caution you should take when experiencing anger. It is really easy to get caught in the trap of blaming others for your anger. What really happens in a blameful attack; not only are you hurting the other person, but you are also being hurt in the process. The language of anger can produce one of the most powerful and impacting hypnotic spells. An angry person will eventually end up destroying themselves if they become too vindictive. They blame everything and everyone for their issues. Blaming others may seem easier than letting go and being non-reactive at the time, but expressing anger is just avoiding facing your own feelings. The end result of this kind of action is further suppression of your feelings. Suppression is always the *real* motive behind expressing anger. Anger is always brought about by the fear of what you might lose: approval, control, being right, or what you have lost in the past that you fear losing again. Sadness, on the other hand, is always about what you fear you have lost or are about to lose. So, you can see that both sadness and anger, or any other non-resourceful emotion, is always fear based. All of which should be considered your greatest gifts—that is, if you use the opportunity to let it go. Every time you experience a non-resourceful emotion of any kind, it is being given to you as an opportunity for self-discovery, self-healing, and self-growth.

It's truly important to know why you experience emotions the way you do. Anger, for example, without the label you give it, is just energy. It is a different form of energy than sadness or hopelessness. Why? The only reason is because you have labeled it differently.

Both are trapped energy wanting to be released. Just like the pen on my desk and the paper I write on are different forms of the same energy. An Oak tree and an Elm tree are both the same energy, just in different forms. When you begin to see each of your feelings or emotions as simply energy—without labels, judgements, or evaluations—you remove their importance and are left with just energy.

Look at it this way. A feeling without a self-created label of any kind, is hardly something you should be frightened of in any way. In fact, without the self-created label you place on your feelings and emotions, there is no feeling at all, just energy moving and changing, coming and going. When you look at it from this perspective, there is absolutely no reason to resist any feeling, because it is just energy coming up to be released back into usable energy once again. Who knows, you might create an Oak tree when you let go of anger—same energy in different form.

The letting go process is not about using effort, willpower, or your brain to change one thing into another—like trying to turn a negative into a positive. That totally misses the point of letting go altogether. When you begin to see your feelings and emotions for what they really are, just energy, you'll then realize that neither positive nor negative exist. These are just more of the same labels you create designed to further suppress painful feelings by means of your own self-judgement.

Letting go should be an effortless process. Hanging on is what uses up all your energy and causes so much pain. Letting go requires no effort at all. It requires observation and making a choice. Letting go is simply a process of releasing restrictive energy that is keeping you stuck in a place you don't want to be. By simply observing the feeling as it is, which is just self-labeled, trapped energy, the experience will basically transform itself. Again, there is no effort involved with letting go at all, only choice. The choice is, you either become self-observant and let go, or you don't. Together they yield self-discovery and personal transformation. Without self-observation and letting go, you stay right where you are; and that's okay, if that's where you want to be.

Letting go is as simple as the statement, "Wow, what a relief!"

TEN

Intention and Faith

The speed of the results you produce is totally based on your clarity of intention without the interference from past or future. Intention and faith are your most important tools in molding and determining outcomes. Faith is simply the tool that gives conviction to your intention. If you have a clear intention that you'll produce a certain outcome, and if there is no conflicting message from your subconscious that produces a conflicting intention, then your intention will become a reality.

Let me offer you a more detailed example. Let's suppose you set out to open your own business. You certainly intend for it to be a super success, otherwise you wouldn't have started it in the first place. Now, let's suppose you've purchased your inventory of merchandise to stock your shelves.

The doors are now open and you offer your merchandise for sale. The problem is, no one is even coming into your store. Your immediate thought may be that you've made a serious mistake. This thought is closely followed by another thought—that you are going to lose a sizable amount of money, which is also accompanied by an intense feeling of fear. And before long, if you don't let go of the doubt and fear and hold true to your original intention of success, you may begin to feel convinced that your business is going to fail. You may even begin to see yourself as bankrupt, with no hope at all, a victim of cruel fate.

Think about it. What would your reaction be if you found yourself in that situation? What would your conviction be, success or failure? What messages would you be listening to? Which would you be honoring the most, your intention to have a successful business, or your fear of failure? If you allow the conviction of failure to be predominate in your mind, you will eventually fail. On the other hand, if you hold true to your original intention, solutions will start to show up. You will only be a success to the degree that you are *convinced* of your success.

Stop for a moment and think about the past year. How many times have you changed directions when you hit the first obstacle? A feeling of either success or failure will back every action you take. That feeling becomes your guidance system that leads you to an eventual outcome. You have got to think and feel successful in order to become so. It is impossible to be a success in any endeavor while thinking and feeling you are a failure. You don't attract results into your life, you create it based on intention. It works the same whether it is in your business, in your relationship, your family, your career, or your health. Whatever you give attention to *grows*. We must have a clear *intention* of what we want to accomplish and have *faith* that it will happen one way or the other.

In the preceding example, the critical point that faith and letting go must be exercised, is the point at which there are no buyers for the merchandise you have in inventory. At this point, refusing to accept your circumstances as a mistake or as an indicator of forthcoming failure is the key. Faith is not about trying to *think positive* or *affirm* the problem away, but by having faith that everything is going to work out, you acknowledge that you just have not yet found the correct formula.

When you stay focused on the problem, you see no solution. When you let go of your fears, you allow new solutions to appear. This doesn't mean you don't take action to change. All it means is you are taking action from a more solution-oriented place instead of acting out of fear.

It is also important to know that it is not always up to you to determine the ways and means and the correct sequence of events by which you will attain success. However, it is up to you to let go of your fears and have faith and conviction that everything is unfolding perfectly—that a solution will appear. It doesn't matter if it is in your business, health, relationship, family or a financial problem, letting go of any feeling that is not contributing to your success is the key.

So, instead of always worrying about tomorrow, develop the understanding that there are no solutions at all in worry. Our real problems in life arise not from what happens to us, but rather from the worries and demands of what we think should be happening, or by what we are concerned may or may not happen.

Imagine, before digital cameras, taking a picture. You loaded the film. You have it focused and perfectly framed for the perfect shot. You snap the camera. Then, right after you snap the picture you open up the camera to see if the picture came out all right. You wouldn't do that, would you? The same should apply to any intention. You create the intention of the end result you want to accomplish, and then trust that the solutions will appear when needed.

There are always two things at work, *intention* and *attention*. Only when you have a clear *intention* do you know what to focus your *attention* on. Intention creates attention. Without a clear intention our attention is focused on the problems, not solutions.

I remember many years ago, having a very clear intention to open a wellness clinic.

I had full confidence that the model I came up with would work. I was excited to get started, and I fully intended to succeed. The only problem was I had no experience running a clinic or with the lab procedures I wanted to perform. I researched it. I talked to medical labs, doctors, nutritionists, and was hitting a dead end everywhere. Then, I got the idea. Why not find the manufacturing company that made the test kits for the procedure? The second person I spoke with about it gave me a referral to the man who manufactured the test kits. It turned out he was only a few miles from me. I met with the man for lunch and told him what I planned to do.

He said with a chuckle, "Let me save you a lot of time and money." He said, "I opened a clinic just like what you are talking about in San Francisco, and it didn't work. I did a total of sixteen hundred dollars in business the first year."

My immediate response was, "What does the fact that you couldn't make it work have to do with my business model?" I respectfully said, "Obviously you didn't have a marketing method that would drive customers to your clinic, but I do."

He asked me what my marketing model looked like, which I told him I wasn't willing to share. Now, I had never used this marketing method, but I was 100% convinced it would work.

As we talked further, he looked at me and said, "You really intend to do this, don't you?"

I said, "Not only do I intend to do it, I intend to have these clinics all over the country!"

He looked at me for a moment and responded. "I believe you are going to be a success, would you like a partner?" He said, "I will handle all the lab set up, create the test kits, and run the office while you focus on the marketing." And he said, "I will also put up all the money to open the first clinic."

I was so intent on doing this, and confident of my success, that it changed his doubt to belief that this model was going to be a success. To make a long story short, we formed a partnership, and within a few weeks, we opened our first clinic.

I wrote the ad to go into the LA Times for the upcoming Sunday main news section; that cost $6,000. At that point, doubt started to creep into my new partner's mind as to whether the ad would work. So, he took my ad to a friend of his that owned one of the top advertising agencies in LA for feedback.

His friend said, "This ad will never pull a call."

All I said was, "Interesting feedback. I'm running it anyway."

When we opened the doors on Monday morning at 9:00 AM, we had already received over 50 messages. The phone rang off the hook for the next four days and for as long as we would stay there at night. The first month, we generated over $200,000 in business off a $6,000 ad. Not only that, but by the end of the first year, we had opened four clinics. He didn't want to expand any further, so I sold my interest to him, and by the end of the second year, I had opened twenty-six clinics—all very successful.

A clear intention will always show you exactly what you need to devote your attention to in order to produce the desired results. In every apparent failure, there lies a greater opportunity, but faith and intention are required to be open to seeing the opportunities.

Maybe he failed in his first business so he could partner with me. Maybe he feared expanding because he failed in his first business. When you let go of fear and have faith and conviction in what you are doing, you will find a market for your goods or a solution to the conflict created perhaps in a totally different manner than originally envisioned.

I know a man who developed a product and was determined to sell it through retail drug stores. After several years of very limited success and eventual failure, instead of giving up, he proceeded ahead with faith and conviction that his product was going to be on the market in a big way. A short time later, he was asked to put his product on television as an infomercial. In less than three years, he had made a net profit of more than $120 million.

Intention is the key. Intention and faith that the correct answer is there if we keep moving forward and continue to honor our intention.

If you choose to feel happy instead of lonely, the perfect relationship will appear to support your happiness. The world you perceive is the world you'll create. Your world is simply a reflection of your intention and faith.

Recall a time in your life when you felt worried about money, anxious about success, a relationship conflict, or a family problem. How did that make you feel?

Here's the real question. Are these problems still affecting you in the present, even though they happened in the past? If so, that is because you are caught in this self-defeating addictive cycle, bringing the past and future into the present.

So, what do you do? What is the answer to handling non-supportive feelings? How do you change a belief that no longer serves you? In most cases we attempt to do so by only changing our thought process. We've been taught to believe that if we can just think positive everything will be all right. Positive thinking to overcome self-limiting beliefs is like walking forward with a giant rubber band around your waist attached to the wall behind you. You may move forward a little, but then the moment you relax a bit, those hidden feelings pull you right back to your starting point again.

Many have become what I call *'positive thinking, motivational, growth junkies.'* They rush from one experience to the next, looking for the hottest new technique, someone with something new to say that will motivate them. They look for that ultimate experience that will recreate that *'mountain top high'* once again. Using positive thinking or motivation to overcome outdated beliefs completely misses the point of letting go.

What does positive thinking mean anyway? What is positive? Where does negative end and positive begin? Who says so? Positive and negative may mean different things to different people. What is positive to one may seem negative to another. It seems we are always beating ourselves up over being *negative* and seeing it as *wrong*, and we try too hard to be *positive,* seeing it as *right*. Of course, *right* and *wrong* is another story, which we'll get into later on.

Positive and negative can be replaced with these two words: 're-source-ful' and 'non-re-source-ful.' The real question is, "Is this action taking me in the direction I want to go." If it is, then it is resourceful. If not, then it is non-resourceful. Success at anything is that simple.

Michelangelo was once asked how he created such a beautiful sculpture of David out of a piece of stone. His reply was, "I simply hold a vision in my mind of what I want to create, and I chip away what doesn't support my desired outcome." That is how you create the life you want. You create the intention of what you want to accomplish and let go of what doesn't fit.

Here's another question I get often: "What about motivation? Isn't motivation important?" Some believe you can't stay focused if you aren't motivated. It is simply an error in thinking to mistake excitement or arousal with staying focused. Motivation and emotional adventures may arouse you, but they will not enhance your sense of clarity. For the most part, it covers up what you need to be chipping away at, what you need to let go of in order to accomplish what you want. Used in the wrong way, motivation can be a form of suppression that feeds your addiction. Motivation can exhaust your vital energy as well as your creative imagination.

Motivation is the tension created when stimulation meets resistance. Stimulation from 'want,' which is based upon a lack of having something in your past, and resistance created from the 'fear' of not having that which you lack. So, what you have is 'want,' which is defined as 'lack' and the 'fear' of not having that lack, all mixed together creating a false sense of *motivation*. It's called 'fear motivation' which produces anxiety, not focus. The motivation ends when either the stimulation ends or the person wears out.

With letting go, on the other hand, there is no resistance. You simply create your intention of a given outcome, trust in the process, then play with whoever shows up to play, knowing that it is the right person. When you let go of what disempowers you, there is no resistance, only focus and flow. If you find yourself out of focus or not feeling right about something, it's simply a signal that there's something you need to clarify and see the truth, or something you need to let go of in order to move past the obstacle and stay true to your intention.

Let's say you have a certain job to do, but you find yourself continually faced with obstacles that hold you back. If you stop and take a closer look, you may find you are experiencing fear or anxiety, or it's your intuition telling you to look for the truth behind what you are feeling.

Motivation and excitement are both rooted in passing desires and instant gratification.

When you are truly passionate and committed to what you want, there is no need for external motivation. When you motivate someone with an addiction, you have a motivated addict!

Another misconception that many have is that we can change a belief through the use of affirmations. The use of affirmations to change a belief, in my opinion, is at best a low-level activity. Affirmations are only effective in changing your mind. Beliefs can only be changed through releasing the feeling energy that keeps the addictions alive. Beliefs are supported and maintained by suppressed feelings. Feelings are in turn created from our experiences, which also support our beliefs. Therefore, there is a mutually dependent cycle that exists. Feelings create beliefs, beliefs create actions, actions create results, and results create experiences which support the original addiction.

As an example, you may experience fear when your belief about financial security is threatened, even if the belief is irrational. The fear is then suppressed, which maintains the belief through the addictive cycle. Thoughts can also support our beliefs. Our beliefs can and do influence our thinking. And of course, our feelings can and do influence our thinking as well. This addictive cycle will continue until it is broken from the release of the supporting feeling and emotion.

So, you see, affirming, *"I have no fear about not having money"* from a mediocre belief will not make you wealthy. It might change your thoughts temporarily, but eventually the feeling that keeps the belief alive will return. Not only that, but it could even support a mediocre consciousness, especially if the feeling of frustration is present while you are speaking the affirmation. For example, let's say you are short on money. You could affirm, *"I have money."* This could trigger a feeling of frustration, a feeling that you are lying to yourself, because you know full well that you don't have any money. If you are going to use an affirmation at all, you should use one that does not confront the feeling directly. Instead, you could say something like this, *"Money is being irresistibly drawn to me from everywhere."*

By doing this, you are now allowing money to flow to you instead of supporting the fear of not having money. You are no longer lying to yourself about having money, which only compounds the problem. However, the underlying belief is still there, living within your addictive cycle. You may have a belief that money is hard to get and doesn't flow at all in your life, and that you have to go out and get it.

Again, learning to let go is the key. Let's say you want to save $25,000 for the down payment on a new home within a certain time frame, but you've never saved that much money before. You have a belief and a corresponding feeling of doubt about saving that amount of money in a given period of time. The key is to focus your attention on letting go of the doubt that keeps the non-supportive belief alive while taking action to save the money.

Here's another example of using affirmations. A man in one of my classes in Nova Scotia carried a written list of all the assets he expected in a woman. He repeated them daily and had for a long time. He knew exactly what he wanted: color of hair, color of eyes, height, weight, age, measurements, etc. She needed to like outdoor activities: hiking, running, biking. He read his list to the class.

Upon awakening every morning, and last before bed, he would affirm, "I have a loving relationship with a woman with dark green eyes, dark hair, etc."

I asked him, "How is that affirmation working for you?"

He said, "Not very well. I have been affirming it for over a year, twice each day, and my loneliness has actually gotten worse, not better."

Next I asked, "How do you feel when you repeat the affirmation?"

He said, "I'm starting to feel like I'm lying to myself. Frustration is what I really feel, even more so than loneliness."

Here is a question for you: do you feel that his feeling of frustration was moving him toward a loving relationship or away from it? Will his feelings bring him closer to his desired relationship, or further away?

Next, I asked, "How would having the perfect relationship would make you feel?"

He said, "Wonderful."

My next series of questions for him was, "Would it really matter if she had blonde hair instead of black? Would it really matter if she was 5'4" instead of 5'6"?"

I went through most of his list and his answers were almost all the same, "No not really."

My suggestion for him was this. First, he was to throw away his list—which he did, on the spot, with great enthusiasm! I then got him talking about how it would feel to have that perfect woman and perfect relationship. Before he finished, half the audience was in tears from the emotions he felt and shared. Thirdly, he was to observe how he felt in his current situation. And finally, he was to let go of any feeling that did not support the feeling of how he wanted his life to be regarding his relationship—which he did in class.

During the lunch break a woman from the class invited him out for lunch. She later shared how much she hated his list and how drawn to him she was after he threw it away and shared his feelings. Within a couple of weeks, he wrote telling of the woman he met *in the class,* and that they were in love and engaged to be married in a few months.

Thoughts, feelings, beliefs, and behaviors create! Thoughts choose the direction, feelings create our beliefs, and behaviors create our circumstances. We all want and attempt to change in many different ways, but with very little success. Here's the reason: changing requires letting go, not pushing against. It requires letting go of the feeling and emotion that supports the belief, so our behaviors take us in the direction we want to go. This young man let go of the belief that the items on his list would produce for him the perfect mate. When he let go of that belief, the perfect mate instantly appeared.

Think of a belief you have that you want to change. Imagine your belief is a brick wall. Got it? Using an affirmation, motivation, or positive thinking to change the belief is like hitting your head against the wall. Imagine that. When you hit your head against it and it doesn't move, it hurts, right! The more you do it, the more it hurts, and the more it hurts, the less you want to do it. Finally, to avoid the pain, you decide it would be a lot less painful to just remain the way you are; but, at the same time, you don't like the way you are. The question becomes, "Do I continue the head bashing and experience the pain, or do I stay the way I am with less pain?" Most decide to stay in the place that creates the least amount of pain.

Picture this: your beliefs are a brick wall. The feelings you hold inside and the emotions that surface to support your beliefs are the mortar that holds the bricks in place. By letting go of the feelings and emotions that support unwanted beliefs, there's nothing to hold the bricks in place. Without the mortar, the bricks will eventually fall, leaving room for a new belief to come forth.

To sum it up, affirmations are used incorrectly when the intention is to avoid or push away what is perceived as unpleasant feelings and emotional experiences. A belief cannot be abandoned, changed, or transformed until the supporting and underlying suppressed feelings have been cleared.

As an example, if a person is hanging onto a feeling of anger or resentment from a break-up or hurt from a past relationship, no change takes place until the feeling is released. No matter how hard you may affirm to the contrary, you will continue to attract a similar relationship that supports your anger. That is what we all do. We go out each day trying to gather information and experiences to prove our beliefs to be correct. Remember, all beliefs are false until you decide they are true. And how do you know if they are true? Are they taking you in the direction you want to go? The whole purpose for an emotional upset is to clear the feeling so you can change a belief.

Look at it this way. Feelings and beliefs are an energy you continually project upon the outside world. You will see, experience, and create only what you are projecting. Your view of the world around you will be based on what you believe to be true. And if you want to know what you are putting out to the world, simply look at your life. For example, if you are hanging onto anger, you will continually be faced with situations that provide you with the opportunity to let go and move past your anger. Because, until you deal with it and let it go, it will surface again and again, and it will be stronger with each surfacing. We project what we feel and believe, and we create what we project. As an example, the expectations of others, the standards they expect you to live up to, are really your own projections given back to you. Think about it. If you want to change how others treat you, all you have to do is change your perceptions of yourself; therefore changing what you are projecting to others to give back to you. Judge yourself by y*our* standards, project them out to others, and then believe they think those things about you.

Let's say that you are depressed, and you judge yourself for being depressed. You then look at your friends and think they hate it when you are depressed. You think they are judging you, when in fact, they may not have any reaction at all. They may not even notice. This is simply a reflection of standards that aren't being met with yourself. What if your friend does notice your depression and judges you for it? That is their problem, not yours—just as it would be your problem if you hated their depression. Whoever sees the problem owns it. It is in *their* head!

Who you are, the relationships you experience with those in your life, and the circumstances you are now living are based solely upon your beliefs, and the feelings that you hang onto to keep the beliefs in place. The secret to living a successful and happy life, in my opinion, is to build up an emotional conviction from the heart of that which you want in life, then let go of that which no longer supports the conviction.

Everything in your life comes to you, or is repelled from you, based upon the vibration of your energy field. It's the Law of Cause and Effect at work. And that energy field is established by what you believe to be true and the resulting behaviors they collectively produce. As an example, think of a time when you were around someone who was angry, anxious, or desperate about a situation in his or her life. How did you feel when you were around them? Did it give you a comforting, uplifting feeling, or did it start to bring you down as well? It is because you were not in vibrational harmony with that person.

Many of the people I associated with in my younger years, I no longer associate with simply because I no longer relate to their vibrational frequency, their way of thinking, or their belief systems.

Doesn't make them bad people. They are just not in alignment with they way I chose to live my life. I'm sure the same holds true for everyone. As you change the people around you will change also. Sometimes they literally go away, never to be heard from again. Once you fully understand this concept, you will see that *nothing* is truly out of place in your life, and everything is perfect based upon your level of consciousness. Your world is simply a mirror of your convictions and core beliefs, stamped out in material form. The question is, do you like what you see? Do you like the world you have created for yourself?

You are your own architect and builder. You have built your world to the exact specifications of your belief system. Even if you ran away from home, left your current job, or changed your circle of friends, nothing would change. Even if you ran away from your present lifestyle, with the thought of starting over in another state or country, in time you would create an almost exact duplication of your former world. You simply cannot run away from your world, because you cannot run away from what you believe to be true.

But here's the good news, you can certainly change your core beliefs. If you truly want to change your experience of life, you must first change the rules by which you've been living by. As an example, if someone gives you money to help you take care of a financial lack, if you don't change the rules that got you where you are—if you don't change how you believe and feel about money—soon you'll be back in the same situation.

I know a man who was flat broke, and a few years later, he had earned over 200,000,000 dollars. The interest alone would have earned him 10 mil a year. And yet, after 20 years, he was reported to be broke again. His former situation of being broke simply returned when enough tension built up again as the result of his suppressed feelings and beliefs about money. It is an addiction! In other words, if at the end of each month a person doesn't have the money to pay their mortgage, they *could* borrow the money to pay it. However, borrowing the money doesn't solve their real problem. They need to examine what they believe about money (or the lack of it), because that is what got them behind on their mortgage in the first place.

In order for your world to improve, your underlying belief about how you perceive the world must change. In order to change a belief, the trapped feeling that keeps the belief alive must be released. You have to let go, start making better decisions, and begin breaking the addiction. To change, you must develop a new understanding of how to function in the world.

In order to be happy, you must develop a new understanding, not of *happiness*, but rather an understanding of what causes *unhappiness* in your life. Happiness is not eluding you. Success and money are not eluding you. It is your idea about happiness, success, and money that eludes you. We should all seek to give up incorrect ideas instead of giving up our happiness, success, or money. Happiness or success can only exist when you begin to see that your unhappiness or success is not connected to the event itself, but rather to how you perceive the event.

The simple key is to develop the ability to let go of the feelings and emotions trapped inside that no longer support the life you want to live. Denying the problem will not make it go away. Letting go is the key. Everyone has the inborn ability to let go of non-supportive feelings. It is simply a matter of choice. We do it all the time. Just look back at your life at all the things you have let go of over the years. It's a choice to let go and grow, or to hang on and stay stuck. Real and permanent growth occurs in your life only when you release the non-supportive feelings and emotions attached to your core beliefs that are the root cause of your conflicts.

A woman called me recently who had attended one of my seminars and had just read my book *Rings of Truth*. She said that as a result of what she learned from the book, she discovered some things she was hanging onto in the form of resentment toward her mother. She explained that the two of them hadn't spoken for almost twenty years.

She said that as soon as she let go of her resentment toward her mother, her mother called and asked if they could get together and resolve their issues. She said that she and her mother were now communicating on a regular basis. She was also surprised by how little effort it required on her part to let go and move past her issue.

The reality is, letting go requires no effort, only a choice. The real effort comes from hanging on! Think about it.

There are many kinds of growth therapies available, and some may be very worthwhile.

However, any therapy that leads you to believe your life is awful, or you are awful because of something you did or something someone else did to you, is certainly very incomplete. We've all had a lot done to us, and we've all done a lot to ourselves. None of that matters! It is all in the past. None of this is happening to us now! What else is there except right now? We should blame no one for our circumstances or lack of happiness, and that, most importantly, includes ourselves.

In order to experience true growth, you must take full responsibility for experiencing life the way it is now, this very moment, not how it used to be or how we want it to be.

You can spend your whole life wanting things to be different, wanting your past to be different, but nothing will change until you do. If you aren't willing to experience life the way it is now, you can never move past your current circumstances. You have to experience it in order to let go. We only stay stuck because we don't want to experience life as it is right now. We want it to be different, but it can't be different. Life today is what it is. It's okay to want something better, but life in this very moment is what it is, and nothing you can do will change that. All the wanting in the world to change what is happening to you now won't change what is happening to you now. This moment cannot be different. It just can't. Because nothing else exists except this moment! There is nothing we can have any effect on except this very moment, so why relive the past or try to live the future. Seeing life the way it is, and then choosing to no longer live under those circumstances, is what will allow you to change.

I'm always reminded of two statements made in the Bible. One is, *"And one day time will be no more."* This simply means, "Someday we will live in the present."

The other statement is, *"Many are called, and few are chosen,"* which means, "Few listen."

Being self-observant and seeing the truth is the real key to listening and knowing. Letting go is the key to living in the present. What else could do more? We can't chase away the past, and we can't grab hold of the future. Letting go and living in the moment is the only way to find happiness. If there was another way, I would sure like to know about it. What do you let go of? You let go of all the emotional distress that drags you through all the unpleasant experiences you have in life.

Letting go allows you to set your mental clock back to zero, where you can live without looking through the filters of yesterday's mistakes or tomorrows worries. Maybe you don't believe letting go will really work for you. Belief plays no part in letting go. You don't have to believe it works in order for it to work. Getting you to believe it doesn't concern me at all. I do know one thing, though. It won't do you any harm to practice letting go. Who knows, it just might work! What if you give it a test for the next 30 days, and if it doesn't work for you, what have you lost? Nothing! It doesn't even require any additional time on your part to try it. If it doesn't work, you'll still be right where you are in 30 days. The important question is, if you don't give it a try, then you'll never know if it would have worked. What have you got to lose?

We can all spend years in counseling, therapy, attending seminars, going to spiritual retreats, or looking for some guru to enlighten us. But until you make a conscious choice to do life differently, you will just keep right on going around in a circle looking for a way out.

Everyone has blocks, destructive habit patterns, stresses, and addictions that keep us in pain. Even physical symptoms can be linked to emotional distresses, both directly and indirectly. Emotional distress is simply a warning signal, an alarm clock, telling you it is time to wake up, to let go. The main purpose for letting go is to help activate growth and experience more self-love and happiness. Whatever it is you think you need to be happy is nothing less than emotional self-healing.

If you want letting go to work, everyday application is the key. It took a lifetime to learn the ways that aren't working, and it will take some time to reverse the process. Even though you will see changes taking place immediately, over time with continued use, you will see significant changes taking place. You'll see things happening in your life that you never dreamed possible before. There is no better time than now to *be* happy. If not now, when?

Your life will always be filled with challenges. All you have to do is decide to let go of the ones brought on by past programming that no longer serve your greater good.

You may feel that your life is just about to get better as soon as a certain thing happens, but there will always be obstacles in the way—something you have to get through first, then you'll be happy. In order to re-discover happiness, you must be willing to open yourself up to pain and work on letting it go. When you open to pain, you also open to joy. When you take off those rose-colored glasses of the past, the first person you will see in the mirror will be someone you love…yourself! Those obstacles are your life. Obstacles are a part of life. Getting rid of obstacles is not the way to find happiness. Happiness is the way. Treasure every moment. Time waits for no one. Don't wait for happiness until you get the right job, find the right mate, lose ten pounds, until the kids are grown, or until you leave on vacation. Don't wait for happiness until you get divorced, until you retire, until summer, until you have a drink, until you have enough money, until you die, or until you are born again and discover that there's no better time than right now to be happy. Happiness is a journey, not a destination.

ELEVEN

Emotional Clearing

I used to believe that reading was very difficult. It would take me sometimes weeks to get through a book. I could only read at about 140 words a minute, whereas the national average was at about 240. I would read a page, then forget what I had read. I *believed* I could never read much faster, and certainly not above the national average.

Then one day, I was introduced to speed-reading. Within 4 lessons, I was reading at about 28,000 words a minute with 99% comprehension. Now I have a new belief. Why? By virtue of developing a new experience toward reading, I basically outgrew the old belief.

As we have discussed, beliefs are held in place by programming and trapped energy patterns that are set off by memory responses. For example, no one walks around full of sadness. They walk around focused upon their surroundings and suddenly something stimulates their trapped energy patterns of sadness—a thought, sound, smell, something someone says.

Let me give you some more examples of trapped energy. This is important. Everything in the universe is made up of energy, or atoms. A tree, a telephone, my clothing, the computer I am using, even my body are all energy, trapped energy. Everything is composed of the same energy, waiting to be molded into something usable, and that is your choice.

Let's say you have a feeling that nobody loves you or you're afraid or lonely. These are all made from the same energy, and they are just as real as the tree outside my window. What would happen to the tree if we set it on fire and burned it to the ground? It would disappear, wouldn't it? Well, yes and no! The physical form of the tree would disappear, but the energy of the tree would still exist. It has been released into usable energy once again.

Another example: What happens if heat is brought into contact with ice? The ice changes its form and becomes water, doesn't it? Now you can drink it. If you apply even more heat than the water can stand, its molecular structure begins to change, and it becomes hot water. All you started with was ice. If you apply even more heat, it begins to boil, and then it becomes steam that could power a locomotive. The ice, water, hot water, and steam change to a higher and higher frequency until it actually disappears into the atmosphere, but it is still energy. As it moves from water to steam, then to vapor, you can even breathe it, but you can no longer drink it or hold it as you could the ice. You didn't add anything at all except a heat source, which in itself is energy at even a higher frequency.

Listen carefully to this:

When heat is added, the water begins to resonate with the heat, becoming as much like it as it can. If you add cold, the water begins to freeze because it resonates with the cold, becoming as much like it as it can. My objective here is to get you to perceive and think of energy in a different way.

Look at it this way. Energy flows where attention goes. In other words, you can change the energy patterns held inside by refocusing your attention. Since everything is energy, there are a lot of energy patterns all around you, and of course inside you. The energy patterns you hold inside not only have an influence on your every action, but also on those around you. You will resonate with your surroundings and your surroundings with you. Birds of a feather flock together. In other words, when your view of the world changes, the world around you changes. For example, if you believe yourself to be a victim, you will resonate with people who tune into your frequency and support your belief.

When you let go of a negative emotion, you actually change your frequency just like adding heat to ice. As you change your frequency, you begin to resonate with those who support your new frequency.

Remember when you used to play 'Make Believe' as a child? Try it now. Close your eyes right now and make believe you are living the life you want. Not so much what you want to have in your life, but rather how do you want to feel. What type of people would you like to resonate with? How would living the perfect life feel to you? What came up? More importantly, how does that make you feel? How do you resonate? What type of people are around the new you?

Let's take two components, *intention* and *vehicle*, and measure what percentage each plays in producing the results you want. Here's what it would look like. Let's say you want to be happy and you think taking a cruise would do it for you. Your intention is to be happy, and the vehicle is taking a cruise. The reality is, the cruise is a temporary pleasure and will not make you happy. Why not just *be* happy? With that, you'll discover a lot of vehicles that will be a pleasurable by-product of your happiness.

Your thoughts choose your direction in life. When a thought becomes in alignment with your intention, and you now know where to focus your attention, a change can occur—just like in the example of the heat and ice. The reason your thoughts don't always produce change is because you have a conflicting intention or belief that you accept as true. In other words, you are mixing two frequencies and confusion is being sent to the subconscious to bring forth in your life.

There are certain things I wouldn't even think of doing. For example, sky diving. I wouldn't even give it a second thought. Why? Because my intention to never sky dive.

I love life too much to risk losing it by jumping out of an airplane at 10,000 feet. I personally don't need to go to that extreme just to have an experience of being alive. But if you do, that's okay too.

We all spend a lot of time, and a lot of energy, trying to label our feelings, thoughts, and emotions. The good ones we try to hang onto, and the bad ones we try to suppress or push away. You'll have a wonderful sense of relief when you begin treating your feelings as just moving, changing energy wanting to be released. Especially when you discover you have absolute control over them.

Let's do a brief exercise. Close your eyes and sit comfortably for a moment and just relax. Take a few long, slow, deep breaths, and just let all your muscles completely relax. Let go of all the tension.

Now, from this relaxed place, in your imagination, attempt to get as angry as you possibly can. Think of a situation in your past that made you really angry. Now, at the same time, try *not* to tense a single muscle. What you'll find is, as long as you remain relaxed, it is impossible to get angry at the same time.

I read a story about a spiritual man who went before his master and said, "I'm a very angry person, and I want you to help me."

The master said, "Show me your anger."

The man replied, "Well right now I'm not angry. I can't show it to you."

The master then replied, "Well then, the anger is obviously not you, since sometimes the anger is not even there."

Anger, like any other emotion, is just energy. It is simply what you are experiencing, not who you are. Any emotion—whether it is anger, sadness, fear or whatever—is only your attachment to, or identification with, a past experience. You have simply trapped it inside and given it a name.

Think of a time when maybe you dented your car or broke something you really liked. It really felt like it was you who got dented or broken, didn't it? You went around all day reliving the upset of the experience. You are not your past experiences. You have only become temporarily identified with them in the present.

Memories of past experiences can be very beneficial, but if recalling a memory also brings forth an unpleasant emotional response that is not released, this can be destructive.

It can be very beneficial however, if you realize that an emotion is simply a signal to investigate what it is you need to let go. In order to more fully understand this, imagine something emotionally painful that happened to you in the past. You, as that person in time, are not in the present moment. In other words, it is not happening to you now, correct? You, and whoever might have been involved in your past situation, are not in the room now, are you? You are only holding the image and the experience of the past in the present moment, correct? In order to resolve this unpleasant experience once and for all, you must let go of the trapped emotional energy surrounding the event. In order to do so, you must first understand that you are the one in total control, not the event or the person involved in the event, as it may feel. You are hanging onto the experience, *it* is not hanging on to you. You are in the driver's seat. Not only that, but you must be willing to re-experience the emotion associated with the event in order to fully let it go.

Many of your past painful experiences may have been brought on by even earlier painful experiences. By re-experiencing and letting go of one feeling, it will weaken and release the energy connected to the other. In other words, when you let go of an emotional response you are having today, it may be linked to a past issue, and at the same time, that past issue may be linked to an issue that goes back even further. When you let go of one, the other is also weakened.

For example, I remember a man in my workshop who was having a problem with anger.

Upon further questioning, he discovered his grandfather was abusive to his father, his father was abusive to him, and as a result, he felt angry toward life itself. He blamed everything and everyone for his lack of happiness and success. When he let go of his anger toward his father and grandfather, his anger and resentment toward life also disappeared.

It is not possible to have an emotional conflict outside of you. You may be thinking, 'How can that be true? My grass is growing like crazy and my lawn mower is broken. How can that problem be inside me?' Let me ask you. Did the grass create the problem? Did the lawn mower create it? No. It is the frustration you are feeling about the grass growing and the lawn mower not working that is the problem. The real question is, "Is what I'm feeling helping to get the lawn mower fixed or the grass mowed?"

When you observe and *experience* the emotion, you stop hanging on, which allows the energy in the trapped feeling of frustration to return to its original form, which is just *free flowing* energy.

Look at it this way. I'll use the example of the block of ice again. We'll call the ice the experience from your past. The ice trapped energy is what we'll call anger. Let's say you realize, through your experience of some past event, you have frozen the water, the usable energy, into ice, or rather in this case, anger. Once you realize this, you can now stop freezing the water, thaw what you have frozen, and let it be just flowing energy once again. First, you take responsibility and stop trapping the energy so it doesn't become an even bigger problem. Second, you re-experience the emotion and let it go, allowing it to return to its original form, which is free flowing energy.

The present time is all there is. There is no past or future. Neither exists. When you recall a past experience, because the past doesn't exist, what you're really experiencing is a psychological response of the past in the present. How severe the experience is in the present will depend on the vividness of your recollection, the impact of the past experience, and how many times you've suppressed the experience over time. Hanging onto and continuing to suppress a past experience can produce the same, if not a more severe, physical and emotional response than occurred when the event first happened.

Even though it is not happening to you now, your reaction can be very much the same.

Once you begin to observe this process, more and more you will realize that reliving an unpleasant experience can drain your energy, make you tense, depressed, and unhappy.

Stop right now and recall a past experience that made you feel sad, angry, or unhappy. Notice how that makes you feel. Now, quickly think of something joyful from your past.

You will notice two things. First, you will notice how difficult it was to switch from the unhappy to the happy feeling. But once you do make the switch, you'll notice how the experience of joy will uplift you.

As we begin to work more and more with the process of self-observation and emotional clearing, you'll see how quickly change can occur.

TWELVE

Suppression and Repression

Let's take a moment and examine the *suppression* and *repression* of feelings and emotions. Suppression is something everyone does to one degree or another. If you've ever known someone who can no longer relate to others, they have merely been more into suppression than the average person. If you know someone who seems more well-balanced, this simply means that person has suppressed less than average.

Let's examine exactly how suppression works. Suppression begins with resistance. What you *resist* grows in strength. Why is that? When you resist, you do so because you don't want to experience the same thing again. This is true, except when you resist, you are focused on the problem instead of the solution. Where attention goes, a result is produced.

Let's say someone says something that really hurts you, and instead of stating how you feel, you say nothing at all and suppress the feeling. After a while, you forget what happened, but the trapped energy pattern created by the experience is still there just the same, because you suppressed it. You see the person again at a later time and recall the experience, but once again you say nothing. The result is further suppression. You have strengthened the feeling by not addressing the issue. Now, keep in mind you can address the issue without having to be with the person, simply by recalling the experience, letting the emotion come up, and letting it go.

The degree to which you hang on to an issue will depend upon the degree of emotional impact you experienced when it was created. As you continue to resist a feeling by suppressing it, you build a shield which blocks the exchange or *flow* of energy. The next time you see that person, they may sense a wall, or a shield, around you, and they won't know why.

To carry it even a step further, a year—even ten years later— down the road, you may find yourself in a similar situation, not even with the same person. Then without realizing it, because the person or situation may remind you of the other person or situation from your past, you put up the same wall and block the exchange. It has become an automatic response.

Through suppression we all build shields, to one degree or another, around our feelings so we don't have to re-experience them. We don't want them to surface because we don't want to experience the pain. What we don't realize is that when we don't let the feeling go, it doesn't go away. It remains trapped within us, waiting for that opportune—or should I say inopportune—moment to re-surface. Over time, the habit of resisting our feelings will result in chronic *repression*.

Repression is slightly different from suppression in that *repression* is an unconscious automatic response. It becomes so familiar to us that we suppress without even knowing it. The reason we suppress or repress is to avoid pain. We also avoid taking responsibility for our own feelings. Responsibility is an interesting word. It is defined as, *"response-ability,"* or to put it another way, *"The ability to respond."* If we don't take responsibility for our own feelings, we have no ability to respond. When we don't take responsibility for our feelings and behaviors, we end up blaming others or our circumstances for how we feel. Which is the ultimate form of repression. Perhaps if we stopped beating ourselves up by hanging onto and suppressing our old experiences and beliefs, there would be no reason to continue the behavior that leads to the beating in the first place.

When you *resist* a feeling by withdrawing your awareness of that feeling, this completes the suppression, which keeps the past feeling alive in the present. When you suppress a feeling, you really don't avoid the feeling as most believe. Instead, you only push it aside allowing it to build strength for a later appearance.

Most believe it is possible to simply close the door on your pain and remain at peace, but you'll find this to be a misconception. You may attempt to forcefully exclude pain from your awareness through all sorts of evasive maneuvers. These may include work-a-holism, over-eating, watching television, going to motivational seminars, or looking for the next exhilarating experience. Most of the time what you are really doing is rejecting yourself, because the pain is still trapped inside. It is held in storage in a state of limbo, waiting for the right time to resurface and give you another opportunity to deal with it. The "feeling energy" is stored in the subconscious. The subconscious is where all past experiences, positive or negative, are stored. If not dealt with, these negative experiences can become like a fragmented hard drive on your computer that has been infected with a virus. You then can become misguided by unconscious urges that lead to self-destructive behaviors. Without even realizing where they originate, you continue to look outside yourself for the answers. What happens then, is that you become attracted to, and even attached to, the wrong people and circumstances, rejecting the right people and circumstances. You can become compulsive, and even addicted to certain behaviors, in spite of your best intentions to change. You don't really want these painful situations in your life, but you will automatically attract them because of your trapped energy patterns keeping the beliefs alive. Your life can then become more stressful, and even confusing, because of feelings that haven't been dealt with properly.

As you create a new vision of something happy and joyful in your life, these visions pass through your fragmented hard drive, or subconscious programming, where the virus is residing, trying to gain support for manifestation. Your new vision then becomes mixed with these old patterns, creating even more stress and confusion. You perceive and experience life in a certain way because that is who you *believe* you are based on past experiences.

When you look at your life in this way, your non-resourceful feelings and emotions are the *gift* that has been perfectly presented to you in order to further your growth. Once you begin to truly observe your unwanted feelings and emotions and let them go, you'll begin to realize the world you have been experiencing has been created by your own projections. And once you change those projections, your life changes with it.

As an example, a person may *perceive* the world as a threatening place, and as a result of that belief and supporting feeling, that person will *experience* the world as a threatening place. A perception is founded by a belief, and a belief is something *you* decide is true, but it may not be at all.

I knew a man back in the early seventies who believed there was a conspiracy to take control of our lives and turn us all into communists. He had gathered all sorts of supporting data from numerous sources, all of which had the same beliefs as he. He had books, tapes, and underground newspapers all claiming the communists would be taking over within the next five years. This was almost fifty years ago! Every year he would push the predicted date ahead another year or two and add some more information to his drama. He is now in his eighties and still claiming that we are all headed for destruction. His latest attempt was Y2K. All computers were to go down, banks would collapse, and if you had money in the banks it would be lost; and the conspirators were behind it all.

I'm sure someone above us is pulling the strings, but I don't choose to live my life controlled by fear and speculation of what *could* happen. Anything *could* happen. The earth *could* get hit by a giant meteor and all of us be killed instantly! My question is, why waste what time you have left living in fear? Why not live *fully* with the time you have left? I'm not saying you shouldn't keep yourself informed and take action when necessary. But this man has lived the last fifty years of his life not living as fully as he might have. And that is okay for him, if that made him happy. That is the direction he chose. We all take our own individual situations very seriously, and we don't even suspect for a moment that we create our own world through what we project, through our own beliefs. The reality is that this man had been taken over by the communists, even before they arrived. But he and his supporters were the only ones. The rest of us escaped the takeover by not buying into his drama.

When any non-resourceful feeling or situation arises from any source, you should automatically assume it is the result of your own projections. Any sort of tension in your life is the result of an unresolved experience you are holding inside. Look at tension as an alarm clock that is telling you it is time to let go and move past this.

When a non-resourceful feeling appears, stop. Observe it with silent strength. The act of self-observation will turn off your alarm clock. Next, take a moment and determine the outcome if you proceed. Look for the truth in the situation. Is it your truth, your belief, or are you about to become the victim of someone else's belief and projection? Realize that the next action you take will be what I call a "seed moment." In other words, it will plant a seed creating a new direction and new outcomes in your life.

Feelings are a lot like rumors. Rumors are the rehashing of something that has happened in the past. And as we all know, the more you pass around a rumor, the less accurate it becomes. It only seems real and true because we are discussing it now. And just like rumors, we are probably doing it with a lot of emotion as well, which makes it seem even more real.

A non-resourceful feeling surfacing is nothing more than the resurfacing of a past experience in the form of an emotion, that needs resolving. Remember, it is not what happens that is important. It is how you perceive what happens, and the actions you take based upon your perceptions of what's happening; that's what really matters.

Let's look at some of our favorite ways of suppressing and repressing our feelings. Read the following list carefully and see if you can identify with any of them. Now, keep in mind that just because you may do some of these things, it doesn't necessarily mean you are using it as a form of suppression. However, if you find you are doing any one of them to an extreme, it may be something you want to examine a little closer.

Excessive television viewing

Over socializing

Excessive use of alcohol/drugs

Smoking

Over organizing

Over intellectualizing

Excessive sleeping

Habitually overeating

Being a workaholic

Excessive cleaning

Unable to be alone and quiet

Always seeking highs

Always blaming others

Procrastination

Being critical of others

Over-spending

Let's look at a few examples of the items in a little more detail.

Television

Begin to notice how much television you watch daily. It is estimated that the average family in the United States watches television more than eight hours a day. Is it any wonder that families have difficulty communicating with one another these days?

I'm not saying television is all bad. It's not. There are a lot of very good programs.

Television is not an intellectual process either, as you may think; it's an emotional process. Virtually all programs are targeted toward reaching our emotions. Even many educational programs, such as wild animal documentaries, are aimed at violence and killing amongst other species just to get your attention.

They are looking for any *emotional hook* they can find that will get you to stay tuned.

Begin to observe the brief news clips that try to hook you into watching. Begin to notice their emotional slant. As you watch television, notice how the television shows target the drama we are all living. They focus on hurt, pain, family problems, sickness. and death.

Begin to notice your own drama as you watch. Begin to notice when you turn on the television and why. Begin to notice which show you are more drawn to watch.

I'm not telling you not to watch TV. All I'm saying is, become more self-observant about what you are watching and why. Are you watching television to support and suppress a feeling and/or to avoid an issue?

Every time you turn on the TV, stop and ask yourself, "Do I really want to watch this program?" If the answer is 'yes,' then watch it without any guilt. All I am saying is, look for the truth behind your behaviors.

Remember, you are the teacher you have been waiting for, and you are also the student that is looking for a teacher.

Socializing

Socializing can be great, unless you feel you have to always be with other people in order to be happy. Should that be the case, you might ask yourself, "What feeling am I hanging onto that causes me to feel the need to always be around people?" You may discover that loneliness is the issue, or maybe a need for acceptance. If you find yourself with a need to socialize a lot, observe yourself in a social situation; begin to notice who you're socializing with, and why. Who have you drawn into your life drama? That's right, through your own projections, you have brought all the players in your drama together.

Work-a-holism

If you are consistently working 12-14 hours daily, you could be considered a workaholic.

Imagine this scenario: You are on your death bed and your last words are, "I wished I had spent more time at the office working." I seriously doubt if that would be the case.

Work-a-holism can create a one-sided life, by excluding all the other areas, family, relationships, personal, health, etc.

I heard it explained this way. Imagine each area of your life as a ball. There is a ball for health, finances, career, spiritual, family, and your relationship. If you drop the ball that represents your career or finances, it can always bounce back. On the other hand, if you drop any one of the other balls, like health or family, it can do irreparable damage. In other words, it may never bounce back. So, it just makes good sense to keep all the areas of your life in balance as best you can.

As you become more self-observant, you will start to realize that being a workaholic is nothing more than suppressing a feeling. If you are a habitual workaholic rest assured there is always a feeling that needs to be dealt with in some way.

Look at it this way. If you are currently in a resourceful state of mind 20% of the time, and you're working 16 hours a day to get your work accomplished, what would happen if you could increase your resourcefulness, to say 40%? Here's what would happen. You would now accomplish your job in just eight hours instead of sixteen. By letting go of non-resourceful feelings, which allows you to stay clearly focused, you could not only eliminate your work-a-holism, but you could actually get more accomplished in less time.

Look at it this way, just by increasing your time in a resourceful, productive state of mind, from 20% to 40%, you could take every other week off and still get the same amount accomplished.

Procrastination

Procrastination is another way that many people suppress their feelings. It is almost always brought on by fear. It could be the fear of success or the fear of failure. You may be fearful of doing it wrong. You may have a fear of not being approved of if it doesn't work out the way you plan. Or maybe a fear of taking responsibility. Or it could be a way to get attention.

Procrastination is most often an unconscious suppression. However, when you suppress through procrastination, there is always a part of you that is aware you are suppressing. Chronic suppression through procrastination can lead to repression, where the act of both feeling and avoiding the feeling becomes an unconscious act. Suppression is basically self-rejection, and repression is a much more serious form of self-rejection. With repression, which is an automatic response, you can become totally out of touch with yourself and your feelings. Eventually, repression can create an addictive behavior, such as anxiety and other self-destructive behaviors and even physical illnesses.

Don't panic. If you lead a fairly normal life, you will always be involved in a certain amount of repression. This is normal and should be no cause for alarm. However, as you begin to practice more self-observation and address your feelings on more of a conscious level, you'll discover previously repressed feelings beginning to surface, giving you a chance to process them more easily.

Our natural instinct is to avoid pain; therefore, we always want to resist painful feelings.

Resistance is just another way we suppress our feelings. We assume that a painful feeling can be avoided by turning away from it, which couldn't be farther from the truth.

Let's say, for example, someone loses a loved one. Their sadness and loss are so overwhelming, so painful, that they don't feel they can deal with their loss. They begin to apply all sorts of avoidance tactics in order to avoid the pain. They read all the time or watch an excessive amount of television. After a while, they become addicted to their act of avoidance.

Resistance to how we feel has become one of the most used causes of suppression and can definitely become a form of addiction. If you want to decrease your amount of suppression, you must become more observant of when you resist and what you do to resist. And instead of suppressing, you can begin to condition yourself to confront and accept and let go of your painful feelings as they arise. The more you actually experience and release unwanted feelings and emotions, the more you'll find your personal boundaries expanding as well. As you become more accepting of your feelings, instead of resisting and suppressing them, you'll discover the very nature of your feelings changing as well.

The more you suppress, the more you'll have to deal with, and the greater the chances are that the feeling will continue to surface more often and with more intensity. As an example, let's take a person with a short fuse. They get upset and angry very easily.

Chances are if you looked back into that person's past, you would discover some sort of feeling of being out of control earlier in life. Maybe divorced parents, the death of one parent at an early age, or maybe even abuse, which left them feeling out of control. Every time a situation came up that left them feeling out of control, they might become angry until they regain control of the situation. And the situation probably doesn't even have anything to do with, or even resemble in any way whatsoever, their earlier experience. The real issue that needs to be dealt with is the feeling of being out of control, or really their *need* to be in control, with everything in their lives. If you heal a present feeling, you will automatically heal the past, without even knowing what happened to cause your feeling of being out of control in the first place. All you are doing by letting go is removing the energy from the memory of the experience.

Blame

Blame is a major way we avoid and suppress our feelings. Blame is our way of avoiding responsibility for what happens to us. In other words, the blaming person is always looking outside themselves for the reason they feel the way they do. When you become involved in blaming any person, circumstance, or whatever, for how you feel, you become blind to how you really feel and to the reality of the situation. You are literally blinded to the truth. The end result is repression of the feelings, which will eventually cause a repeat performance of a similar circumstance at a later time, or at least a circumstance that will trigger the same emotion to arise once again.

As an example, if you continually blame an outside circumstance, your job, education, government, kids, etc., for your poor financial condition, you will remain blinded to the real issue. The first step to curing your condition is to let go of the blame that blinds you from seeing the truth of your situation.

Most often we think that whatever triggered our feeling is the cause of our problem, so we look for someone or some "thing" to place the blame upon. Whatever triggered your feeling, and your need to blame, has really just offered you an incredible opportunity to let go. But if you are not self-observant, you will never see that you are the one in control and the one creating your drama.

In certain cultures, a person who blames another for his/her problems is considered unconscious. To become fully conscious, you must move past blame into truly understanding the real cause of your issue, which certainly has very little, if anything, to do with the other person. Understanding the problem does not eliminate it. It simply lets you see more clearly what work truly needs to be done. The very first step should always be to *see* the truth, otherwise you will continue to perpetuate the lie you are living. Besides, without first *seeing* the truth, you can't see the real problem.

When a problem arises, simply stop for a moment and ask yourself, *"Is this true."* As an example, let's say you are upset because your children don't do a certain thing. When you feel the upset and the need to control their behavior, stop and ask yourself. "Is this true? Are they really causing my upset?" Without knowing the real problem, how could you possibly know what needs to be done to correct it?

It is extremely important not to get into self-blame either. Blame should never be the issue. Seeing the truth is the issue! The way to handle blame is by seeing the truth behind the blame. So, when you feel the urge to blame, either an outside circumstance or yourself, stop! And drop the blame. Then, look for the feeling supporting the blame. Observe it and let it go. Only then is it safe to move forward. When you feel the need to blame, stop, determine the outcome if you proceed, then move forward in the appropriate direction.

Forgiveness is also a major part of releasing blame. True forgiveness is realizing that the other person is not responsible for how you feel. Forgiveness is not even about the other person. It is about you and the feelings you hold about the other person. No one can make you feel anything. Your feelings are simply the trigger point that shows you what you need to let go of. The real question you should be asking yourself regarding forgiveness is, "Does the feeling I am holding toward the other person support my happiness and peace of mind, or not?"

Often times, we try to force ourselves to forgive another. We believe that if we forgive, we are now being more loving toward the other person. But this type of forgiveness is just another attempt to avoid or suppress painful feelings. The other person is not the one you should be concerned about. It is your own peace of mind that is important. The reason we think we need to forgive the other person is because we continue to believe that the other person is responsible for what we are feeling. Nothing could be further from the truth. No one can make you feel anything. Only you can make yourself feel a certain way. We think that through forgiveness the problem will go away. But until we let go of the feeling, nothing will be resolved.

Forgiveness toward the other person is only intellectual and defeats the purpose of letting go all together. With this type of forgiveness, you can become more out of touch with your own feelings, which causes further repression. And at the same time, no real forgiveness takes place. True forgiveness comes with the understanding that the original blame was misdirected in the first place. Most often you create the experience as a result of your own beliefs and perceptions. That may be hard to understand and believe, but if you will just take some time and look for the real truth behind your situation, you'll begin to see that the real problem may have started inside you. Again, it is not possible to have a problem outside yourself. That is where the problem starts, and that is where it will be resolved.

Often times you are told to forgive without the understanding that you should take full responsibility for your own feelings. Here's another way to look at it. When you blame another for how you feel, what you are really doing is taking on the burden of the very issue you are blaming them for in the first place! If someone did something wrong that made you angry, and you blame them for making you feel that way, your anger actually supports the issue and keeps it alive! Get over it! Look for the truth. Let it go and move on.

Blaming yourself for how you feel is not the answer either. Taking full responsibility for letting go of your resentful feelings toward yourself is the key to forgiveness. Remember that *self-blame* and *taking responsibility* are not the same thing. You are responsible for your experience, and as a result you may fall into the trap of blaming yourself rather than the other person. It's true, you do create your own experience, but no one is to blame. It is just something that happened. Get over it and move on. It is not happening to you now. It is just something that happened. Regardless of whether you place the blame on someone else or yourself, you are still rejecting yourself, and therefore blocking your own development and peace of mind. Self-blame is just another form of avoiding or suppressing your feelings instead of taking responsibility for them and releasing them.

Even the *expression* of feelings can become another form of suppression. As an example, the expression of anger does not release the anger, as most believe. When you express anger toward another just to get it off your chest, it is both harmful to the giver as well as the receiver. Once you become aware that the other person is not responsible for how you feel, or what you experience, it becomes obvious that taking out your anger on another is not the correct approach to getting rid of it. It may feel as though someone is making you angry, but what is really happening is the person is showing you a way to better understand yourself and take full responsibility for how *you* are feeling. Blaming someone else or yourself for how you feel is a distortion of reality and leads to further avoidance of the real truth and to more suppressed feelings. Expressing your anger may appear to be the correct thing to do. It appears to be much easier than not reacting at all. But think about it. Who really wins in an argument? Who wins with anger? The answer is no one! Nobody wins. Both parties lose! It is just a temporary release that does nothing at all except strengthen the original feeling that triggered your anger in the first place.

One evening my wife and I were out to dinner with some friends. A woman was talking about how much she and her husband argued. She asked my wife how often we argued.

My wife thought for a moment and said, "We've never really had an argument that I can recall." She said, "We've had disagreements and discussions, but never an argument."

The woman asked, "How is that possible? Every couple argues."

She said, "We've never argued because I didn't have anyone to argue with, because Jim refuses to get upset."

The true motive behind anger or arguing is always suppression. Expression by arguing or being angry may feel like a release, when in reality it only strengthens the feeling for a later appearance. What's really important to know is that when you hurt another in blameful expression, you are also hurting yourself. The attack is just as harmful to the sender as it is to the receiver. Angry people eventually end up destroying themselves.

Another thing you should realize is that *mentally blaming* someone is the same as verbally blaming, because you are still carrying around the anger. Whether you express it, or just simply think and feel it doesn't really matter. The damage is being done either way. The damage actually takes place inside the person who is mentally blaming the other. Both ways you are still expressing the emotion, rejecting yourself, and suppressing the real feeling.

Motivation

Another area that should not be overlooked regarding suppression is *motivation*. You may wonder what motivation has to do with the suppression of feelings? Most often the feeling of needing motivation from an external source is based upon a sense of lack. If you define the words 'lack' and 'want,' you'll discover that 'lack' is defined as *'want,'* and 'want' is defined as *'lack.'* Basically, they are both based in fear—the fear of lack and the fear of not having.

To put it another way, motivation is where the stimulation from *wanting* something meets the resistance from *lacking* it. When the stimulation is gone, all you are left with is lack, leaving you unmotivated. Motivation is fear based and takes us out of the moment where the real experience or real life is taking place. The reason motivation is short term is because it has no basis for reality. When the stimulation is gone, the motivation ends. Then a new resistance begins—one that triggered your need for motivation in the first place. Thus, an addictive cycle is born.

Most of us are not even aware of what we are being motivated by in the first place. We think getting the money or the trip or whatever will restore a sense of balance into our lives. We need to become more self-observant as to what is truly motivating us. We only seek motivation in order to avoid the feeling of pain or fear that has caused us to think we need motivation. When in reality, all we really need to do is let go of our fear.

We feel something is missing. And something *is* missing. It is our willingness to see the truth behind the unwanted feelings we need to deal with. We all think we have certain needs. Something is missing. Something we must achieve to finally make us happy. We rationalize our behavior, but the real truth is we are trying desperately to avoid our own feelings. For example, let's say you are depressed and very lonely. Out of habit, your basic response is to suppress the feeling through some sort of diversion, such as being around people, entertainment, or perhaps alcohol and other recreational substances.

In this case your *lack* of happiness is really motivating you. You are being motivated by the fear of not having. While seeking the motivation to avoid your loneliness, you then reject yourself, which only compounds your feeling of loneliness. Using avoidance may give you temporary "short-term patchwork" relief from your loneliness, but that is the only motivation it will provide. If you simply face your fear of loneliness and let it go, the need for motivation would eventually go away completely. It may not go away immediately, because you will likely need to observe and release your suppressed feelings about the issue more than once. You may even need to investigate further as to why you are lonely in the first place. Over time, with repeated observation, eventually it will go away.

When you don't allow your unwanted feelings to surface, allowing you to release them, you can be faced with all sorts of self-destructive behavior patterns. The answer is to increase your observation and awareness of your unwanted feelings—to not suppress them, but rather to accept and experience them and let them go. You can resolve them, not by opposing them or being motivated by them, but by releasing them. And be patient. It may take some time and practice, or it could happen quickly. Being impatient with yourself is an insidious form of self-rejection that most completely fail to notice. Impatience is simply the rejection of what is happening now in this moment. It is rejecting reality. You can never be in the moment when you are experiencing impatience.

Being impatient with others is also being impatient with yourself. You are simply projecting your impatience upon the other person. You are trying to control someone else's behavior which is something that is totally beyond your control! Trying to control another's behavior is like telling your neighbor which day he should cut his grass or what time he should eat dinner or leave for work.

Right now, in the moment is where all experience takes place. When you are out of the moment, it is impossible to be in touch with reality. When you are out of touch with reality, you are out of touch with the truth. Impatience is equivalent to anxiety. Both are the absence of relaxation. Being anxious means you are not accepting what is happening. Anxiety actually causes you to reject what is happening, thus rejecting reality…rejecting yourself! When you reject reality, you reject life as it is happening. When you are always anxious to get somewhere or to get something done, you lose our ability to live life as it happens.

By becoming self-observant, you can see beyond impatience and anxiety to suppressed feelings that need to be released—the fear, depression, and anger that surround anxiety.

Think about it. What do you most often want to do when in a state of anxiety? You feel like speeding up, don't you? It seems like going faster is the only thing that makes any sense. We feel behind, therefore, the only way to catch up is to go faster. Right? Wrong!

Anxiety creates confusion. And speeding up only adds to the confusion. When in a state of anxiety, the only sane thing to do is *stop*. As you stop and observe, you'll discover that the solutions you are anxiously searching for will magically appear. When you slow down, you'll discover the solution you were running so quickly away from, trying so hard to find was hidden by anxiety.

Be patient. Work on one thing at a time. Defeating self-rejection and anxiety requires only three things—*courage, patience, and trust.* It requires courage not to avoid and suppress pain when it arises. It requires patience to slow down and release the feelings one layer at a time.

It requires *trusting* that the answers you are seeking will be there for you when you slow down and open yourself to receive them.

Letting go is a life-long process, not something you do once, and then you're all done.

However, the value of every release of any non-resourceful feeling will stay with you for a lifetime. When you let go, what you are really doing is discovering more of who you are. Respect for yourself, for others, and for life overall will begin to grow as you develop the courage to face your unwanted feelings, beliefs, emotions, and behaviors.

Again, remember, you are the teacher you have been waiting for all your life. You have all the answers you've been seeking. Just listen, observe, and apply the lessons. Look for the truth before taking action and know that truth will always be kinder to you than your own story. You are the answer to your freedom, and no one can keep you from that.

THIRTEEN

Releasing Attachments

Imagine for a moment how much time is required to travel 250,000 light years. That is, traveling at the speed of light, 186,000 miles per second, for 250,000 years. That's hard to imagine, isn't it? A single galaxy is estimated to be that far across, give or take a few miles. Now, imagine a galaxy that is four galaxies away from earth. That is 1,000,000 light years away. Imagine there are billions of galaxies within the universe. It is even harder to imagine, isn't it? I find it fascinating and mind blowing.

Envision our galaxy within all the galaxies of the universe. Look at the Milky Way. We are in there some place. Visualize the center of our galaxy as planet earth. Compared to the universe, or even our own galaxy, Earth is pretty small stuff, right? Now, imagine yourself *on* Earth. Even smaller stuff, right?

You are probably thinking, *'Okay enough of the universe stuff. What does this have to do with me?'* Here it is. I want you to imagine the problems you try so hard to control.

When you compare your problems to the galaxy or the universe, they pretty small stuff, right?

I have a theory. When you arrive here on Earth, you are given an allotment of…let's call it "cosmic energy" to burn up, and when it's gone, your *trip* gets canceled. The good news is, you get to choose how to burn up your energy.

Let's say you are traveling down the freeway at seventy mph. You are going to an appointment five miles away. If you continue at the same speed, you will arrive on time with 5 minutes to spare. All of a sudden you get cut off by someone who decides to travel at only sixty mph. You begin to get uptight. "How could this idiot be in front of me? Doesn't he have a brain or what? Come on let's go!"

If you continue at the same speed for the remainder of your five miles, that idiot will have cost you about thirty seconds. The thirty seconds is not the issue. The real issue is, how much of your cosmic energy allotment have you used, attempting to control something that is beyond your control. To what degree did your need to control something that is not within your control shorten your time on earth?

Imagine this, you go into the bathroom, and at that critical moment, you realize there is no toilet tissue. You get upset because your child did not replace it when needed. So, you lash out. "I can't believe this. I told him a thousand times to replace the TP when it runs out." Question is, do you want to burn up some of your cosmic energy allotment for this? It's alright if you do, but think about this. What if your cosmic energy allotment runs out while you are sitting there? What if that's where they find you. You have to think about those things. My point is this: Is it really worth the upset? Is it helping you live a stress-free life?

Let's say you are having an argument with your spouse, and you're both getting pretty angry. There are two things you might want to consider. First, you might want to ask yourself, "Who really wins in an argument?" The answer...nobody. The second thing you might want to consider is, "Do I want to burn a portion of my energy allotment for this, or is there a more sane, stress-free solution?"

We suffer *physically* when something is not working properly in our bodies. We suffer *emotionally* when something is not working in concert with our beliefs. We suffer *mentally* when we don't get what we want, or when we feel forced to live with something we don't want. Either type of suffering shortens our time here on earth by burning up our allotment of cosmic energy. That is my theory anyway. At the very least, it decreases our ability to experience the level of happiness that is available to us.

Let me ask you. If you didn't hang on and experience something as non-resourceful, would it be?

Think about it. Anything that you become attached to, a belief, an upset feeling, anything you are determined to be right about, will be an area in which your inner peace is affected. Anything you become attached to will eventually cause you pain. You can become attached to feeling fearful.

You could become attached to being angry, and feel that if you let it go, a part of you would die as well.

Some attachments cause more pain than others. The attachment you have toward those you love is a life-long attachment and is much harder to let go of when someone passes on, for example.

When a loved one dies, you feel as if a part of you dies as well. You feel pain, heartache and sadness, but eventually you deal with the loss and move forward with your life savoring the memories of the past.

I remember a woman in one of my workshops who had lost her son about fifteen years before.

She refused to let it go. She wanted to hang on to the sadness she felt, hoping in some way it might bring him back. I asked her why she had been celebrating his death for over 15 years instead of celebrating the memories of the time she had with him.

She said, "Oh my God, I never ever thought of it in that way."

With this new realization, you could see the pain lifting from her face as she spoke. I worked with her on letting go of her attachment, assuring her that her special memories would not be lost. After some time, she finally let it go. When she did, she stood up crying tears of joy, repeating over and over, "I finally let <u>him</u> go! I finally let him go!"

For more than fifteen years she had been unwilling to face the truth that her son was dead, and there was nothing she could do about it. As a result, she spent fifteen years not living her life fully, but rather attached to something over which she had no control. *Anything* you become attached to will eventually cause you pain, whether it is an emotion, feeling, physical addiction, money and other material things, a person, a job, etc.

Your prison lies within you. It is in your heart and mind. We all lock ourselves in addictions of our own making. All our pain and sufferings are based on ignorance. We don't see our situation for what it is. We don't see the truth, and therefore we can't see how to deal with it. We are blinded to solutions. We pass by the joys and happiness in life, not realizing we have missed a lot. We are like fish swimming toward a net knowing we will be trapped. But because of our unwillingness to see the truth, we continue heading in the same direction hoping something will change before we are trapped in the net of our own making.

When you see truth through self-observation, that the net is there, you can simply lower the net and move forward with ease. The real problem is that because of our beliefs about how things "should" be, we disregard what we see as truth. We think there should not be a net there in the first place, so if we ignore it, maybe it will go away. We all want our situation to be something other than what it is. We want to control something that is not within our control. Everything, everything, is what it is. You can't change what is, but you can change how you respond to it.

Inner peace, happiness, love, and joy are connections to your resourceful nature. In order to achieve inner peace, you must have nothing to defend, nothing that you are attached to, and no need to be right. A crisis only becomes a *breaking point* when you fail to use it as a *turning point* in your life.

Letting go does not mean giving up control of your life. Letting go of attachments simply lets you live from that peaceful place inside while taking action and moving forward with greater ease.

Think of something in your life you would like to feel peaceful about, something you have been hanging on to, something you are attached to, or something that causes you pain. Now, take a moment and get in touch with how it makes you feel. Observe yourself feeling the way you do.

Now say to yourself, "The only reason I can't be at peace with this is _____." What keeps you from being at peace with this issue? When you find out, you will have discovered what you need to let go of. You will have discovered the truth. The question is, are you trying to control something that is beyond your control? Are you attached to having a certain outcome? Letting go puts your mind in a state of receptivity for solutions, and at the same time provides you with an opportunity to see other issues that may need attention. You will see relationships that need healing, past mistakes that need to be forgotten or resolved, emotional wounds that need healing, and much more.

New solutions to resolve issues in your life cannot come forth if the old issues are taking up all the space. It is necessary to let go of old beliefs, habits, attachments, opinions and even some friends, in order to allow in the new. Letting go doesn't require any additional time on your part, whereas hanging on does. Hanging on consumes at least 90% of most people's time and energy. If you don't handle non-resourceful feelings and negative issues quickly, on the spot, when they arise, you will always suppress or repress them. This in turn creates a pattern of behavior which will create painful conditions again in the future. Hanging on wastes your time, burns your energy, and lessens your ability to experience happiness and all the other things you want in life.

When a feeling is released, five things are achieved. One–the suppressed feeling itself is weakened or completely resolved. Two–the belief that supports the action pattern is weakened and eventually undone. Three–the action pattern is weakened with every release of a feeling. Four–your happiness and ability to perform at your optimum is increased. Five–you have weakened your addictive cycle.

Remember, you can *make* yourself unhappy, but you can't *make* yourself happy. Because, when it comes to being happy, any effort will be in vain. Why? Because we cannot pursue happiness. It can't be caught. Happiness is simply the natural by-product of letting go of those things that make you unhappy.

The most important thing to remember is to always deal with the problems at hand first, before taking action. If there is a non-resourceful feeling present, this represents an immediate problem that needs attention. If you are about to take an action you know will lead you down the wrong path, this is an immediate problem that needs attention.

By letting go and living in the present moment, you can simply observe your problems with silent strength, instead of being swept away by them. When you make a choice to not let go when you know you should, you are making a decision to chase the solutions—or should I say to chase the problem? Because that is what ends up happening. On the other hand, when you let go, you are detaching from the problem so you can give birth to new solutions. Learning to let go and simply having the courage to just leave it at that will leave you open to receive the solutions to your problem.

Our biggest obstacle in life seems to be trying to figure out how to *handle* our problems rather than getting rid of them once and for all! Pushing forward, trying to forget your problems, is not only hanging on to them, but it is suppressing the issue, allowing it to return later, even stronger.

When you let go, everything seems different, even though nothing outside you has changed at all. The change actually took place inside, and all you did was stop resisting. And when you stop resisting, you will also find others around you not being resistant as well.

Another caution is not to attempt to analyze a feeling. Analyzing a feeling only strengthens it. The key is to simply observe the feeling, and if it is not supportive, let it go. It doesn't matter where a non-resourceful feeling came from. What matters is, it is there and does not need to be.

Although many believe it to be so. It does not require expressing a feeling, like anger, in order to let it go. *Expression* of a feeling such as anger only creates more resistance, and actually enhances the feeling rather than resolving it. It truly does not make any difference as to who is at fault in a given situation. The real point should be to solve the problem at hand, not to find fault.

You cannot solve a problem as long as anger is present. In most disagreements, both parties are so busy blaming the other person and defending their own position, that they forget to solve the problem anyway. Now you have two problems. The one that did not get resolved and the one created by anger. Think about it. If an emotion such as anger did not have any energy in it, would it be a problem? Of course not. If there were no energy in it, there would be no emotion at all. The trapped energy is the problem. If people would simply understand this fact, there would be no reason to fight because there would be nothing to win! There is nothing to become attached to except the emotion, derived from past experiences. And a past experience has nothing to do with right here, right now. So why not just relax and let go? It certainly won't make matters any worse, and it just might make them better. Whenever we allow a feeling to become conscious without resistance, it begins to clear.

Begin to simply sit back and observe your own actions. Begin to experience emotions such as fear or anger as just energy that comes and goes. Just be observant without attempting to express or suppress the feeling. Simply observe it and let it be. Observe it without letting it consume you, without identifying with it. Just observe it as "a" feeling rather than "your" feeling. In other words, I am "feeling" anxious rather than I "am" anxious. Just be with your feeling and allow your exploration of the feeling to go deeper.

If there is a fear of letting go, then let go of the fear that keeps you *from* letting go. Closer observation of any painful feeling or situation is the first step to letting go. See your feeling like an onion, each layer represents a different experience you have had in your life with a feeling attached. And know that each time you observe it, you are peeling off layers, one by one. When the layers are all peeled away, what do you think will be left? The real you, that's what!

Experiencing more love and happiness in your life is an unlearning process, not a learning process. When you allow yourself to become motivated by a non-resourceful feeling, by hanging onto it, what you are doing is actually reinforcing its power over you. When you do this, you are also reinforcing the addiction which allows it to return again at a later time with reinforcements!

Perhaps if we would stop abusing ourselves by hanging on, there would be no reason to continue the type of behavior that leads to the self-abuse in the first place.

You don't pay a large price for your development, but rather for clinging to your old ways. I know this approach may go against your conditioning. Not reacting to a situation is difficult when you feel threatened and you want to defend your beliefs. But what you'll find is that by letting go, by not reacting to a situation, your life will become much more effective in every way. The reason you will become more effective is because your emotions will not be in the way when taking action. In other words, you can now take action from a place of clarity and resourcefulness.

Not reacting does not mean you become passive to anyone's aggressions. You simply realize that if someone is upset with you, the upset is not about you. Their upset is just their drama, they are acting out, and you just happened to be there at the time. You can choose to be a victim in their drama, or not. If you want peace of mind, you will always encounter those who try to upset you.

Peace of mind will not arrive in a limousine or on a silver platter as you might hope. Instead, you'll run into situation after situation that lets you practice not becoming involved and maintaining peace of mind.

Another example: if you want to have more money in your life, and at the same time you are in frantic pursuit of money, trying to do ten things at a time is not the answer. With that kind of anxiety toward money, there will be no capacity to create more. In order to create more money, first and foremost, you have to let go of any anxiety toward money. Otherwise, all you will attract is more anxiety. You get caught up in the chase. Anxiety is fear based. So, the question becomes, can you have anxiety toward or fear money and have it?

If you are in desperate search for a perfect relationship, coming from a position of trying to overcome your loneliness, what you get instead of a loving relationship is more loneliness. Why? Because that is your focus. What you pursue or chase will always elude you. What you *become* you will create. If you *become* the perfect mate, you will attract the perfect mate! On the other hand, if you *become* perfect loneliness, what you create in return is more of the same. So, the answer is to let go of the loneliness, not to overcome or push it away, but to let it go and move past it.

Here are some of the most commonly asked questions regarding letting go.

Question: How does letting go compare with other forms of self-improvement?

Answer: It doesn't really. Most self-improvement programs are intellectual. They are targeted toward changing one's mind through learning and applying a certain *system* or *technique*.

Letting go, on the other hand, is not trying to force your mind into learning and applying a technique or system. In fact, letting go is not trying to force your mind to do anything at all.

When you attempt to force your mind to do a certain thing, you are actually feeding the problem you are attempting to overcome. Self-improvement definitely works, but only to the degree that you can change your non-supportive belief systems and break the addictive cycle so you can move forward. The only way to change an outdated belief is to first release the emotional energy that's keeping it alive in the first place.

Self-improvement is self-addition. Self-improvement without letting go will result in an endless addictive cycle of frustration going nowhere! Letting go is really very simple. There is no system to follow. Letting go is as simple as observing your non-resourceful feeling as it arises, acknowledging it and saying, "Here I am feeling that way again." Then, without buying into the illusion, without self-judgement, returning to the moment where the real action is.

In the beginning when you start to practice letting go, you may catch yourself after the fact. You may catch yourself saying, "I can't believe I just did it again." That's okay. Don't beat yourself up because you didn't catch yourself in time. Just let that feeling go and move on. Let it be a reminder for the next opportunity. After a while, with a little practice, you'll begin to catch yourself while you are right in the middle of the act.

You'll say, "Here I am again, right in the middle of being angry," or whatever. That is okay too. If you caught yourself, just know you are making progress. Then, after a little more practice, you will begin to catch yourself before you get into it. The more you let go, the easier it becomes. Remember, the simple act of self-observation in itself is letting go.

Question: What does "being in the moment" really mean?

Answer: Being in the moment simply means this: "Wherever we are, be there!" If you are caught up in a past mistake, you cannot be in the moment because you are lost in the past. In one way, you are in the moment, but what you are really doing is re-living a past experience in the moment, which destroys the moment. You really can't escape the moment, but you can chose what you do with it. If you are worrying about your future, you can't truly "be there." You are bringing worry into the moment.

If you are cleaning the house, just be there, cleaning the house. Observe the feelings you have that interrupts that work. "I don't like this. The vacuum is noisy. I shouldn't have to do this work, because I have a college degree." The reality is, you are doing it, and you have three choices. Pay someone else to do it. Do it without complaint. Or continue complaining while doing it. Either one is okay. It is just what works best for you.

If you are cutting the grass, driving the car, or whatever, you should try to be right there, not hating what you're doing, but being with the job at hand. When you are in the moment, you become more efficient, more effective, and happier overall.

If you hate your job, for example, you'll get caught up in the hate for your job, and as a result, find yourself closed to new possibilities and opportunities for a better job. I remember my first job. I worked in a gas station. I believed I was the best gas station attendant in the whole world. I was really good, and I took pride in my job. When a customer came in, I gave them the best service they had ever gotten anywhere. I would greet them with a smile, check their oil, check the air in their tires, wash their windshield, sweep out their car, etc.

One day, after I had gone through the whole routine with a customer and brought back his change, as I walked away, he got out of the car, and said, "Excuse me young man, but could I ask you a question?"

I said, "Sure."

And he said, "What are doing working in this gas station?"

I said, "Well it's my job."

"And you are very good at it," he said. "But you have a lot more on the ball than working in this station." He said, "You ought to be working in the factory."

"The factory," I said, "I could never qualify for that job because I don't have a high school diploma."

He explained that he was one a supervisor, and he could arrange for me to be hired, which he did. After about a year working in the factory, I became the number one worker out of about 9,000 employees.

They rated us with an efficiency program, giving us a certain amount of time to do a certain job. My best month was 457% efficiency, which meant I did the job of 4.57 people. Every month, I tried to beat my record from the previous month. Not to be THE best, but to do MY best.

One day, someone approached me and said, "Hey Britt, are you going to work in this factory the rest of your life? You should join me in a business." Long story short, in less than a week I was working full time in my own business in a direct sales company.

I struggled for over a year and just couldn't make any money. In fact, I ended up losing everything I owned trying to figure out how to succeed in business. I refused to give up though. As a result of my persistence, a man from the company came by one day and showed me what I was doing wrong and what I needed to be doing instead. Within six months, I was number one in the company.

My point is, when you are striving to be your best at whatever it is you are doing, you are open for other opportunities to come forth within your view; opportunities that could move you to the next level of success.

On the other side of the coin, John—a man who worked with me in my first job at the gas station—was a habitual complainer. He complained about everything. When a customer came in, he would complain, "It's too hot. It's too cold," or "Don't they know that it's closing time?" etc. Several times daily John would say, "One of these days, I am getting out of here."

Twenty-five years later, I was back in that town. While I was there, I decided to stop by the gas station where I used to work. To my surprise, guess who I discovered still working there. John! After twenty-five years, he was still complaining. "One day I'm going to get out of here." What do you think the odds are that someone will come by and ask John, "What are you doing working in this place? You've got a lot more on the ball than pumping gas."

Here's the moral to the story. If you do what you do with love, you'll eventually have only what you love in your life. This doesn't mean you necessarily have to love what you do, but what I'm saying is to do it with love; and there's a difference. In other words, if you are going to do a job, or anything else, why not be the best you can be at whatever you are doing? If you are going to do something, it takes a lot less energy to do it well instead of doing it and complaining about not liking it. When you are at your best, you are in a resourceful state, which leaves you wide open for new possibilities or opportunities. Nobody is going to promote a complainer or one that does not perform productively. When you are the best you can be at whatever you are doing, the universe steps in and provides you with a better opportunity to encourage further growth.

I never even had a thought of leaving my gas station job, but as soon as I had become the best gas station attendant in the world (at least in my opinion), the universe went to work for me, because I had reached my full potential in that job. The way I see it, if you have not discovered and learned all you can where you are currently, you don't get to move on to bigger and better things. That is the reason some feel stuck while others seem to be always moving on to better opportunities. This can hold true in any area of your life: work, relationships, spiritual, personal happiness, and so on. Again, when you do what you do with love, you eventually have *only* what you love in your life.

If you observe your thoughts, feelings, emotions and behaviors drifting in any way from being the best you can be, simply return to the present and put forth your best effort. This should apply whether you are mowing the lawn, having a conversation with a friend, or having dinner with the family. If you observe yourself drifting away, then *return to the present*. In other words, if you are at work, you should be working. If you are playing, you should play! If you are spending time with the family, you should be there with the family. Wherever you are, be there! That is what is meant by *being in the moment*.

Question: What are feelings made of?

Answer: Energy! Everything in the universe is made of energy. The computer that I'm using, the clothes I'm wearing, the chair I'm sitting in, my body, and even my voice are all energy. Everything is made of energy, the same energy. The pen on my desk is someone's idea of what to do with usable energy. The pen is what you might call "trapped energy." In other words, the energy is already being used for some purpose. You can't use the pen as a key to start your car. Just like you cannot use negative energy to create something good in your life. It's already being used for something negative.

All energy is both expansive and usable, or it is restrictive and already being used for some other purpose. As an example, *"I am lonely"* is energy that can't be used for anything else until you let it go. *"I feel loving toward myself"* is a different use of the same energy.

Let's look at it in another way to make it even clearer. Let's say that everything is made out of snow. And let's say that snow is energy, which it is. Now, we pick up some snow and make a snowball. Now, the snow is solid. It no longer can float like a snowflake. It's more like a ball of ice, and we can throw it. It is no longer in its original form. If you spread it out, it becomes snow once again.

Another example is turning water into ice by freezing it. The water is energy. The ice is also energy. Both are the same energy, only one is trapped in place as ice, while the other is flowing.

This is like 'lonely' and 'love.' One is flowing, the other is trapped in place. Both are use of the same energy. All the upsets you experience can only exist if you keep them trapped in place. When you let go, you neutralize the trapped energy, allowing it to flow once again.

Question: Why can't we just love more? If we love more, won't these feelings eventually go away?

Answer: I've heard it said many times that if we all just become more loving toward one another, everything would be just fine, as if being more loving can be done intentionally. We try to be more loving, then we fail. We then feel guilty and beat ourselves up because we can't love more. The next thing we do is develop a non-resourceful attitude toward loving, thinking that we cannot do it. The reason we can't be more loving is that we are going about it in the wrong way. We approach it through the mind, and the mind never produces love. No matter how hard you try to mentally convince yourself to feel love, you can never succeed. By trying to mentally talk yourself into being more loving, what you are really doing is setting yourself up to fail, which will in turn cause you to feel more incapable of loving. Your love will merely be a creation of your mind, which has no basis for reality. Only by no longer being motivated by loneliness, fear, etc., by letting those go, can will we truly discover how to give and receive love. When you begin to feel lonely, or any other negative emotion, simply observe it and release the pain and fear, which will allow real love—the real you—to show through.

Remember, the pain is nothing more than a signal, a mental alarm clock, alerting us that it is time to let go. It's just restrictive energy being used for something else coming up to be released. It is telling us that it is time to wake up! The pain is actually your greatest gift of self-love. Every crisis, every non-resourceful feeling or situation, is a perfectly planned opportunity for you to let go and experience more love.

And now, the most asked question of all is:

Question: What exactly is fear?

I'm not talking about the type of fear you experience when a wild bear is chasing you. That is real fear! I am talking about emotional fear.

Answer: Fear is also trapped energy—nothing more, nothing less. Because so many experience it so often, let me explain in a little more detail. It is good to know where fear comes from. Fear is the expectation of pain. Fear is the result of taking a negative past experience and projecting it into the future, with the anticipation of it happening again; then re-experiencing it in the present. Fear is simply using your imagination to make up an experience of pain. Fear is never about the present. It is only about the future, based on the past. It only appears to be happening to you now, because you bring it into the present. Whatever you allow into your mind is treated as though it is a present moment experience. Therefore, anticipating pain is the very same thing as experiencing it.

When you begin to let go more and more, you will begin to understand that the past only exists for the purpose of utilizing the practical, useful knowledge you have gained over your lifetime. It is really good to know not to jump out of a ten-story window or stick your hand in a flame. That is good practical knowledge.

Never, ever should you allow the past to become a source of pain in your life. It should only exist as a source of experience. You should be very observant when listening to past programming that does not support your current circumstances. In other words, do not let a past negative experience influence a current decision, unless it supports it.

When you are operating in fear, you tend to over analyze everything. And often times, when you over analyze, you are creating a cover-up that is supposed to keep you safe in your own make-believe world.

We also fear letting go because we are afraid that we will not know who we are if we do. We think that when we let go, we will be totally out of control; actually, the opposite is true.

Often times you may need to let go and have faith in order to find out what you really need to let go of. In other words, you may need to let go of your fear in a relationship in order to realize that the real issue is not the fear, but rather commitment. You may need to let go of the fear of losing your job to find out that your self-doubt is the real issue.

Anything you cling to will eventually cause you pain. When you cling to your fears, you have trapped the energy and given it a name—fear. And as long as you hang on to it, it will cause you pain. Why? Because fear is trapped pain, trapped energy that can be used for nothing else until you let it go. Fear is absolute proof that we as humans have the ability to create! Wow! What a concept! We are afraid of our own creation! Amazing!

If fear is the expectation of pain, then its opposite must be the anticipation of pleasure. When you let go of your fears, you can shift your focus to what you want in life. The only way that fear can have any power over you, is when you identify with it and allow it. For example, thinking you are eight feet tall will have no effect on you at all, because you do not identify with being eight feet tall. You know it is not you, so there's nothing to hang onto. On the other hand, if you think, "I am lonely," *that* has a hook, an emotional *link* to a previous experience. When you have a hook, you begin to identify once again with the pain from your past. When you identify with something, it becomes like glue. It sticks to you. If you challenge your fears through self-observation, instead of becoming identified with them, they will lose their hold on you—or should I say, you will lose your hold on them.

The more you ask yourself, "Where does this fear come from," you'll soon find your fears appearing less and less often, with longer and longer space in between. When you let go of fear, you begin to see the truth behind it, and therefore break its addictive cycle. You will also begin to realize that the space between your fears is who you really are. The more you let go of your fears, the greater the space between them becomes.

When do you let go? Do you set aside time to practice, or do you have to go away to practice?

Here is when you practice letting go. You practice all the time! You practice it every waking moment of your life.

When you are in a traffic jam.

When you are in a corporate meeting.

When you are having a meal.

When you are disciplining your children.

When you are in an argument with someone.

When you are stressed.

When you are feeling anxious.

When you are caught in a fear storm.

When you are stuck and don't know what to do next.

When you meet someone new.

When you cannot sleep.

When you need answers.

When you feel nervous.

When you are worried.

You practice letting go anytime there is a non-resourceful feeling present that is moving you further away from what you want in your life.

Letting go is about taking action from a position of strength. Letting go is about "high action" and "low attachment." Letting go lets you take solution-oriented action, instead of problem-oriented action. You should also avoid the temptation to be hard on yourself for feeling negative. Getting rid of outdated habit patterns, beliefs, and emotions should be guiltless. Look at negative feelings and emotions, not as your enemy, but rather as an ally that is providing you with a wonderful opportunity to experience more love, success, happiness, and pleasure in life.

Anytime you hear that familiar voice inside your head speaking to you, if it's not speaking with love and compassion, simply say, *"That's how I used to be. That's not me now."*

You see, being open to a new way requires being able to view the old, not with anger or resentment, but rather with love and compassion. You should never let your past dictate how you live your life in the present. Just do the best you can and do not concern yourself over whether it was good enough. Remember that every present moment is always brand new, and you can make of it what you want. What happened to you in the past is not happening to you now, unless of course, you allow it.

In addition to the basics (food, clothing, shelter, water, sunlight, and oxygen) needed to sustain life, there is one other element most of us completely overlook, and that is love. We need love in order to survive. Not feeling any love actually threatens our very existence, just the same as not having oxygen would. Carrying around self-hate or non-loving feelings is simply a slower way to die. Every time you let go of a non-loving feeling, what you are really doing is changing cells and re-balancing the body and brain. The more you let go, the more the real you will appear—the one who is full of joy, happiness, self-confidence, and peace of mind.

Starting today, allow every unplanned experience, every unexpected mishap, every non-resourceful thought, every unwanted feeling and emotion—no matter what it is or how much it hurts—to have a life of its own. Allow it to come up, be released, and become free flowing energy once again. Begin today to view your life with this higher understanding, an understanding that everything under the sun—from emotions and thoughts, to thunder and lightning—has its own birth, life and death. The only reason that any part of your painful past exists at all is because you refuse to let it die its own natural death by letting it go.

Living with pain and disappointment is not a requirement. Letting go of what no longer supports your happiness and success is not a requirement. It is simply a way of ending pain and unhappiness in your life.

FOURTEEN

Language and Feelings

Let's discuss the power of words; because the language you use has an effect on you and those you are speaking to. Words carry power.

Consider the phrases, "I hope," "I'll try," "I think," "I believe," and "I know." Which of these phrases do you feel has more power to influence you or others?

I *hope* I can do it.

I'm going to *try* to do it.

I *think* I can do it.

I *believe* I can do it.

I *know* I can do it.

Each phrase produces a different feeling and a different result, even though many people assume they have the same or similar meaning.

How do these words feel to you? Feel them as you say each. "I *hope*, I'll *try*, I *think*, I *believe*. I *know*." Which one of these words do you think carries the most power?

Let's say, for example, that you want to write a book. Do you hope to write a book?

'Hope' is defined as, *"To entertain an outcome."* You are only entertaining the idea of writing a book. You have not made a decision to do so. What if you set out to try to write a book? What do you suppose happens? Would you ever finish the book? Probably not. Why? Because the word 'try' is defined as, *"To struggle."* Not a very inspiring approach either, is it? You think you will write a book. To 'think' is defined as, *"to contemplate."* Still not a very inspiring approach to getting the job done. You believe you will write a book. To 'believe' is defined as, *"To hold an opinion of."* Most think that to believe in something is the most powerful. But, when you look at the definition of 'belief' it is not enough to get the job done. I mentioned earlier that all beliefs are false, until you decide they are true. You know you are going to write a book. To 'know' means, *"To be certain."* Only when you are *certain* do you make the decision and commitment necessary to move forward and complete the job.

How you choose your language greatly influences your feelings and emotions, and at the same time, your feelings and emotions can influence your language. You express yourself based on how you feel, and how you feel will influence how you express yourself. If you use language casually, you will create casualties.

Only when you know, when you are certain, will you truly take correct action to get the job done. Why? Because *knowing* is the basis for making a firm decision that nothing less than writing the book will do. Knowing is having clear intention. It is the foundation for change. Intention creates the passion, the why, behind the decision to get the job done.

Most of us have been programmed to live in our rational minds instead of our feelings. We are actually taught to suppress how we truly feel, to suppress our intuitions, our imagination, and creative abilities. The fact is that the words we use and hear are such a part of our everyday language and thought process that we tend to believe them without question, and often times use words haphazardly.

All words are hypnotic. You are literally hypnotized by what you say and what you hear others say to you. For example, we tend to believe what we see and hear on TV is presented as factual. However, the messages are twisted and organized in a way to trigger your emotions—to hypnotize you. Remember, in the book of Genesis, the origin of all things, the *source,* was "the word."

A few thousand years ago, humans heard only a few words daily. Only in the last 200 generations or so has this increased to sometimes tens of thousands of words being processed through the average person's brain every day. For example, the dictionary on my shelf has about 3,000 pages with an average of 50 to 75 words on each page. That is about 200,000 words, all of which have multiple definitions.

Words are not just sounds you can choose to ignore, especially if you speak them. Words influence the behavior of both the person speaking and the one listening. When the ancients referred to hypnotic spell casting, it was not their superstitions at work. They were recognizing the hypnotic power of words and how they communicated to influence another's behavior. This is the reason, as I mentioned earlier, that the organization of letters to form a word is referred to as *'spelling.'* Words cast spells! In fact, that is the only purpose for a word and for speaking them. They cast a spell.

For example, when you arrange a series of letters in a different order, it means something totally different. Same letters, different spell. For example, *"eleven plus two"* also spells *"twelve plus one."* Both have the same meaning, but the letters arranged differently. Let's try *"Mother-in-law."* The same letters re-arranged spell, *"woman Hitler."* Funny uh? Dormitory also spells, *"dirty room."*

Words are stored in the brain like an erector set. Take the word freedom, for example. Your concept and my concept of freedom include words, images, feelings, thoughts, and so on, that have been stored in our minds and are associated with the word or concept of freedom. However, your concept of freedom is probably totally different from mine. When one person thinks of freedom, it may differ greatly from someone else's thought of freedom. To one, freedom might mean having lots of money. For another, freedom might mean taking a walk on the beach every morning. To another, it may mean being free of fear and experiencing more love. Either way, whenever we contemplate the word 'freedom,' we become hypnotized by it to one degree or another. Even thinking a word can be hypnotic. In addition, you may be able to influence another's concept of freedom simply by communicating your concept of freedom to them.

We wonder why so many people suffer from emotional distress these days—such as worry, fear, depression, and anxiety. It is because we have so many words to communicate and to assimilate daily, words that hypnotize us into *this or that* state of mind. Think about it. If you did not have all those words and all that input to process, would you even have stress?

Look at it this way. All words carry a vibrational frequency which is either loving or fear-based depending upon their use. Each word you speak and hear influences you to move either toward what you want in your life or further away. Words such as, "I can't," "I don't care," "What's the use," or "It's too late," all create conditions that move us away from our desired life. On the other hand, words such as "I can," "I know," "I am confident," "I am receptive," and "I will," are resourceful and supportive and will move you toward your desired life.

Words are not just arbitrary sounds you should ignore. They either expand your possibilities or they become restrictive. Words are verbal expressions of how you feel, of the person you imagine yourself to be, of how you perceive the world. The words you choose to use are the result of how you experience the world. And, how you experience the world will have an influence on the words you choose to use.

A passing thought, for example, may not necessarily create a result, but when you think it, feel it, and then verbalize it, the universe goes to work to create it. The stronger the emotional conviction is behind the word, the greater its effect.

For example, if you have a serious illness and you fear you won't recover, you start to believe you're going to just have to live with it. You may say things like, "I've got the illness, and there's nothing I can do. So what's the use?" If you speak those words, the universe will go to work to honor and assist you in creating your wish. Not only that. You are communicating with the 75 trillion cells in your body. They work for you. They will do what you tell them. It is their job. They will thrive for you or they will die for you. And your directive to your cells is, "I've got this illness, and there's nothing I can do about it. So what's the use?"

This type of thinking will and does limit your range of possibilities, because you are using the power of words and energy to create a hopeless feeling. As a result, you will create more of the same. On the other hand, if you have a serious illness and you are open to finding a solution to your problem, instead of being consumed by it, you are now open for solutions.

Look at it this way. Every word you speak is like a prayer. If you believe that happiness is impossible for you, you definitely don't want to verbalize it! In other words, don't pray for it! When you are in this state of mind there are two things you might want to consider.

One is to keep your mouth closed! And two, don't verbalize your problems, unless it is to someone that can help you find a solution! Idle chatter is simply a waste of time and energy that will only accentuate the problem.

A good starting point to transform your fears and the feelings that limit you and separate you from the life you want is by creating a new language—a language that expresses how you want your life to be. A language of caring for yourself and respecting others.

Since words can disempower you and those around you, begin to observe and choose your words with care. Look for ways to say things that leave the recipient empowered and feeling better as a result of having contact with you. By doing so, you will leave yourself feeling empowered as well. Begin to select words that affirm life, that affirm abundance, that affirm love, integrity, commitment, and a heart-felt connection to everyone you meet. Your vision becomes reality. The words you choose create a vision of how you perceive your life and the world around you.

Next, let's discuss the internal/external connection. We assume there is only a causal connection between the internal and the external. We believe some outer event actually caused us to feel a certain way. Although it may be difficult to perceive, the inner event and the outer event actually happen at the same time. One does not cause the other.

Here's an example. Let's say someone says something that makes you angry. What really happened is that you already held a feeling trapped inside in the form of anger. It may not at all be related to the current anger you are experiencing or to the person whom you believe is making you angry. Simultaneously, the act brings up your anger.

If you have anger and resentment toward another, about something that you believe they are doing to you, the act you *believe* they are doing against you and the resentment created by some past event are meeting at this place and time. Without the trapped anger, the event probably would not have occurred at all. And if it did occur, you would have perceived it differently. Why? Because you see and experience what you feel inside, which influences your view of the world around you. If you are not holding anger, you will not be projecting anger; and if you are not projecting anger, you will not have the experience that triggers anger.

For example, my wife is structured and organized, while I operate more without structure and am less organized. Our children growing up, of course were less structured and organized by their very nature. As a result, my wife was more bothered by our children's disorganization than I. We perceived it differently because we *felt* differently about disorganization. It is not that either one of us was right or wrong, it was just perception.

In fact, if you put a thousand people in the same exact situation, they will all have a different experience. The situation might be exactly the same, but each person's perception and experience will be different. Understanding this concept removes the tendency to blame others for their behaviors or how they make you feel. It makes self-acceptance, as well as accepting others, much easier.

The feelings you hold are not always accompanied by outside events. A feeling may be triggered by a thought. Let's say you experienced the death of someone close to you.

Later, you remember an experience with that person, and as a result of that thought, you experience a sad feeling. The thought serves to bring up the feeling just as an outer event might do. However, it is not the thought that needs processing, but rather the feeling.

A behavior can also serve to bring up feelings that need to be released. If you are compulsive, for example, about keeping your house clean or having something a certain way, becoming self-observant allows you to see the feeling behind your compulsiveness. If you can back away and objectively observe, your compulsiveness can become the gift. It offers you a signal in the form of an emotion, telling you there is something you need to deal with and release. Your feelings and emotions are not something to be feared, or to suppress in order to avoid the pain. They are truly a gift.

It is also important to know the difference between thoughts and feelings. When you are working with feelings, you are working with stored or trapped energy. Whereas a thought doesn't have a charged feeling or any energy behind it.

Emotions are always based in past experiences which can create energy blocks. A lot of therapies attempt to go back into the past to uncover suppressed feelings and their cause.

Going into the past is not really necessary. It is okay if it comes up, but it is not necessary in order to let go. When you are working with a present emotion that was created from a past experience, letting go of the present emotion will automatically begin healing the past. The past experience is what's causing you, either directly or indirectly, to feel what you are experiencing today. When you let go of a present feeling or emotion, you are automatically healing a past pain or experience.

There is also what is known as "pure feelings" that are not filtered through your past experiences. For example, you may *feel* happy, alive, or loving. These are all pure feelings with no emotional connection to the past. They are based in love which operates in the present. If you are aware of a "pure feeling," there is no need to let it go because with pure feelings you are already in the experience of the moment. Also, with a pure feeling you will not experience stress. The only way stress gets into the moment is when we bring a past issue or experience into the present and re-experience it. Stress comes from emotions, and emotions are created in present time from a trapped feeling as a result of a past experience.

Looking at the present can also be looking at the past. In other words, you think you are looking at the present, but in reality, the past has been brought into the present and re-experienced. Looking at the past is not *ever* living in the present. It is simply re-living the past all over again, which has absolutely no value at all in the present.

Imagine you are taking a walk out in nature. Everything feels perfect. There is no feeling of stress. There is just you and nature. You are feeling wonderful! Then suddenly you remember a stressful situation you are dealing with at the office. The next thing you know, you are feeling stressed out, and everything no longer seems so perfect. This is called bringing the past and future into the present. There is no stress in the moment. The only time stress exists is when you bring the past into the present, reliving it in the moment. Or you bring the anticipation of a future event based on a past experience into the present.

Now, let's examine worry. Worry is a unique fear condition. Worry is thinking about what you are feeling instead of just feeling the feeling. Instead of feeling what you fear, you are thinking about what you fear. Worry is always directly or indirectly based on a past experience and some related belief you hold about that experience.

Let's say you grew up with not much money in the family. There was always a lot of talk about not enough money. Today you have a great job that pays you a lot of money, but you are always worried that it may not last, or that you are going to lose your money for some reason. In this case, your worry is different than your direct experience, but at the same time directly related.

Another example: Let's say you are worried about your teenager going to the senior prom. You are afraid he/she is going to stay out all night, possibly drinking, partying, and getting into trouble. The reason you are worried is because you may have a belief that that is what teenagers do at senior proms. And why do you suppose you feel that way?

You feel that way, maybe because of what you did at *your* senior prom, or maybe what you have heard happens at senior proms, which has created your belief system. And based upon that belief, you feel the fear, and then you think about your fear over and over, producing worry. In this case you may have never had a direct experience at all about the issue. You are in fact basing your belief on what someone else believes or just hearsay.

Worry is the ultimate need-for-control issue. It is trying desperately to control something that is beyond your control. If you are a worrier, the question you should be asking yourself is, "Is the worry I'm experiencing supporting the safety and well-being of my teenager, or does my worry contribute to the problem?" It may not contribute to the perceived problem directly, but it certainly contributes to your problem, which is your need to control the uncontrollable.

The real problem worry creates is inside you, in the form of restricted free-flowing energy. It then sets your focus on the restriction. Your teenager comes home right on time, but you have a headache from loss of sleep and worry. Remember, what you focus on is what you'll create! You hand out worry, you create stress.

Worry in itself uses a lot of emotional and physical energy. And that is not all. In an attempt to recover your lost energy, you can literally become addicted to the worry. Let me give you an example. Let's say you are worried about not having the money to pay your bills on time. You begin to feel the worry will somehow help you to earn money faster, when in reality, the exact opposite is true. Worry can and does become an addiction.

Let me offer you a four-step program for eliminating worry.

1. Become aware of yourself worrying.
2. Observe yourself worrying. Consciously realize that you are trying to control something that is beyond your control.
3. Make the conscious effort to drop your thoughts about what you are worried about and your need to control the outcome.
4. Embrace your worry. Observe yourself worrying and no matter how difficult it may be, allow your emotion to surface, then take a deep breath, and when you exhale, let it go.

Worry is a killer. It can lead to many types of addictions such as alcohol, overeating, drugs, and many other forms of escaping behaviors. What you are really doing when you worry is identifying with your fear of what might happen—somehow thinking it will help you escape the pain. If you do not accept your worry and allow the attached emotion to surface, you will choose to suppress it. Or you my judge your feelings as bad and beat yourself up for feeling that way. By judging yourself, you resist experiencing the feeling, which in turn will allow it to re-surface as some other worry or emotional issue.

You have four choices about how you handle your non-supportive feelings and emotions.

1. You can suppress them.
2. You can express them, which is really suppressing in disguise.
3. You can repress them, which is a totally unconscious response—a habit that most have become very good at (which is also suppression).
4. Or you can let them go.

We have literally buried our happiness with our unhappiness. And when we do, we also bury the cause of our unhappiness along with it. It is absolutely impossible to be truly happy and cling to what makes you unhappy at the same time. As long as you are looking outward for answers to your happiness, you are not looking in the right direction. Only when you begin to observe and understand all the evasive maneuvers you use to create your unhappiness, are you free to choose happiness.

Let's say you lose your job. Of course, you may feel hurt, angry, betrayed, and even fearful (unless, of course, you wanted to get a new job in the first place). In that case, you may be relieved. But the point I want to make is this: You have a choice as to how long you want to hang onto your upset feelings over losing your job. Here is a good question you should consider. Does hanging onto the feelings about losing your job support you in finding a new one?

Does hanging onto the feeling about your breakup in a past relationship help you to find a new one? Wouldn't it make more sense to just let it go and move on sooner rather than later?

Of course, you may feel awful about losing your job or your relationship. Anyone would, and that is normal. But feeling bad for a very long period of time is a choice you make.

Letting go of the upset you feel about losing your job or your relationship is not a requirement. It is simply a way to end the suffering sooner.

As long as you are clinging to any fixed thought or feeling about how your life or circumstances should be, you will always suffer to one degree or another. A great deal of the time, life just simply will not be the way you expect it to be. So, you might as well just relax. You might as well let go. What have you got to lose? It just might work! And you certainly will not know until you give it a go! The moment you let go of your expectations about how things "should be," everything changes, even though nothing external changed at all.

When you let go, your view of the external changes. Consider for a moment where the change actually occurs when you let go. The change occurred inside, and all you did was let go of your resistance. When you attempt to make things be the way you want them to be, you become tense, and you live in a state of resistance. You then come to a false conclusion that you are in control. But that conclusion is only an illusion. If you are hanging on to any sort of upset, until you let it go, you are out of control. If you observe yourself closely, you'll discover that all you are really controlling is keeping your upset in place by hanging on. When you hang on, you are keeping new solutions out of sight. When you let go, only then are you free of the pain your resistance has created.

Absolutely nothing can take away your peace of mind, you have to voluntarily give it up!

And we all tend give it up so easily—for just about anything. Red lights, people's opinions, traffic, old hurts, when things are not going your way, when the toilet paper roller is empty, when others don't act the way *you* think they should, and on and on.

Here's a formula for discovering and handling fears and other non-resourceful feelings and emotions in your life.

1. Take a look at what you are experiencing as an obstacle in your life, in your business, relationship, family, or personally.

2. What belief are you clinging to about how life *should* be that makes your obstacle an obstacle?

3. How did this belief originate? Is it yours from experience, or was it a result of someone else's experience or opinion?

4. What do you have to gain by *having* this obstacle or belief that is not painful or stressful?

5. What do you have to gain by *not having* this obstacle or belief in your life?

Take some time. Take a sheet of paper and draw a line down the middle from top to bottom. Make a list of what you have to gain by *having* it on one side, and a list of what you have to gain by *not having* it on the other. Then, notice which list is longer.

6. What would happen if you let go of what you *believe* you have to gain by keeping this obstacle in your life?

A few years ago, in one of my workshops, I led a woman through the above process. I asked her for a goal she had that she wanted to share. She said her goal was to lose 180 pounds. She said she had been on every diet program imaginable—about 30 total—and nothing worked. She weighed about 300 pounds.

Now, I want *you* to think of something you have been wanting to accomplish but have struggled to do so—something that has been completely eluding you. Got one? Now, as I go through the process I did with her, use the same process with your goal. Grab a sheet of paper, write your goal across the top, and draw a line down the middle from top to bottom.

On one side write, "What I have to gain by accomplishing my goal." On the other side write, "What I have to gain by not accomplishing my goal."

I started by asking, "What do you have to gain by losing the weight?"

Her response was, "I would look better."

Next question, "What do you have to gain by keeping the weight on?"

Her response, "Nothing."

Again, I asked, "What do you have to gain by losing the weight?"

She responded, "I would feel better."

Once again, I asked, "What do you have to gain by keeping the weight?"

Again, she responded by answering, "Nothing."

We continued with the questions until we had completely filled several pages on the left side with what she had to gain by losing the weight. Look better, feel better, smaller dress size, fit into a bikini, live longer, and so on. On the right side, under what she had to gain by keeping the weight on, we hadn't listed a thing.

Once again, I asked her, "What do you have to gain by keeping the weight on?"

She hesitated for a few moments without answering, looking down. Her hands were shaking. I let her think for a moment and asked her again, "What do you have to gain by keeping the weight on?"

Finally, with a great deal of emotion, she quietly answered, "I wouldn't have to have men touching me."

Again, I asked, "What do you have to gain by keeping the weight on."

She answered, "I wouldn't have to commit to a relationship." Next, she said, "I have something very difficult that I want to tell you about." She said, "This is something that I have never told anyone, not even my parents. Twenty years ago, when I was thirteen years old, I was the school football queen. One night after a game, I was walking home alone, and was attacked and raped by four boys. I went home that night and vowed never to tell a soul. I made a commitment to myself, for the rest of my life, to never let a man touch me again. Then, I began to eat and eat and eat until I had gained more than 100 pounds. As time passed, I continued eating excessively until I had gained 180 pounds."

Within the next 20 minutes of working with her, she let go of her anger, her fears, and her resentment toward men. From creating the list to the point of letting go was a process of over 90 minutes. It was a very emotional experience for her, and for the entire audience, as we began to peel off the layers of years of suppression. She got really clear that this was a past issue; it was not happening to her now and had nothing to do with the present. She was only bringing it into the present. She made peace with herself and the past experience.

She reported back to me monthly with her progress. Within six months, and only by letting go of the emotion created from a past experience, she had lost a total of 80 pounds without dieting. Over the following year, she had lost a total of 180 pounds. All she did was *let* the emotion and experience go. She let go of her resistance to losing weight by letting go of the reason for keeping it on.

Use this concept on a few of the obstacles that are keeping you from reaching your goals. See if you can discover what you have to gain by not having your goal, and what you have to gain by having it. If you are honest with yourself, you'll be amazed by the results.

FIFTEEN

Letting Go of the Need for Acceptance

When you need *acceptance* from others, what you are giving up is your *freedom*. Needing acceptance from others will lead you to take actions that are based on what others want, not what you want.

You may be doing something for someone else, and that is alright. But if the real reason you are doing it is because *they* want you to do it, or you think they would be more accepting of you if you do it, then you have lost your freedom.

Let's go over the following list of questions to see how much of a *need for acceptance* you may have. Check off the ones you can relate to.

1. You feel that you should give up your own interests in order to please others.

2. You need the acceptance of others in order to feel good about yourself.

3. When someone strongly expects you to do something for them, you more often than not feel you should do it whether you want to or not.

4. You feel that your value as a person, greatly depends upon what others think of you.

5. If someone dislikes you, you feel less worthwhile.

6. If someone disagrees with you, you generally take it personally.

7. Before you confront someone about a sensitive issue, you begin to imagine all that could go wrong and what they may think of you.

8.   You get upset with yourself when you do something you feel was not right.

9.   If you can't settle a difference of opinion with another, you try to avoid them altogether.

10. When you are criticized for your performance you get upset.

If you answered *"Yes"* to seven or more of these, this indicates that you suffer from excessive addiction to the need for acceptance.

If you answered *"Yes"* to three or more of them, this generally indicates that you often look down on yourself.

If you answered "Yes" to less than three of the questions, you have a fairly healthy sense of self-worth.

Let's look at some of the ways you may use to gain acceptance from others. See if any of these fit you.

~Always competing, trying to be better than others.

~Feeling guilty so that others feel sorry for you.

~Being a martyr and letting others walk on you.

~Trying to please by always rescuing others.

~Always complaining, trying to gain support.

~Using excuses so that others think you are perfect.

~Pretending so that you look good in the eyes of others.

~Being a workaholic so that others notice your value.

~Always giving advice so that others will think you know it all.

~Justifying your position to keep from admitting you are wrong.

~Criticizing others so that others do not expect too much of you.

~Flaunting money so people will notice you.

~Being shy so that people give you more attention.

~Always suffering so people give you more attention.

~Losing so others will feel sorry for you and give you more attention.

~Sacrificing so others will feel sorry for you and give you more attention.

~Gossiping so others think you have the inside scoop.

~Over talking for attention, so others will think you know it all.

~Saying, "I'll try" so you appear able to help everyone, without commitment.

~Procrastinating, so that you get attention for not getting the job done on time or waiting until last minute so you look really busy.

Let's look at a few of these in greater detail.

Saying, "I'll try":

Let's say that someone invites you to a party and you say, *"I'll try my best to be there."*

By saying, *"I'll try,"* you don't have to fully commit, just in case you can't make it, or a better opportunity comes along. You say you are going to *"try"* to attend the party, then you don't show. When asked why you didn't show, you simply say something else came up. This is an indirect way of gaining approval. "I tried to be there, but just couldn't make it, so will you keep liking me anyway?"

So, the next time you hear, "I'll try," from your own lips or from another, stop! If it is from you, say a direct 'yes' or 'no.' If you hear it from another ask, "Is that a '*yes*' or a '*no*?'"

Remember that your words carry power. They are hypnotic. They can empower or dis-empower. For example, 'try' is defined as, *"to struggle."* So, when you either *say* or *accept* an "I'll try" you are setting yourself up for struggle. An example: You say, "I'll try to be there," then you plunge into a non-resourceful state of struggle, *trying* to figure out an appropriate way to get out of the commitment you really didn't want to make in the first place. The reason we put ourselves through all these gyrations is because of our need for acceptance from others. We are afraid of what the other person might think of us if we simply say, "No, I can't make it."

I was preparing to present a workshop in New York, when I received a call from one of the people inquiring about the program. He was a representative for the company to which I was presenting. He explained he was starting a new sales organization and wondered if I would suggest what he could do to get his team off to a fast start.

I said, "What I would do if I were you, is attend the program along with five of the new sales people in your organization." I asked if he could do that.

His response went something like this: "Yes, I'll be there if I can. I'm going to really try. And if nothing comes up, I'll be there for sure. If I can make it, I will probably try to get some of my new salespeople there as well."

I interrupted him and said, "Wait a minute. Was that a 'yes' or a 'no?'" He, once again, went through some of the same answer as before. I stopped him once again and asked, "Was that a 'yes' or a 'no?'"

With some stammering and difficulty, he finally gave me a, *'no'* that he couldn't have five new people there. Then, he gave me a doubtful *'yes'* that he himself would be there.

He did attend, and after the program, he came up to me and said, "I wish I had committed to having ALL my new salepeople here as well." The reality was that he was afraid they might not like the program and blame him for convincing them to attend.

He was more than willing to say, "I'll try," but he was not at all willing to truly make a commitment, or even say, "I'll discuss it with my people and get back with you tomorrow to let you know for sure."

Relationship conflict:

I'm sure you have heard it said, "Opposites attract." You have also heard it said that, "Like attracts like."

In a relationship, although not very often, you may find two people together that both need acceptance. On the other hand, you may occasionally find two controlling personalities together. But neither of these types of relationships typically lasts for very long, if they ever come together at all. In fact, they are not even attracted to one another, unless it is purely a physical attraction, or they just want someone to argue with, or to feel sorry for each other.

There will always be some degree of opposite needs within even a healthy relationship.

One partner may be a little more controlling, and as a result may be more organized or outspoken. Their partner, on the other hand, is more acceptance-oriented and may not be as well organized and doesn't speak out as much. In other words, the two personalities together can make up a well-balanced relationship. It is when they become extreme opposites that conflicts arise.

The following is an example of an extremely out of balance relationship and what was done to remedy the situation.

A woman in her mid-forties attended one of my two-day workshops in San Francisco.

As she was registering the first morning, I noticed she had a black eye she had attempted to cover with makeup and several bruises on her throat and wrists. She also had a busted lip. It was very apparent she had been severely beaten.

Later that day, as I discussed issues around the need for acceptance and control and how it applied in relationships, she shared the problems she was having.

She said, "I have been involved in a total of seven relationships in the past 25 years. Three of which were marriages, and the other three were men I lived with for a couple years each. All six relationships were extremely physically abusive, and this includes the one I am currently involved in." She said, "When I left this morning, my boyfriend said, 'If you try to leave me, I will kill you!' He meant it too."

During one exercise, she discovered she had a very strong *need for acceptance*, brought on by some traumatic childhood experiences. Her father had been physically abusive to both her and her mother.

As she shared information about her current boyfriend, she discovered two things. One was that her boyfriend had a very strong *need to be in control*. The second thing she discovered was that the man she was with, as well as the other six prior relationships, were all exactly like her father. By choosing this type of person, this gave her the perfect opportunity to work out the differences she was still holding onto regarding her father. They made a perfect match as long as she was hanging onto her need for acceptance.

I worked with her individually following the exercise.

I began by asking her, "Do you like feeling that need for approval?"

To which she answered quietly, "No." Then she said, "But I must like it, otherwise I wouldn't keep doing it, but I'm not sure why I would like it." I worked with her for a moment, asking her to really dig deep inside for the truth. Finally, after a couple minutes, she came back with a definite, "No, I don't like feeling this way."

My next question, "Is your feeling for the need for acceptance helping you live a better life?"

She said, "No, obviously not."

My next question, "Do you want to let go of always needing acceptance?"

She answered, "YES! YES, I DO!"

My next question, "Are you willing to let it go?"

To which the answered, "I don't know if I can."

I said, "I didn't ask you to, only if you are willing to." I said, "If you are willing, when I ask the last question, and you say yes, you will no longer have a need for anyone's approval." Again, I asked, "Are you willing to?"

She came back immediately with, "Yes. Yes, I am willing to let it go"

I said, "My final question for you. When are you going to let it go?"

She could not answer. She just had a blank, fearful look on her face. I gave her a moment to think. Tears started running down her face. I waited.

After a few minutes of silence, I asked once again, "When are you willing to let go of your need for acceptance?"

She said, "I don't know if I can."

I repeated the process several times looking for that definite, "yes,"—that commitment to let it go. I got a multitude of answers that ranged from, "maybe," or "not right now. I need to think about it," to "later today," and "maybe by the end of the class."

I didn't give up on her. And kept repeating the process. After about an hour she said, "I'm afraid."

I asked, "Afraid of what?"

She said, "I'm afraid I'll just die when I do."

"You are correct, I said. "A part of you will die when you let go. Your need for approval will die." I said, "It's your choice to hang on and keep living the drama you are now living, or you can let go and start living the life you want and deserve."

Again, I asked, "When are you going to let it go?"

She burst into tears. Sobbing, she finally yelled out, "NOW! I am letting it go now!"

The whole class felt her release and gave her a standing ovation! I explained to her and the class that this process may or may not have released her entire approval issue, and that she might have to spend some time working with it on her own to completely clear it.

She immediately jumped up and responded with, "No, I am finished with it. I know I am." She said, "I feel free for the first time in my life. I no longer need approval from anyone, especially my boyfriend."

She had apparently cleared her need for acceptance. The only thing she hadn't cleared was her boyfriend. I encouraged her not to attempt to figure out the potential outcome, or how she was going to get rid of her boyfriend. I told her to just allow the outcome to unfold. I told her to just give it a little time and see what happens before taking any action.

The next morning, upon arriving at class, she could not wait to share with the group what had happened. As soon as the class started, she ran to the front of the room saying, "I have something to share and I can't wait."

She explained in some detail the abuse she had experienced over the past two years. He had even threatened her life if she made any attempt to leave. She went on to explain, that when she got home the night before, she felt there was something different even before going into the house. When she walked in, she expected to see him in front of the television with his beer or yelling at her to get him another. But he was not in front of the television. She figured he was in the kitchen getting his own beer, so she went to the kitchen. He was not there either. She thought he was probably already passed out on the bed, which he did often on weekends. He was not on the bed either. She then ran to the closet and found that he had taken his clothes and belongings and left a note saying, "I will never be back."

What happened was a result of her letting go of her need to be accepted by him; she cut the 'chain of pain,' and he intuitively felt the cut. Or, if you'd rather, you could call it a coincidence. Or you could call it her seeing the truth and choosing to no longer live her life under those circumstances, and he intuitively felt that he no longer had someone he could control, so he was off to find a new victim.

A few months later, she called to share with me that she had met the love of her life and there was no abuse present in their relationship. I spoke with her over two years later, and the two of them were married, living a happy, non-abusive well-balanced, life together.

Letting go in advance is also a concept worth applying. This is a method you can utilize every day that will help you avoid setting yourself up for new problems that you will have to deal with at a later date.

As an example, let's say you need to make a telephone call to someone to confront an uncomfortable issue. Stop for a moment and think of a real situation you might have. Maybe one that you are currently experiencing. Now, notice how it makes you feel. We have all felt it. You know, the fear of what the outcome might be. In this kind of situation, you basically have one of three options:

Option one- is to *not* make the call, so you don't have to confront the issue; maybe it will just go away. With this approach, here is most likely what will happen. By not making the call, you have now satisfied your need for acceptance and replaced it with a need to control. In other words, "I have decided to control my fear instead of making the call."

But here is what you are really saying, "I have decided to *honor* my fear, and my *need for acceptance,* instead of making the call and resolving the issue." In reality, what you really did was further suppress the issue for a stronger, return later.

Option two- is that you can hang on to your fear, hang on to *your need for acceptance*, make the call, and hope for the best. With this approach, here is what will happen. When you approach a situation in a non-resourceful state of mind, you create more of the same in return.

Option three- is to let go of your *need for acceptance*, thereby not giving any energy to your fear. Watch it go away, then make the call with no attachment to or a need to control the outcome.

It is always your choice. You can hang on, honor your fear, and come from a non-resourceful place, push their control button, and hope for the best. Or, you can let go of your fear, come from a resourceful, loving place, and move past, or rise above your fear.

When you come from the heart by letting go, you will connect heart to heart, therefore, bypassing both the need for acceptance and the need to be in control. With this approach, you will never be disappointed with the outcome, because you will never be attached to the results.

Over talking is another example of how we seek acceptance from others. I remember a woman in a class in Los Angeles. Every time I asked a question of the group, she was always first with the answer. At every table discussion, she dominated the conversation with her opinions and advice. If someone else got a chance to share, she always added to their response with her "expert advice." She would talk, talk, and talk, endlessly. She was really disrupting the whole class. In fact, during the break, several people made it a point to make a comment to me about how distracting and disruptive she was being.

So, I decided to resolve the problem in a resourceful way and help her too. Right in the middle of her next interruption, I interrupted her and asked, "Would you mind if I asked you a question?"

She said, "No, not at all."

I knew she would love the chance to answer a direct question, so she could give her opinion. So, I said, "Here's the question. Do you know that you talk a lot?"

"Yes," she said, without hesitation. "People tell me that all the time."

I asked, "So you know you talk a lot?"

She said, "Yes."

Then I asked her, "Do you feel that your desire to talk a lot comes from your need for acceptance or your need to be in control?"

After some inner reflection, a couple minutes of silence, she answered, "I guess my need for acceptance."

With further investigation she found that this need had been created by a repeated experience she'd had as a child with her father. I helped her let go of her need for acceptance. And with that, she also let go of her need to talk so much in class.

Six months later, I received a card from her telling me how her life had changed after the letting go process. She said she now felt truly in control of her life for the first time.

She explained she had much more time to listen and think now that she wasn't so busy talking all the time. She said her sales business had also grown for the first time in years, because she listened more and talked less.

Over talking, is oftentimes the expression of our urge to think. But in our culture, those who seem to think, rather than talk, tend to be considered uncooperative, or not very knowledgeable. This belief encourages talking and discourages listening or thinking.

Talking too much is not usually motivated by our desire to discover the truth, but rather from our search for acceptance and to avoid the real truth. We believe that acceptance is given to those who say something that appears to be the truth, because they talk a lot.

When we tend to speak more and more out of our need for acceptance, we will actually see less and less of the truth. As we seek to offer more and more clever words to make us look smarter, the deeper our need for acceptance becomes.

As you begin to observe yourself with these two needs, notice how you truly are and what is at the bottom of all your needs, then begin to let them go. You'll notice two things:

1. You will notice these two needs beginning to wither away from lack of attention.

2. You will notice your resourceful feelings being enhanced and your life working better overall.

Remember, the more you feel the need for acceptance or control, the less of each you have. When you let go of your need for acceptance or control, only then will you have any level of control or acceptance in your life.

In order to become more fully aware of this automatic behavior response, it will require your close and persistent self-observation. The next time you experience feelings such as, anger, fear, sadness, anxiety, or feeling stuck in any way, take a minute, observe yourself feeling this way, then ask yourself, "Is this my need for acceptance or control?" It is *always* one or the other. You'll be amazed at the results you experience and how different your life becomes.

Take a moment right now and consider some of the negative feelings you may be experiencing in your life. Ask yourself, "Does this feeling or emotion I'm experiencing stem from my need for acceptance or my need to be in control?" You can rest assured that it is always one of the two needs. But if you just cannot decide, don't upset yourself over the issue, just observe the feeling, let it go, and move on.

Here is a simple exercise that will be very helpful. Pick a day and become self-observant. Observe your every action that day. Just watch yourself, like you are observing someone else. You know what I mean. You can always see what others are doing wrong, can't you? Observe your every word, your tone of voice in a conversation. Observe your gestures, your actions, thoughts, and feelings. Observe your beliefs. Do not let any part of you go unobserved. Do this for just one day and see what happens.

As you observe and catch something, ask yourself, "Why did I do that? What was the root cause of that behavior? What was my motivation for speaking or acting the way I did? Was I seeking acceptance or control?" You will discover that many of your daily actions have no real value, except to allow you to be approved of or to feel more in control. Through persistent self-observation and letting go, you will quickly begin to strip away your addictive programming, and your need for support from others in order to feel good about yourself. Only through self-observation and seeing the truth will you truly know the appropriate action to take in any given situation. Only through self-observation can you know reality. In fact, self-observation creates reality.

The real effect of this process will be life progressive. First, you will begin to catch yourself after the fact. In other words, you will catch yourself after an upset. But don't beat yourself about that. Instead, celebrate your discovery. Just stop for a moment and ask yourself, "Why did I do that?" Look for the deeper meaning. After some time and with more experience you will begin to catch yourself in mid-action, and you'll say, "Why am I doing this?"

As you get better and better at self-observation, after you practice it for a while, you will begin to catch yourself before you take action, and you'll say, "Do I really want to take this action?"

Remember, anytime you attempt to cling to either side of a duality, such as needing acceptance or control, you are also clinging to its opposite. When you cling to someone else's drama, you become the victim in their drama and the victim in your own drama as well.

Clinging and pushing away become the same. We attempt to hang onto someone we love, and they leave us. We hang onto the need for acceptance, so we remain in control, and instead we lose both acceptance as well control. When you try to push something away, you can't seem to get it out of your life. You want only pleasant people in your life and all you seem to attract are arrogant people. Your need for acceptance and control has brought both together. You want more patience and all you seem to attract are people and circumstances that make you feel more impatient. Patience does not arrive on a silver platter, you know. It comes from situations that trigger your impatience, so you can let it go and be more patient.

When you begin to accept that life is simply life and that different types of people are just a part of life—sometimes you get the good, and sometimes the bad—only then can you truly be free.

SIXTEEN

Letting Go of Control

All conflict is self-conflict, and all self-conflict originates from the two needs. One we discussed, the need for acceptance. The other is our need to be in control. When you need acceptance, you get none. When you need control, you are out of control. These two needs often work hand-in-hand. In other words, the need to be in control can be the need for acceptance in disguise. Let's discuss the need for control in more detail.

We get hurt not by what others say or do, but rather by our own need to control what others say or do. When we let go of our demands about how people should be acting, people can act as they wish, and we can remain at peace. Another way of saying it is, when you take your hand out of the fire, it will quit burning!

You may be asking yourself, "How can I be in control without *needing* to be in control?" And, if I let go of my need to control, won't I then be out of control?" You don't actually let go of control. You only let go of your need to be in control. There is a difference.

None of us has any control over what happens to us next, what others might think of us, the decisions someone else might make, or the action they will take. When you let go of your *need* to know what's going to happen next, what others may think of you, what you are letting go of is your attachment, or your expectation of the outcome. In short, when you let go of the *need* to control an outcome over which you have no control, you are detaching from your own drama and allowing the outcome to simply happen, instead of trying to force it to happen. If you are always living your life trying to second guess what's going to happen, or being upset when things aren't going your way, or worrying about what others might think of you, you are living your life out of control.

Ask yourself, "Who would I be without the need to control?" What if you simply allowed an outcome to be an outcome? Here is a question for you. Does trying to control an outcome provide you with a faster solution, or keep you away from seeing a solution? Does it contribute to stress or relieve it? We seek acceptance, so we can have more people around us. We seek control, so we have influence over others; therefore, having more people around us, so we can gain greater acceptance. Those who feel a *need* to be in control, do so because of their *need* to be accepted. The reality is, the more you seek acceptance or control, the less you actually have in your life.

I met a woman in my workshop who was raised by an alcoholic parent. She felt out of control as a child and as a result she became a perfectionist, so she felt in control. She wanted everything to be perfect around the house, not a speck of dirt and everything in its proper place all the time. She wanted her kids to be perfect as well. She did not allow them to be just kids, she wanted them to be perfect little adults. Her feeling of being out of control was now manifesting itself as the need to have everything under control. When you look at her control issue on a deeper level, you can see that her control issue as an adult was created by her need to be accepted and loved as a child.

For the sake of better understanding both the need for control and the need for acceptance, let's look at the two of them individually.

Let's first discuss the need to be in control.

If you look back over your life, you could probably come up with a long list of people whom you believe hurt you in some way. We all have our list: the parent, the school teacher, the husband, the wife, the child, the best friend. The list is endless. Because of our list of hurts and pains, we develop patterns of avoidance, which cause us to develop a conditioned way of thinking and perceiving life. We develop behavior patterns of avoidance, trying desperately to avoid our pain! We then begin to judge others based upon how we judge ourselves. We form opinions about anyone or anything we fear might cause us any sort of pain. We then project that pain outward with our judgement of others, hoping it will somehow ease our own pain. In fact, most of us spend our whole lives attempting to move in a direction that avoids any discomfort or pain.

Deep down inside, we believe we are the victims, so we attempt to arrange our whole life so that we are in control. But without even realizing it, what we are really doing is setting up a life that is totally out of control. We've become so obsessed with not being hurt and remaining in control, our real life is just passing us by without even noticing it. We spend 90% of our time, energy, and creativity defending our needs instead of living our lives.

Our methods for avoiding pain and protecting our needs have become almost endless.

When we are threatened in any way, we instantly react by putting up a barrier of some sort that we hope will keep us in control. But in reality, what is really happening is we are clouding our vision and living *out of control* because of our *need* to be in control.

And, because most of us are in a reactive state every few minutes, or even seconds, our vision of how we want our lives to be, or how life really is, is completely out of focus.

We become completely caught up in the drama that we have set up as a form of protection to keep us feeling in control, when in reality, we are getting further *out* of control all the time.

For example, you have an idea or a belief about how something should be. Let's say you want your house to be absolutely spotless all the time. With this in mind, you are always looking for ways to clean the house. There is nothing wrong with wanting to keep a clean home, but let's take it a little further. Suppose you have a family with five children under the age of twelve. Your belief is, *'I need to have a spotless home all the time.'* This produces a behavior derived from your need to be in control, instead of a behavior stemming from a real need. If you have five children who are under twelve, the reality is your home is not going to be spotless all the time. Maybe never! Unless, of course, you place a great deal more importance on having a spotless home than on your family. This is called the need to be in control. "My home must be clean all the time. This is my belief. Homes should be clean, no matter what." If you believe that it is 'bad' for your house to not be clean at all costs, this is known as your control drama. On the other hand, if you are concerned about what others will think of you if your house is not clean, this is known as an acceptance drama.

Most of the time, they both work hand in hand. You want to be in control so you can gain acceptance from others. Or, to take it even another step further, you want a clean house so you can gain acceptance from your parents when you were ten years old. You are acting out the past drama of needing to be accepted and loved by your parents. You need to have a clean home, thinking that will satisfy your need. Until you investigate your own story and see the truth behind it, you are stuck with it.

Ask yourself:

"What am I trying to control that is leaving me out of control?"

"What is my story?"

"Is it true?"

"Is my story really true, or am I bringing the past into the present trying to make it into something it's not?"

"Is it true today, or am I simply reliving the past experience over and over again?"

More importantly, who would you be without your story?

The way to begin to release your concerns about having to always have a spotless home, or whatever, is by letting go of your need to be in control of something over which you have no control. The key is to learn to identify those things you *can* control, from those you *cannot*. In other words, learn to identify the difference between *controllable* and *uncontrollable* circumstances.

Can you control the past? No. But you can sure control whether you chose to relive it in the present moment. Any circumstance that is beyond your control, is *not* your responsibility. If, however, there is an action that could be taken, you should first, let go of your need to control the outcome, then take action.

As an example: If you want to get a child to clean a messy room, instead of making the child wrong or getting angry because the child has not cleaned his room, first let go of the need to control what they did or didn't do, the anger, then take action. By doing so, you truly remain in control. You remain in control of your thoughts, feelings, emotions, and behaviors, which is the only thing you really have control of in the first place.

Let's say the child is gone for the day and there is no action you can take at the time. Then simply let go of your need to control, maintain your sanity, and have the courage to leave it at that until you can take action. Concerning yourself over having a clean house, or what others think, or about how something should turn out, or what a child *should* have done, is a non-resourceful 'leak' of your resourceful energy reserve. It is really not your job to seek happiness. It is your job to deal with your story as it arises, and out of that your happiness will unfold.

When you let go of the need to control, you don't give up control as some believe. You don't give up using any of your skills. What you really give up is using your skills to manipulate the world and the people in your life, trying to make them the way you would like them to be instead of letting them be who they are. When *you* change, those around you will change. You can watch it happen.

A good example of that was a woman in one of my workshops who was having a lot of difficulty with her seventeen-year-old son. She said he had become totally uncontrollable. He was using drugs and alcohol and in the habit of coming home stoned or drunk; that is, when he came home at all. He had the habit of staying out until three or four o'clock in the morning and would never call. Sometimes, he would stay out for two and three days at a time. She explained they were always in some sort of a battle about his behavior.

One day, she'd had all she could take, so she joined a tough-love group. She explained that tough love was when she would tell her son she really loved him, but could no longer tolerate his behavior—that he could no longer live in her home. She basically locked him out of the house. The next step for the mother was that she had to attend support meetings two times a week in order to help her handle the guilt she was feeling for abandoning her own son. I asked her how she felt about the situation and about her son.

She said, "I feel very guilty about what I am doing to my son, and at the same time, I feel very angry toward him for his behavior and what he is doing to me and the family. I just want him to stop. I just want us to love each other again."

I asked her what she was feeling. She said, "I feel angry and frustrated." I then asked if she felt that her anger and frustration were a need to be in control or a need for acceptance?

She said, "I think it is my need to be in control." I asked if she would mind if I asked her some questions. She said, "No, I don't mind."

I asked, "Do you like feeling the way you do?"

Looking a little perplexed that I had asked such a question, she answered, "No, of course I don't."

The next question I asked was, "Do you think that the way you feel contributes to having a better relationship with your son? Will it help resolve the problem?"

Her answer was, "No."

The next question I asked was, "Do you want to let it go?"

To which she answered, "Yes, I do."

Next question, "Are you willing to let go of your need to control your son?"

She answered hesitantly, "I think so."

I said, "I'm not asking you to let it go, but rather, are you willing to let it go?"

I asked her once again, "Are you willing to let go of your need to be in control of your son's behavior?"

She said, "I'm afraid to say yes."

"Afraid of what?" I asked.

She said, "I'm afraid that if I let go of the control, he will keep doing what he is doing."

I said, "Well, how is that working for you so far?"

She said, "It's not working."

Once again, I asked, "Are you willing to let go of your need to control your son's behavior?"

With some hesitation, she finally answered, "Yes I am."

The last question I asked her was, "When? When are you willing to let it go?"

She said, "Maybe a little later, or tomorrow. I want to think about it."

I asked, "Do you really want to solve the problem, or just keep on doing what is not working? The only person you are in control of is you. You have no control over other's actions. When are you willing to let go of controlling someone over whom you have no control?"

She said, "I see what you mean." She breathed a big sigh of relief, as she answered, "I will let it go now."

After processing her feelings about the situation several times, in different ways, and recognizing her need to control her son's behavior, she discovered that the most important thing she could do for her son was to stay in a resourceful and happy state. After some more time working with her, and as she gained a deeper understanding of the part she played in the situation, she completely let go of her need to be in control.

Only when you detach from the drama can healing to take place. In fact, the only way healing can take place is when one or the other let's go and changes the story. Up until then, they were a perfect match, the victim and the victimizer. We basically keep people in our drama by our own projections. And when you stop projecting, the drama has to stop.

A short time after the workshop, she called me to share her good news. Her son had moved back into the house. He joined a drug and alcohol rehab program. He started coming in before midnight, and if he was going to be late, he called to let her know where he was and when he would be home. And to top it off, he joined the peace corp. She said earlier that day, she sat down with him for a heart-to-heart talk. She asked him why he had changed so quickly? He said, "Mom, you are the one who changed."

Consider for a moment where the healing actually occurred. She thought her son was the cause of her feeling the way she felt. Nobody can *make* you feel the way you do. It is your choice. When she let go of her need to control the situation, the situation healed. Why do you suppose that is? Because all conflict is self-conflict. All the conflict was within her. It had nothing to do with her son, but rather her need to control him. Her son simply wanted to feel that he was in charge of his own life, while she wanted to be in control of his every action. That creates a conflict. When she let go, she was now in charge of her life and her son was in charge of his, and now they are both happy. When you hang onto your need to control, you create resistance.

Remember you see and experience *only* what *you* are projecting in life. When you project resistance, you get resistance from others. When you have a need to control another person or circumstance, you have set up an invisible emotional connection that creates resistance between you and that person or circumstance. If you are feeling angry toward another person, not only is your anger having an adverse effect on you, it is also having a negative effect on the other person, even though you may not be verbally expressing it. If you feel frustrated about your current circumstances in life, you are actually creating a wall around you that will keep you imprisoned in your current circumstances.

Here is a good rule to follow. We live in a black and white world, not a gray world. Every act is either an act of *love* or an act of *violence,* either toward another person or yourself. There is really nothing in between. Look at some of your habits and evaluate. Are they love or violence? Anger, resentment, judgement, are all acts of violence. That is pretty easy to see. How about something like being late all the time? Is wasting their time waiting on you an act of love or violence? How about anxiety? That is an act of violence toward yourself. Disciplining a child while in an angry state is an act of violence. Any action toward another that is not love is, to one degree or another, an act of violence.

Imagine this scenario. Two world leaders get upset with one another, and out of that upset there is some sort of political conflict that needs to be resolved. As it progresses, they begin to threaten one another. Next a small conflict breaks out. Now some of the allies of each country decide to get involved. We send some of our troops to help stop the conflict, but instead it accelerates into a full-scale war. Some of our troops are killed in the process. Then the families of the soldiers who were killed get angry and begin to express their anger toward others and our government leaders. The news media gets involved and accelerates the problem even more. We begin to protest out of anger to stop the war, which in turn upsets the police. The police then get angry and begin fighting against the people who only wanted peace in the first place. Sort of sounds all too familiar, doesn't it?

Instead of becoming a part of the on-going drama, or the "chain of pain," why not let go and break the chain. Then, if there is action you can take to improve the situation, do it from a place of love not violence.

Letting go of the need to control is like sailing, surfing, skiing, or even living your life to the fullest. What is required is a subtle blend of control through your skill and knowledge, and at the same time, letting go of your need for control and allowing an outcome be an outcome—an outcome you had no control over in the first place. Does that not make sense?

Letting go of your need to control simply means letting go of your attachment to the outcome, then taking action from that viewpoint. If there is no action you can take, just simply let go and have the courage to leave it at that. Anything you cling to will eventually cause you emotional pain. When you are experiencing emotional pain, you set up a "chain of pain" affecting those around you.

When we discipline a child, for example, our tendency is to *demand* that they act a certain way. What would happen if you demanded that your friend across the street acted a certain way? Maybe you demand that they mow their lawn when you want them to.

They would probably tell you where to get off, wouldn't they? Wouldn't you if they demanded that of you? When you *demand,* you push the *resistance* button of the other person, whether it is your friend, your teenager, or whomever. When you demand, you will always meet with resistance, which in turn pushes your need-to-be-in-control button—escalating the matter into a full scale argument, until someone decides to let go and break the chain of pain.

Do you have anything in your life where you feel out of control? If so, let go of your need to be in control and see what happens with the situation. Might as well try it. You have no control over it anyway. And what have you got to lose? Who knows, it just might work.

Letting go of your need to control puts you in control and allows you to live resistance free. When you make demands of your children, you raise demanding children. On the other hand, when you let go of your need to control them, you are coming from a non-violent, loving place where the two of you can connect heart-to-heart. As an example, you could say, "Go clean your room. It looks like a pigpen. Don't you have any pride at all?" On the other hand, you could connect heart-to-heart by saying, "Honey, your room looks a little messy, would you mind giving it a good cleaning today? I would love that."

The most important thing in the world to each of us should be to maintain our own peace of mind. Because if you are not peaceful, those around you cannot be fully at peace. Taking action from a resourceful, peaceful, loving state of mind is the key to remaining peaceful.

I was having dinner one night at a networking club where everyone at the table was sharing their goals and visions for their life's work. When it came time for the woman next to me to share, she said she was very upset because she didn't have a vision for her life's work. She said that everyone told her she needed to clarify her vision and find a meaningful project to work on.

After everyone had shared, I turned to her and asked, "What do you want to do?"

She said, "All I know is I want to make a difference for others, but I don't know what that would look like."

I asked her, "How is the rest of her life was going?"

She said, "I am very happy." She said, "I am financially secure. I have a wonderful relationship with my husband and basically everything in my life is great…except for not knowing what I could do to contribute to the lives of others."

I then asked, "How does it feel to not have a clear vision about how you might make a contribution?"

Her answer was, "Frustrating and a little depressing."

I asked, "Does your frustration come from your need to control or your need for acceptance?"

She thought for a minute and said, "I think it is my need to acceptance."

I then asked, "Does your depression, frustration, and your need for acceptance contribute to anyone else's life?"

She said, "No, I don't think it does."

I then asked, "Do you think that being satisfied and happy with your life as it is now would make a contribution to others?"

She answered, "Yes, I believe I set a good example for others to follow."

I said, "You see, by letting go of your frustration and your need to control, you are contributing and setting an example for others to follow. You will now contribute to everyone you come in contact with."

All she really needed to do was create a vision of wanting to know her purpose, let go of her fear and frustration over not knowing, then simply have the courage to leave it at that and see what appeared. The simple truth is, if you don't know, you don't know. How *could* you know what you don't know? You cannot control an outcome especially if you don't know what direction to take in the first place. If you're stuck in a state of frustration, there is no room for the right solution to come forth. Inner conflict can always be resolved if the first step is letting go of your need to control the outcome. As long as you are hanging onto the control drama, there's no room for solutions—just the rehashing of old problems. What you try to control, actually controls you.

Let's explore some of the ways you may use *the need to be in control* in your everyday life. As you go through the list, see if there are any in which you find yourself identifying.

~Not forgiving someone for a past mistake.

~Thinking that you are better than others.

~Blaming others to make yourself look good.

~Putting others down to make yourself look good.

~Getting even so that you feel in control.

~Being late just to show that you are busy and in control.

~Being impatient to show others how important you are.

~Blaming others to avoid seeing the truth.

~Holding grudges in order to stay in control.

~Being rigid, *doing it your way,* in order to take all the credit.

~Undermining others to make yourself look better.

~Always having strings attached in order to exercise your authority.

~Exercising aggressive behavior in order to be first or the best.

~Judging others to make yourself look better.

~Saying, "I'll try" so you won't look bad if you don't follow through.

~Being a workaholic to show others how important you are.

~Using manipulation in order to look better in other's eyes.

Now, let's review a few of these, and see how they can become a need to control.

Manipulation:

Defined as, *"To alter a situation to suit your own purpose."* That about sums it up, doesn't it?

Let's say you are in sales, and you are about to make a really important sales call—one you've been waiting on for months. It is a really big account, one that you really want to acquire. So, you plan and scheme and try to think of every tricky technique in the book to close the sale. You become obsessed, fearful, and anxious about getting the account. It is alright to plan, to be prepared, and to make an effective, well-organized presentation that leads to the sale. That is skill! But what doesn't work is being obsessed, fearful, and anxious, wanting to control or manipulate the outcome for your greater good. What I'm saying is, let go of your need to control the outcome, so you can keep your attention on the presentation at hand instead of trying to manipulate the end result.

Another example is, some people get so obsessed with their goals and dreams, doing affirmations, visualizations, story board, etc., that they completely lose track of the moment where the action takes place. My approach is to make the decision about what you want to accomplish, and then move on it. All the rest is just mental gymnastics. If you are passionate about what you want to accomplish, you are not going to forget it.

Being rigid:

Another way we try to control is by being rigid about how to create a certain outcome. A while back I was thinking I would like to give some lectures at a local college on entrepreneurship. I asked a business associate if he knew how I might go about it, or who I might contact. He suggested that I call the college and ask. What a concept! So, I wrote down in my day planner to do so the next day. That evening, I stopped by my favorite health food restaurant for dinner.

I was by myself, so I sat at the counter to eat. The server had just brought my meal when a woman sat down next to me. She said, "Hello."

She then asked me what I was having for dinner. We continued our conversation, sharing with one another what we did professionally. As it turned out, she was a professor at the college where I wanted to speak and in charge of the marketing department. When she found out about some the topics I spoke on, she got really excited. She then asked if I would be open to being a guest speaker at the college for some of her entrepreneurial students. I couldn't have created that situation in a million years out of my need to control, or by being rigid as to how it was to come about. A clear vision is very powerful, as long as you don't place restrictions on how and when it will happen. Here's a great way to remember that: "Create your vision and play with whoever shows up to play!"

Here is another example.

Many years ago, I was consulting for a seminar production company in Phoenix. At the time, I was living in Sedona—about two hours away. The company contracted with me to assist them in hiring and training some instructors to teach their courses. I was sitting at my desk thinking about who I might know that would be a good candidate for the job.

I suddenly thought about a woman I knew in Southern California by the name of Mary Johnson. I could see Mary teaching this course. She would be perfect. My second thought was that I had lost touch and had no idea how to reach her. This was before the internet. I thought, *'I will keep her in mind, and somehow I'll figure out how to reach her.'* I looked at my watch and it was 3:00 PM. I remembered that I had to be in Sedona at 5:00 PM for my son's baseball game. I left for the day, not giving Mary another thought.

The next morning when I arrived at the office, there was a fax on my desk addressed to: "To whom it may concern." The fax read, "I am a graduate of your course from about eight months ago. I was very impacted by your program. I have a background in speaking and conducting workshops. Because of my background, and the impact your program had on me, should the opportunity ever arise, I would like very much to be considered as one of your workshop leaders. Sincerely, Mary Johnson."

My first thought was that there was no way it could be the same Mary Johnson.

I immediately picked up the telephone and called the number on the fax, and to my surprise, it was the very same person! During the course of our conversation, I asked her exactly when she started thinking about contacting this company about becoming an instructor.

She said, "Well, I was just sitting around yesterday thinking about what I wanted to do with my life. I felt a desire to make a change. Then suddenly, I began thinking about the workshop I attended several months before, and how much of an impact it had on me. I thought, 'Wouldn't it be great to be able to teach the course?' So, I sat down and wrote the letter and faxed it to the company."

The next question, that I could not wait to ask was, "About what time was it when you wrote the letter?"

Her reply was, "I started thinking about it around 3:00 PM the day before, and faxed it around 5:00 PM." Call it a coincidence, but that was the exact time I was thinking about her teaching the course.

Another great example of letting go of the need to be in control, was with my son Warren, when he was around four years old. One day, I was just walking out the front door of my home when I saw Warren running across the street to retrieve the mail from the mailbox. In his excitement to get there, he did not take the time to look for cars before crossing the street. Just as he made it to the other side, a car traveling at a pretty good speed just missed him by a few feet. It was sort of a blind hill. He did not look for cars, and the driver couldn't see him until he was right on him. You can imagine how I must have felt. I was experiencing a combination of fear, relief, and anger all at the same time.

Once I saw that he was all right, there were two approaches I could take to educate him on the correct way to cross a street. Here is one approach I *could* have taken. "Warren! Are you stupid or what?

Didn't you see that car? You could have been killed! Are you too dumb to know to look both ways before you cross the street? What if that car would have run over you? Think about how your mother and I would feel! How could you be so unconscious? Don't you ever do that again, you got it!"

Here is the approach I chose instead. I walked out to the street and said, "Hey, Warren. What are you doing?"

He said, "I'm getting the mail for you and Mom."

I said, "Thank you. That is very nice of you." I said, "Do you have a minute to talk?"

Looking somewhat surprised, he said, "Sure Dad, what for?"

I said, "Why don't you come over here, and let's sit on the curb and talk. But, before you do, be sure to look both ways before you cross the street." We sat down on the curb, then I asked, "Warren, do you see this street in front of us?"

He said, "Yes I do."

I said, "Do you know what the street is for?"

He said, "Sure Dad, it's for cars to drive on."

I asked, "Do you see that hill right there?"

He said, "Yes."

I said, "You know Warren, when cars come up over that hill, it is sometimes hard for them to see a little guy like you crossing the street." Then I asked, "Do you know how much Mom and I love you?" I said, "We love you a lot, and we wouldn't ever want to have anything happen to you. So, would you do Mom and me a big favor?"

He said, "Sure, what do you want me to do?"

Well, I said, "The next time that you come and get the mail, would you stop right here at the curb and look both ways for cars before you cross the street? And before you come back, do the same thing from the other side? Could you do that for Mom and me?"

He said, "Sure Dad, can I go now?"

Which approach to the situation do you feel would be most effective—getting your point across from a place of love or from a place of fear and anger? Would it have been better to satisfy my anger and *be right* and to make him *wrong,* or simply to *do* the right thing?

Our children rebel against us because we push and discipline, instead of correct and love.

Letting go of the need to be in control before acting puts you in control of your emotions and your emotional reaction to situation.

Saying, "I'll try":

This is another method most of us use to one degree or another to stay in control.

When you say, *"I'll try"* to another, they want to believe you have made a commitment to them. But by saying, "I'll try to come to your party," if what you promised doesn't happen, you can then say that you only said you would "try," and you did your best, but just could not make it. So, you're off the hook with a good excuse, for not doing something you knew you were not going to do in the first place. The real question is, how does the other person feel? Was that an act of love or violence?

Just about 100% of the time, when a person says to another, "I'll try," they have already decided not to do what they said they would try to do. Wouldn't it be easier on both parties to just say what you mean…yes or no.

Blame:

The last controlling action I want to review, and possibly the most common, is *blame.*

Not blaming, doesn't mean we become incapable of knowing what appropriate or inappropriate behaviors are in others. But when your energy is twisted and unfocused by always blaming, you become incapable of thinking, speaking, and acting in a resourceful way in an effort to always appear right to others. You can become literally blinded by your blame toward the other person. Blame puts you into a state of mind, where the real issue remains hidden. Blaming is brought on by suppressed anger.

When you're in a blameful state, there are two things that take place. First, you begin to look outside yourself for the answers. You blame your circumstances, or others, for how you feel. Second, by blaming, you suppress your anger even further. The act of blaming will keep your power *outside* you. Blaming will basically keep you out of control and the real truth hidden. When you blame, you see yourself as a victim who is powerless to make a change. Someone else is always doing something to you. The blaming person thinks that everyone is out to get them. It is the ultimate control drama. *'My kids won't behave or clean their room because they want me to suffer.'*

So remember, the next time you catch yourself blaming, the thing you feel you need to control is actually controlling you. When you allow yourself to be controlled by outside circumstances, the controller, or the one who blames, only grows more afraid of losing control; and as a result, becomes more out of control. The reality is, the only thing you lose by letting go of your *need* to control, is your fear of not being in control—which was just imaginary control in the first place. What you really gain with blame is only the illusion of control, which comes from your fear of being out of control. See what we do to ourselves by trying to control things beyond our control? Remember, that which you attempt to control actually controls you, and when you let go of the need to be in control, only then are you truly in control.

SEVENTEEN

What is Love?

I believe we all have some misconceptions about love. The first misconception is that it comes from outside us, and second, is that it is secured through relationships. If you narrow love down to these two things, you are cheating yourself out of the endless possibilities that exist within the power of love. Love is always present. Love has no opposite. It is an energy that travels so fast it's everywhere at once. Even in the darkest moments, love is always present. The unloving feelings you experience comes from not being present with yourself, right here, right now, and bringing the past and future into the present. They come from looking outside yourself, or into the future somewhere, or from looking to someone else as a source of your happiness.

Love is a word that many of us find difficult to comprehend. It is sometimes used to explain pleasure. "I love chocolate chip cookies." Or to express an intention. "I'd love to have that new car." To measure how much we care for someone. "If you really loved me, you wouldn't treat me this way." Or in some of the songs we hear, to express an addiction. "I'm hooked on your love." Or to express pain. "Love hurts." Being "in" love doesn't ever hurt us; being "in" anger, fear, and anxiety is what hurts us. What you really get from being *in* love is joy. To be *in* love means to be full of joy, to be deeply connected to source, where ALL things originate. And the depth of that connection becomes stronger as you let go of the fear, doubt, anger, and blame that you allow into your life. The love you are searching for is always present inside you. It has only been covered up by all the fears and conflicts.

Love is the spirit that lives within each of us. It has been said that love is the most powerful force in the universe and it can overcome all obstacles. If love does travel so fast that it is everywhere at the same time, then love should relieve us of all our problems. And if love can truly solve all our problems, then perhaps we should begin to look at it in a whole new way.

What is the true definition of love? It is defined as, "God's benevolence toward mankind." I'm sure if you asked 100 people for their definition of love you would get a hundred different answers.

Some might say:

Love is happiness.

Love is caring for another.

Love is sharing.

Love is caring for yourself.

Love is having empathy and compassion.

Love for some might be friendship, kindness, or believing in God.

These could all be how some define love, and I'm sure we could come up with many more like them. Yet, you asked the same hundred people to share with you their experience of love, what do you think you would hear? Do you suppose you would hear a story of happiness, sharing, caring, kindness, and self-love? I would think not. From a great deal of them you would hear a story of heartache and broken hearts.

The truth is, either we do not know the correct definition of love or we simply don't know how to experience it. Maybe we could gain a better understanding if we looked at love from a different point of view. For the moment, I would like to ask you to put all your beliefs aside and just consider another approach to understanding love. I am not asking you to believe me here, just to have an open mind and see if this rings true for you.

I don't mean to get religious, but maybe we could begin by asking, "What or who is God?" I bet that if you asked the same hundred people that question, a good portion of them would say that, "God is love." Certainly, if you asked most of the religions and spiritual teachers from around the world, I am sure you would find that at least one thing they all agree upon is that, "God is love." If God is love, then love was there in the beginning, it is still here now, and it shall be for all time; it is everywhere at once. If love is now, has always been, and will always be for all eternity, then it must surely be everywhere. Love is not reserved for a chosen few. And we should not have to go to some chosen place to experience it either. It is okay if you do. That is everyone's choice, but we should not have to, not if love is everywhere.

If love is everywhere, then love must be present in Europe, in Africa, in the Middle East, in China, North Korea, behind prison walls, and inside every home. If love is everywhere, it must be inside the church as well as outside the church. And even in the body we live in. It must also be inside every atom. If love is inside of every atom, and we are made of atoms, then we must also be made of love. If love is in every human being, then love must be equal for every person on earth. Wouldn't you agree? It must be equal for the prisoner and the guard, the priest and the congregation, the parent and the child, for the enlightened and the ignorant, even for the Christian and the atheist. It must even be the same for those you love and those you hate. Love is the same on Sunday as it is on Wednesday, and December or July wouldn't matter either.

Love would also have to be present when you are happy or sad, rich or poor, sick or healthy. If love always is, is always equal, and is always present in all things, then maybe the truth is that everything exists "in" love. Love is not only "in" us, but rather we are "in" love. And if love is everything, then perhaps love is, of course, everyone's love. In other words, your love and my love are equal. I know it to be true—at least it is my experience—but it does not have to be your truth.

If this is so, then we must ask the question, how do we become more aware of, or experience, more love? You see, joy and love are one in the same. One cannot exist without the other. When you enjoy something, you might say you are "in" love with it as well.

Source is defined as, "Where all things originate." Not some things, but all things. *Source* is also defined as, "Love." So, when you fall *in love* with what you want to accomplish, that is when it begins to materialize. The only other option is fall into fear. This is the exact reason we have so many definitions of love. We may call it compassion, caring, giving, sharing, sex, making love. This is perhaps the reason we love so many things.

I love my boat.

I love my cat.

I love fishing.

I love my BMW.

Because joy and love are inseparable, we have an experience of love anytime we enjoy something or even look forward to enjoying something. I enjoy fishing, therefore I am in a state of joy, or love, when I am fishing. The problem arises though, when we begin to believe that the things we enjoy (like our BMW) are the source of love itself. Love then turns into an attached form of love. "I love chocolate. I love cars."

When you become romantically involved in a relationship, it is because you enjoy certain things about that person. Since they are the source of the joy, you then believe they are also the source of the love; so we say, "I am in love with you." If you want to experience more love, then learn to experience more joy and work toward things that will create more joy in your life. If you want the other person in the relationship to be more loving, then simply help them to experience more joy. You don't even have to be involved in what brings them joy.

Maybe you can relate to this. When I take the time to exercise in the morning, it helps me to relax and be more productive. I enjoy doing it, and as a result, I am almost always more loving. When either person in the relationship does something they truly enjoy, they naturally become more loving and lovable. Then, the other person will experience more love as a result. This is because their enjoyable experience, whatever it might be, will make the person more aware of the experience we call love. And he/she will naturally share that experience with everyone in their presence without even trying.

The wife does not need to go fishing with the husband in order to experience the joy he experiences while fishing. It is simply that when either experiences something they enjoy, they become more of a joyful person. If you want to experience more love in your life, do more things that you enjoy. And let go of the things you do not enjoy—beliefs, incorrect thinking, old habit patterns, feelings, emotions, etc.

You've heard it said that when you give love, you receive love in return. I personally think it should be the other way around. When you receive love, you can give love.

You have to first be open to receiving love, before you have any love to give. And when you are doing the things you enjoy, you are receiving love and giving love, and it happens automatically. Fortunately, there are so many ways for us to enjoy: laughter, flowers, fishing, a smile, sunshine, clouds, rainbows, snow…did I mention fishing?

Many traditions and religious disciplines teach that getting in touch with the spirit aspect of your true nature is a long, drawn-out process that requires a great deal of discipline and special techniques. The fact is that it is simple and easy. The thing you should realize is that nothing is so intimately a part of you as your own spirit. The love we are all seek is right there all the time. It cannot be lost. It cannot be separated from you. In fact, it *is* you!

Many believe that we, as human beings, are imperfect and need to develop ourselves into perfection, when the opposite is really true. We are already perfect. All you have to do is let go of your beliefs about your imperfections, which then allows the real you to shine through. Love and happiness are our natural states, and for that reason we continually search for them. We intuitively feel the pull toward love and happiness because they vibrate within us. That longing we feel is simply home sickness. The search will end only when we release the layers of fear and conflict that create our resistance in the first place. When you resist the natural flow, by giving your attention to fear, you are really resisting your own natural state.

Trying to "earn" love by acting or being a certain way will always end in failure. Because, once you stop behaving in these conditioned ways, you are still left with self-doubt—which is exactly where you started in the first place. In order to end the search for real love, you have to go beyond behavior and start looking inside. When you do, you'll discover your real self, the self who knows on a soul level that love is all there is. When you uncover the layers and reveal your outdated beliefs for what they really are, you discover the most basic truth of all—that compassion, happiness, peace of mind, and love are your natural state. However, before you can fully realize this fact, before you can experience being filled with love and happiness, you must first be emptied of all that is not love. In order to be reborn into a new way in any area of your life, you must first die to the old ways and let go of the beliefs that keep you searching outside yourself for love.

One of the most basic fears that most people have about letting go is fear of the emptiness they believe will be there when they do. But in reality, when you die to the old, a vacuum is created for the new. That empty space is instantly filled with love, where all things originate. Trying to chase love is like trying to vacuum the carpet with the bag full. When you surrender a false belief, the vacuum is emptied and then filled with love, and it happens without any effort whatsoever.

We seem to be constantly looking back into our past, hoping to find some kind of guidance that will provide us with more love and fulfillment in the future. When you stop viewing the future through the filters of the past, only then do you have freedom from it and no anxiety for the future. Because only then, do you truly exist where everything happens—including love and happiness—in the present moment.

When you begin to see that every seemingly painful event is truly a gift designed to show you the power of love, the real you will step forward and take center stage. What you pursue will always elude you. What you become is what you will create. If you *pursue* love, it will always be out there somewhere—in the next relationship, job, or outside event. When you *become* love through the process of letting go of unloving feelings, behaviors, and emotions, you step into the universal broadcast of love. When you exist "in" love, you discover it in everything. You will transmit it in all you do, through your touch, thoughts, words, eyes, feelings, handshake, smile, and your very presence. With one act of real love you can cancel out thousands of acts of non-love. When you give love in this way, you actually raise your own vibration, and in turn bring more love into your life.

Remember, in order to truly give love to another, you must first be open to receiving it; because how can you give something you have not yet received? Receiving comes first, then giving. As you receive and give to others, you also give to yourself in return. And of course, the reverse is also true: what you withhold from yourself, you withhold from others.

One day, many years ago, out of the blue, my four year old, Will asked, "Dad, do you know how much I love, love?"

Curious, I answered, "No, I don't Will. How much do you love, love?"

He said, "I love, love, more than anything."

So, intrigued with the dialog, I asked, "What is love?"

He said, "It is getting hugs and kisses from you and Mom and my brothers and also from Grandma and my uncle Rick." He said, "I miss them a lot when I don't get to see them. I also miss getting hugs and kisses from Grandpa, and I miss giving them to him. But someday I'll see him again in heaven with God." He then looked at me very seriously and said, "Dad, when I die, I don't want to be put into a box in a hole in the ground, with one of those markers on top of my head. I want to go back to God. God's love is the love I like best, so I want to be with him again someday, okay?"

What could I say? From the mouth of a four-year-old.

Think of someone you would enjoy giving love to today. By simply considering giving love to someone, you will automatically open yourself up to receive love, so you can then give it. And when you give it, you receive it back. With no effort at all! Here is the most important point of all...love only operates in the present. And by living in the present, you send love into your future, while also healing your past. When you exist "in" love, your whole life will become an endless stream of miracles.

We spend a great deal of our time pondering two questions. The first is, *"Will I get something out of this?"* And the second is, *"Will this cause me pain?"* We may seem to be calm, but under the surface, these two questions are always lingering. And in order to avoid the pain, and find happiness, you take the same old subconscious habit patterns you've used all your life and attempt to create a new framework from which to live. It is like putting dry clothes on over wet ones and expecting to get dry. We continue this life-long habit of running after something. We run around in our self-created circle-eight trying to find the beginning or the end.

What do you think will help you find happiness and avoid the pain of life? Is it position? Money? Would that do it? How about the perfect relationship? Is that it? Power? Would that be the key? Enjoying each moment is the key. Each and every moment is complete and full just the way it is. Right now, what does your moment hold? Happiness, anxiety, pleasure, discouragement? Each moment is just as each moment is. Your real mission in life is to truly exist in that moment whatever it may bring. Another way to say it is, "Wherever you are, be there!" When you are willing to just *be* there, exactly as you are, life is always okay. If things go right, that is okay. If things go wrong, that is okay too.

The moment is what it is, and you can't change that. However, by letting go of the need to control the moment, you change some moment in the future. We only think of the emotional upset we experience as problems, because of the pain it creates. And we want to avoid the pain, so we try to make the moment into something it is not. The pain you feel is the result of your expectations, which are created by remaining focused on a past mistake, projecting it into the future with the anticipation of it happening again. When you replace your expectations with aspirations, you see things from a completely different point of view. With aspirations, you can have the courage to remain in the moment, remain resourceful, and accept the results that moment brings.

I'm not suggesting for a second that you shouldn't take action to improve your circumstances. What I am saying is, if you don't get the results you want, you should accept that fact, instead of continuing to experience the pain of not getting what you wanted. You cannot manage results. It has already happened. All you can manage is how you handle it and what action you take next to change your circumstances at some point in the future. This moment is all you have. When you have *expectations*, your mind wanders into the past and the future. On the other hand, when you live your life with aspirations, you can gently return to the present moment, where the real action takes place.

Getting rid of this false belief structure we have created is the key. Actually, we are not getting rid of it so much as we are simply seeing it for what it is. As you begin to see through your false beliefs and discover the truth of who you really are, and the power you have, your outdated beliefs and programming begin to lose their hold on you, or rather your hold on them.

Our stories and drama literally run the world. Everyone has a story, but the good news is you are not your story. One of the most common stories is, "Never enough. This isn't it. I want more." Before long, if you are not careful, other people's stories become part of your story. You can become a victim in someone else's drama. In reality, there are only about six stories in the whole world! We just pass them around our circle-eight like a relay team trying to win a race that cannot be won. It is a race with no finish line!

If you take your story personally, you'll get hung up in all the little hardships of life.

Just remember to let go. Your story is not you—just a passenger you picked up along the way that can be dropped off at the next bus stop.

Simply create your vision of the life you want and play with whoever shows up to play.

Hold your vision, remain in the moment, and let your non-supportive beliefs and programs wither away from lack of attention.

Let me ask you. Who is the most important person on the planet? It is me! At least to me it should be me! To you it should be you! In order to help another, you must first help yourself.

Remember, that every action you take is always based on your desire for acceptance. Your need for acceptance from others always stems from your need for self-love. This deep-seated desire can cause you to seek power, money, fame, and a need for acceptance or control. Unfortunately, love cannot be obtained in these ways. Only by letting go of these needs, existing in the moment can you truly know love and happiness. In other words, if you want to help the world, you must first help yourself. You cannot show others the way unless you know the way first.

As you use the power of letting go more and more, your life will take on a whole new meaning. Stress will become a thing of the past. And, if you are not already, you will begin to laugh at your own drama. After a while, you'll look back and wonder how you ever thought and believed the way you did. And one thing is for sure. Once you make the shift, you will never be able to go back to your old way of living.

When you do what you do with love, you will eventually have only what you love in your life.

EIGHTEEN

Loverage

I can trace my personal and business success back to a word I heard someone use recently. Not only was this the defining concept of my early success, it has always been the driving catalyst in my life and business since.

The driving force of my life is "LOVERAGE." Say it out loud. L-O-V-E-R-A-G-E— Using love and leverage to help others help you. You won't find it in the dictionary, but it is the visible, yet invisible, thread of success and personal fulfillment that has been trying to help humanity throughout the ages. Unfortunately, most don't care to listen or really hear.

I've built my career on leading by example, going first. Serving. Giving value. Looking for ways to help others. If you want to live life to the fullest, or explode your business, loverage is the answer you've been looking for. Loverage is building your life and business through the success and fulfillment of others!

Some go through years of abnormal self-centeredness, extreme selfishness, and you can visibly see it not working for them. I'm not sure about you, but I know it's never worked for me! Using loverage is a way of life. It is actually a LAW that goes back thousands of years and has been taught to each generation, decade after decade, century after century. And those who have achieved and lived lives of success, fulfillment, happiness, and peace of mind, have heard its truths.

It's the *"Law of LOVERAGE."*

Loverage is about building yourself up and giving yourself away to benefit others.

Loverage is about becoming a person of value.

Loverage is about helping others help themselves.

Loverage is about loving yourself.

Loverage is about loving others.

Loverage is about living a life that your great grandchildren talk about.

Loverage is about leaving a legacy as a path for others to follow.

Loverage is about asking the question each day, "How can I go the extra mile and do more?"

Loverage is about treating others as you would like to be treated.

Loverage is about becoming an inspiration and resource for others.

Loverage is about giving away something you have and knowing what is left will multiply.

Loverage is about seeing the good in others.

Loverage is about using the power of love and leverage to help more people and help yourself.

Loverage is about realizing that people are important, that the greatest need people have is to be loved, wanted and recognized.

I'm not perfect by a long shot. I've made a lot of mistakes in my life. But I do know that every time I have tapped into the awesome power of *loverage*, great things happen, and I know they will for you too.

Become somebody for someone else. Smile. Send a note. Share a good book. Share your talent. You know you'll reap what you sow. Plant seeds of success in others' lives and watch the harvest grow in yours. And don't allow yourself to think for a moment that you have nothing to give. You do! Start small. Every time you meet someone new or run into an old friend, ask yourself, "What can I do to help this person?"

Do something today. Today! Jump on the loverage band wagon. When you do, your happiness and success will soar like an eagle!

Afterword

As I close, I would like to say that you are amazing! I want to leave you with this final message.

We are all amazed by the movie superstars—who's the greatest, who's the best, who has the most. And although we may be mesmerized as we watch them, we are also reminded of all that we are not. We are not good enough. We don't deserve more. We are not smart enough. We didn't get the "lucky" breaks. I don't see you that way at all. I want you to take a moment out of your busy life each day to celebrate you, the real hero in your life, and remind yourself that the greatest hero in your life is not in the movies, it is you!

A real hero is a person like you, with character and courage. One that is willing to step up, step out of the crowd, and make a difference by doing something different. With discipline and dignity each day, you will play that heroic role to the best of your ability without background music, the right lighting, or a script to follow. With no props, you step to center stage every day and give life your best performance. No stunt doubles. You know your life is not a pre-written screen play. It is lived out moment by moment, with no rehearsals or editing.

I may not know the details of your life, but I do know that you are here for a reason. I know that at some point you made a calculated decision to improve your future, to write and create your own success story, and be the star of your own production! While others stand on the sidelines and wish, you work! While others make excuses, you make changes! The reason others quit is the very reason that you are unstoppable!

So, in moments that you are not "up" or you are not feeling so great, moments when you feel everything and everyone is against you, I want to remind you of your greatness. You are smart enough and strong enough. You do have the talent and discipline to achieve your dreams.

Look within and see just how special you really are! You are truly amazing! Believe it with all your heart! Thank you for joining me. I look forward to hearing your new story.

Remember, when you do what you do with love, you will eventually have only what you love in your life. And loving yourself is the greatest gift you can give to the world.

Have a wonderful life!

Stay in Touch

I would like to encourage you to do three things.

One, is to stay involved with my websites.

www.jimbritt.com

www.CrackingTheRichCode.com

www.JimBrittCoaching.com

You will find support for this work and many other areas of your development both personally and professionally, all designed to help you to further your growth and self-discovery.

Two, stay in touch on social media where I'll be posting lots of valuable life enhancing tips.

Facebook: www.facebook.com/jimbrittonline

LinkedIn: www.linkedin.com/in/jim-britt

Instagram: www.instagram.com/jimbritt.official/

And Three, if you haven't read my book Rings of Truth, I would encourage you to do so right away. It is my story about how My philosophy began. You will love it. It will take the process of letting go to a whole new level.

If you would like more information about other audios, books, workshops, and retreats, or if you would like to get a friend involved in this work, you can direct them to my website at www.jimbritt.com.

If you would like to schedule Jim Britt as a keynote speaker at your special event. Get details by emailing to support@jimbritt.com.

www.ingramcontent.com/pod-product-compliance
Lightning Source LLC
Chambersburg PA
CBHW071227080526
44587CB00013BA/1525